The Olympics, Media and Society

When the general public follow the Olympic Games on television, on the internet, even in the newspapers, they feel like they have themselves experienced the performances of the athletes. This book explores whether it is ever possible to experience the Olympic Games as an athletic event without considering the effect of the media. It addresses a multitude of ways in which the intermediary of media production alters the experience of the Olympics.

Spectators watching Olympic events from the stands are less subjected to the language of the commentators, journalists, and even the athlete interviews as they form impressions and understandings of the games. However, even those who sit in the stands for the opening ceremonies or walk down the streets of the Olympic Village and the host city are treated to media spectacles that are intentionally produced to display the attitudes, values, and beliefs of the host country and its Olympic Committee. This book performs the important task of analysing ways in which the media serves as both an integral component and an arbiter of the Games for society.

This book was originally published as a special issue of *Mass Communication and Society*.

Kim Bissell is the Director of the Institute for Communication and Information Research, and the Associate Dean for Research in the College of Communication and Information Sciences at the University of Alabama. She has published more than 30 research articles in peer reviewed journals and several book chapters. Her research interests include the intersection of media, health, and sport in the context of media effects and media messages.

Stephen D. Perry is the Editor of *Mass Communication and Society*, and is the Mass Media Coordinator and Professor at Illinois State University. He is co-author of *Communication Theories for Everyday Life* (2003) and author of *A Consolidated History of Media* (2005), as well as many book chapters and research articles in peer-reviewed journals. His research interests include media effects on society, and media history.

The Olympics, Media and Society

Edited by
Kim Bissell and Stephen D. Perry

Routledge
Taylor & Francis Group

LONDON AND NEW YORK

First published 2013
by Routledge
2 Park Square, Milton Park, Abingdon, Oxfordshire OX14 4RN

Simultaneously published in the USA and Canada
by Routledge
711 Third Avenue, New York, NY 10017

First issued in paperback 2015

Routledge is an imprint of the Taylor & Francis Group, an informa business

This book is a reproduction of *Mass Communication and Society*, volume 15, issue 4. The Publisher requests to those authors who may be citing this book to state, also, the bibliographical details of the special issue on which the book was based.

British Library Cataloguing in Publication Data
A catalogue record for this book is available from the British Library

ISBN13: 978-1-138-94432-9 (pbk)
ISBN13: 978-0-415-81596-3 (hbk)

Typeset in Times New Roman
by Taylor & Francis Books

Publisher's Note
The publisher would like to make readers aware that the chapters in this book may be referred to as articles as they are identical to the articles published in the special issue. The publisher accepts responsibility for any inconsistencies that may have arisen in the course of preparing this volume for print.

Contents

CONTENTS

Citation Information

The chapters in this book were originally published in the journal *Mass Communication and Society*, volume 15, issue 4 (2012). When citing this material, please use the original page numbering for each article, as follows:

Chapter 1
Introduction: Olympics, Media, and Society
Kim Bissell and Stephen D. Perry
Mass Communication and Society, volume 15, issue 4 (2012) pp. 481-484

Chapter 2
The Olympics, Jesse Owens, Burke, and the Implications of Media Framing in Symbolic Boasting
Mike Milford
Mass Communication and Society, volume 15, issue 4 (2012) pp. 485-505

Chapter 3
Fans, Nonfans, and the Olympics: Predictors of Audience's Multiplatform Experience with the 2008 Beijing Games
Roger Cooper and Tang Tang
Mass Communication and Society, volume 15, issue 4 (2012) pp. 506-524

Chapter 4
The Expediency of Hybridity: Beijing 2008
Robert Moses Peaslee and Shu-Ling Chen Berggreen
Mass Communication and Society, volume 15, issue 4 (2012) pp. 525-545

Chapter 5
Media Reports of Olympic Success by Chinese and American Gold Medalists: Cultural Differences in Causal Attribution
Mei Hua and Alexis Tan
Mass Communication and Society, volume 15, issue 4 (2012) pp. 546-558

Notes on Contributors

Shu-Ling Chen Berggreen (Ph.D., University of Tennessee, 1989) is an Associate Professor of Journalism and Mass Communication at the University of Colorado. Her research areas include children and media, media and identity politics, media, culture and globalization, and media institutions and economics in Asia.

Kim Bissell is Director of the Institute for Communication and Information Research, and the Associate Dean for Research in the College of Communication and Information Sciences at the University of Alabama.

Roger Cooper (Ph.D., Indiana University, 1992) is an Associate Professor in the School of Media Arts and Studies at Ohio University. His research interests include media uses in convergent environments and the personality attributes that enhance success in the creative industries.

Jennifer Greer (Ph.D., University of Florida, 1996) is an Associate Professor in the Department of Journalism at the University of Alabama. Her research interests include media effects and online news.

Marie Hardin (Ph.D., University of Georgia, 1998) is a Professor of Journalism and Associate Dean in the College of Communications at the Pennsylvania State University. Her research concentrates on diversity, ethics and professional practices in sports journalism, including new media.

Mei Hua (M.A., Washington State University) resides in Minneapolis, Minnesota. Her research interest focuses on intercultural communication.

Helen Hyunji Kang (M.Sc., University of Toronto, 2005) is a doctoral candidate in the Department of Sociology and Anthropology at Simon Fraser University. Her research interests include cultural studies, health humanities and science and technology studies.

Amy Jones (Ph.D., University of Alabama, 2011) is an Assistant Professor in the Department of Languages and Literature at the University of West Alabama. Her research focuses on media effects.

Mike Milford (Ph.D., University of Kansas, 2005) is an Assistant Professor in the Department of Communication and Journalism at Auburn University. His research interests include the rhetorical dimensions of sports, allegory and popular narratives, and Burkean considerations of communal identity.

Robert Moses Peaslee (Ph.D., University of Colorado, 2007) is Assistant Professor in the College of Mass Communications at Texas Tech University. His research interests include international communication, media industry studies, media anthropology, and discourse analysis.

Karen-Marie Elah Perry (M.A., Simon Fraser University, 2010) is a doctoral student in the Department of Anthropology at the University of Victoria. Her research interests include visual anthropology and the anthropology of science and medicine.

Stephen D. Perry is the Editor of *Mass Communication and Society*, and is Mass Media Coordinator and Professor at Illinois State University.

Kelly Poniatowski (Ph.D., The Pennsylvania State University, 2008) is an Assistant Professor in the Department of Communications at Elizabethtown College. Her research interests include race, gender, and nationality in mediated sports.

Alexis Tan (Ph.D., University of Wisconsin, 1970) is University Faculty Fellow in the Office of the Provost and Professor in The Edward R. Murrow College of Communication at Washington State University. His research interests include communication and prejudice.

Tang Tang (Ph.D., Ohio University, 2008) is an Assistant Professor in the School of Communication at the University of Akron. Her research interests include audience research and the impact of new communication technologies.

Bu Zhong (Ph.D., University of Maryland, 2006) is Associate Professor in the Department of Journalism at The Pennsylvania State University. His research interests include decision-making theories studying judgments and decisions regarding information use, ranging from news to sports information and social media.

Yong Zhou (Ph.D., Renmin University of China, 2008) is Associate Professor in the School of Journalism and Mass Communication at Renmin University of China. His research concentrates on media effects, especially TV news media.

Introduction
Olympics, Media, and Society

Kim Bissell

Institute for Communication and Information Research
University of Alabama

Stephen D. Perry

Department of Communications
Illinois State University

When we think about the Olympic Games, the facets of those Games that touch media and through the media have an influence on society, are many. Submissions for this special issue spanned topics from how doping problems and policies are covered, to concerns with accurate portrayals of the security of the Games, to the relationships between journalists and their home country athletes, to how documentaries on the Olympics present a one-sided, rose-colored view of the Games. In the end, none of those topics made it into this publication, but several of the original 40-plus topic submissions were accepted. The wide range of interests that were represented by the initial submissions suggests that the field of Olympics, Media, and Society is one ripe for additional research. We are happy to produce a venue where some of that research can be presented.

Submissions for the special issue often focused on more recent Olympiads. The 2008 games in Beijing are represented by four of the articles selected for publication in this issue. Three manuscripts focus on the 2010 Olympic Winter Games in Vancouver. But only one manuscript was accepted from earlier Olympiads—and that was much earlier. The 1936 Olympics, known mostly for the successes of Jesse Owens in track and field, provided the background for an analysis of how an Olympian's image is not necessarily his (or her) own to control. Owens' story became larger than the reality, in many ways, and the person of Owens may have been lost amidst the larger cultural understanding of the mediated Owens. That story is told well in the work of author Mike Milford.

Of those articles covering the Beijing Olympic experience, one addresses the audience's consumption of the games through both traditional and newer media platforms. Authors Roger Cooper and Tang Tang argued that there are two types of consumers for the Olympics. They look at the fan and the non-fan separately and find that non-fans were as likely to consume the Olympics in the online mediated platform as were fans. Delivery methods of Olympic Games frequently require much consideration from broadcast networks serving a country half a world and several time zones away from the games. This research is useful in understanding how different dissemination methods may in fact serve different purposes for audiences.

Robert Moses Peaslee and Shu-Ling Chen Berggreen examined what is perhaps the grandest spectacle of the Games each quadrennium, the opening ceremonies. They analyzed their importance at the 2008 Beijing Summer Games from three perspectives: the artistic selections and planning that represented China, the publicity surrounding the opening ceremonies as extolled by the Beijing Olympic Committee, and the discourse of the NBC broadcast that commented on the ceremonies as they unfolded. Their analysis clearly articulates the intentional national image that the event was designed to reveal—a discourse of harmony between the old and new China. Their findings also reveal the use of the opening ceremonies as an attempt to dissolve national boundaries between China and the rest of the world.

Many scholars approach questions of the Olympics and Media with an eye toward promotion of national image. Some would probably call this a manipulation of national image. In fact, that is the picture that Peaslee and Berggreen paint well, though they suggest no ill intent in that manipulation. Mei Hua and Alexis Tan include a look at how national pride and cultural values are portrayed through the interviews with gold medalists, showing stark differences in portrayed causes of victory. They show that for American winners there is often a nod to their own motivation to win, personal characteristics like athletic ability, and their individual style. National pride is frequently mentioned, but is less pronounced than personal characteristics and falls far short of its frequent mention by Chinese victors. Chinese athletes are more likely to reflect the collectivist thinking common in Asian countries, attributing their success to social support structures including their national pride most often, followed in frequency by the expectations of others, training, and the support of their coach and teammates.

The fourth manuscript related to the 2008 Olympic Games is authored by Bu Zhong and Yong Zhou. They look at an unstudied area of the effect of weather and pollution on journalists' reporting of the Games. Zhong and Zhou find that journalists are more likely to use positive words when the weather is better and the pollution is lower. As these conditions decline, journalists can be seen to write more negatively, using terms that may reflect negative personal moods that may be experienced by the journalists personally. This finding, while specific to the Olympics here, has implications for understanding journalism at large.

Studies of the Winter Olympic Games have received comparatively less attention than the Summer Games; however, three of the articles in this issue examine different aspects of the Vancouver Winter Games. Karen-Marie Elah Perry and Helen Hyunji Kang investigate the potential negative effect created by the Olympic committee's control of published images of the Games and of the host nation. In this work the authors studied the efforts to silence anti-Olympic speech and demonstrations held in the area of the Games. Their critical analysis acknowledges compelling questions about where an appropriate balance might lie between protecting the interests of countries, investors, and the Olympic brand vs. the rights of local residents, businesses, and sub-populations that are physically, legally, and through hegemonic power, pushed into the thin margins of society to have any place at all to express their viewpoints.

Amy Jones and Jennifer Greer address perceptions of masculinity and femininity of winter sports—sports where athletes' bodies are less of a focus since they are usually wearing significantly more clothing than sports played during the Summer Games. This piece contributes to the body of work in gender and sport communication because of their study of a sport not often included in earlier studies—the sport of snowboarding. They found that camera angles and commentary often followed traditional gendered expectations with men shown from low camera angles and described as powerful while women were shown from high angles and described as more graceful. However, they found that the audience was not as discriminating. Heavy viewers were more likely to apply the commentary about the sport to athletes of both sexes, saying both male and female athletes were more graceful as well as more aggressive. This finding was unexpected.

In a similar study, Kelly Poniatowski and Marie Hardin examined the commentary during women's ice hockey at the Vancouver Olympics. This study, added to this special issue after being accepted through the normal journal review process, noted that hockey is a traditionally violent sport where women are often seen as intruders into a male world. The commentary compared women to male role models, but never compared men to female role models nor rarely to other men, revealing the continuation of a masculine hegemony. Women were often noted as playing for college teams after starting by playing with boys' teams. Ultimately, they conclude that gendered expectations were reinforced, marginalizing female hockey players in the Vancouver games. While the findings of the coverage are similar, though perhaps more severe than those identified by Jones and Greer in

3

the coverage of snowboarding, Poniatowski and Hardin do not look at the audience's resulting perceptions. It would be interesting to know whether the audience applies attributes of the commentary to players of both sexes as happened with snowboarding, or whether they maintain a distinction between women and men players in this more violent team sport.

We would like to thank the panel of reviewers who reviewed multiple manuscripts in a short window of time to critique and rate them for publication in this special issue. They include Lindsey Mean, Andrew Billings, Phil Chidester, Marie Hardin, Erin Whiteside, Bryan Denham, Michael Butterworth, Lawrence Mullen, Scott Reinardy, and Bradley Schultz. Several others reviewed individual manuscripts, and many of those same people regularly review other manuscripts for the journal. As always, the service of reviewers is crucial to the successful peer review process that our manuscripts must undergo in order to be properly vetted for publication in the academic environment.

This special issue on the Olympics, Media, and Society displays a wide breadth of contribution to the field. The notions of how iconic athletes of the Olympic Games become an image and a representation beyond the actual person could only have been studied using someone whose memory has stood the test of time. But the ability to otherwise present several areas of study that converged on a single Summer and Winter Game set should prove useful to scholars in the field. It is our hope that this special issue will provide a strong reference point from which others will study the 2012 Olympics and beyond.

The Olympics, Jesse Owens, Burke, and the Implications of Media Framing in Symbolic Boasting

Mike Milford

Department of Communication and Journalism
Auburn University

One of the most enduring figures of the Olympics is Jesse Owens, the track and field athlete who won four gold medals at the 1936 Games in Berlin. Although Owens's athletic achievements were impressive, he is more remembered for being the athlete who singled-handedly brought down the Nazi's theories of Aryan supremacy. This aspect of Owens's identity owes less to his performance and more to the Olympic media's ideological framing. Over time Owens was transformed from a world-class athlete to a transcendent hero. The Olympic media framed Owens as a communal hero, boasting of his accomplishments as if they were their own, infusing him with ideological significance. A Burkean examination of the media's framing surrounding Owens shows that the ideological image eventually outshined his identity.

INTRODUCTION

At the 1936 Olympics Jesse Owens single-handedly dismantled Nazi ideology in 10.3 seconds. Owens was an African American track and field athlete who claimed the title of "world's fastest man" en route to four gold medals in the 100 meters, 200 meters, 4 × 100 meter relay, and long jump at the 1936 Olympiad in Berlin. Through media accounts that combined his remarkable performances with his race, Owens's achievements were transformed into a refutation of the Nazis' theory of racial superiority. As Schaap (2007) summarized, "While the western democracies were perfecting the art of appeasement, while much of the rest of the world kowtowed to the Nazis, Owens stood up to them at their own Olympics, refuting their venomous theories with his awesome deeds" (p. xv). Through of the mediated spectacle of the Olympics, Owens's performance was conceived as an ideological victory, one that promoted dominant social and political beliefs. The Olympic media framed Jesse Owens as a communal hero, and the nation boasted of his accomplishments as if they were their own, infusing Owens with considerable ideological import. A critical examination of the media's framing of Owens shows that the ideological image eventually outshined his identity.

Central to Owens's apotheosis was the Olympic setting. It is oft assumed that the Olympics were created as an apolitical international competition, but this is not the case. D. C. Young (1984) argued that the Olympics were created to promote amateurism as a form of socioeconomic elitism disguised as idealistic competition (pp. 25–27). Over time, through the lens of the Olympic media, the competitions became less about amateur ideals than competing national ideologies. As media outlets "exaggerated ideological rifts" in an effort to dramatize events for readers, the Games were transformed into a cultural competition (Eagan, 1955, p. 266; Pope, 1997, pp. 46–47; C. Young, 2008, pp. 87–88). The American press in particular worked to transform Olympic athletes into "middle-class icons who showed the decadent Old World the strength of an emerging world power" (Pope, 1997, p. 41; Riggs, Eastman, & Golobic, 1993, p. 254). In this manner the athletes' performances became enactments of their nations' mythologies, using the medal count as the scorecard (Butterworth, 2007b, p. 232; Pope, 1993, p. 329). Because of this history the Olympics are perhaps the strongest confluence of media, sport, and ideology (Kraft & Brummett, 2009, pp. 11–12; Schultz & Sheffer, 2008, p. 181).

The 1936 Summer Games in Berlin are among the best examples of this integration. These were the first Games to generate significant worldwide media attention because of the spectacle provided by the image-conscious Nazis (Farrell, 1989, pp. 162–163). For example, the torch relay from Olympia, now a staple of the Games, began in 1936, a product of the Nazi propaganda machine (Large, 2007, p. 4). This attention to pageantry combined with the significance embedded in sport and ideology established the Berlin Games as a powerful event. Within those Games the representative example was Jesse Owens, "an emblem of democracy juxtaposed against Hitler's racist call for Aryan triumph" (Riggs et al., 1993, p. 254; Spyropolous, 2004, p. 70). Although other Olympiads have had their share of political intrigue (the Mexico City Games of 1968, the Munich Games of 1972, the Moscow Games of 1980, the Los Angeles Games of 1984), few matched the ideological power of the Berlin Games. Heeding Butterworth's (2007a) call to "engage more critically with the discourses of sport as they intersect with global culture and international politics," I offer as a case study the symbolic boasting of Jesse Owens at the 1936 Olympic Games in Berlin (p. 199).

The Owens's case not only provides insight into the ideological forum of the Olympics but also elucidates the construction of the communal hero in mediated sport. Kenneth Burke makes a strong case for understanding collective identification through the symbolic boasting of a communal hero. Communal heroes are a powerful rhetorical tool for the creation and reinforcement of ideological principles because their performances can be used as models of social and political beliefs. Symbolic boasting, the celebration of another's accomplishments as one's own for ideological purposes, is the means by which a community asserts its principles through a hero's actions. This is often displayed in how media storytellers engage in apotheosis, the raising and maintaining of heroes. However, as the case of Jesse Owens will show, the creation of a communal hero has serious side effects on the individual's identity. Reducing the hero to an ideological enthymeme effectively erases the individuality of the person resulting in rhetorical fossilization. I begin by examining symbolic boasting as a unique variant of identification and its implication on a community's ideology through the creation of a communal hero. Then by examining the mediated Owens I demonstrate how symbolic boasting functioned to reframe a historical event into a powerful ideological statement. Finally I discuss the fossilizing effect that framing had on Jesse Owens's life.

SYMBOLIC BOASTING

Identification is the central term in Kenneth Burke's rhetoric. Burke (1969b) argued that it is endemic in symbol use, incorporating both explicit and "unconscious" factors that shape a community's substance (p. 21; Hochmuth, 1952, pp. 7–8). These factors coalesce around symbols that create "substantive identification" between the community's members (Gaines, 1979, p. 200; Heath, 1986, p. 209). Burke (1937) wrote that people identify "with all sorts of manifestations beyond" themselves, that the "so-called 'I' is merely a unique combination of partially conflicting 'we's'" (p. 264). This desire to be part of something beyond ourselves "reflects our fundamentally social, political, and historical makeup" and acts as the impetus for communal identification (Wolin, 2001, p. 93). Hence the "ultimate condition sought by rhetorical endeavor" is corporate identification, a rally around communal symbols (Carpenter, 1972, p. 19).

Symbolic boasting, then, is the development and repetition of symbols that provide consubstantiality to the corporate unit through a sense of collaboration (Burke, 1969b, p. 58). Burke (1937) wrote, "He identifies himself with some corporate unit (church, guild, company, lodge, party, team, college, city, nation, etc.)—and by profuse praise of this unit, he praises himself," celebrating the "I" via the "we" (p. 267; 1969b, p. 21). This is achieved by "*acting-together*" through the communal property of "common sensations, concepts, images, ideas, [and] attitudes" in the "context of social action" (Burke, 1969b, p. 21). Because the corporate symbol comes to represent the totality of the community, groups target "symbolic structures that embody the ideal," resulting in powerful icons (Wolin, 2001, p. 94). Boasting of these corporate icons simultaneously praises both the group and the individual for joining it.

Often these corporate icons are manifested as a communal hero who enacts the group's ideology. Ideology in this case refers to the "political or social doctrine" inherent in the political language of a community "exploited" to justify actions (Burke, 1931, p. 161; Burke, 1947, p. 195; McGee, 2000, p. 458). The communal hero is a figure whose performance is used to represent these doctrines as an exemplar of communal principles. The hero provides a means to consubstantiality by allowing members who share a common ideology to vicariously partake in the hero's activities without "paying the costs entailed by participation" (Walsh, 1986, p. 8). Then, by symbolically boasting of the hero's accomplishments, the corporate unit is able to take on the hero's actions, motives, methods, and results as their own and use them for ideological purposes. For example, in Butterworth's (2007a) analysis, the Bush administration's appropriation of the success of the Iraqi national soccer team allowed Bush to "condense" his message of success in Iraq into their achievements on the pitch (p. 195). Through a celebration of the soccer team the Bush administration was able to praise their agenda. As this example demonstrates, the corporate unit is able to revamp its identity and history by constructing a hero that manifests the ideology it espouses.

Framing theory provides a good example as to how symbolic boasting is manifested in communal discourse. In framing an event, a rhetor highlights certain "aspects of a perceived reality and make[s] them more salient," encouraging facts to be "interpreted by others in a particular manner" (Entman, 1993, p. 51; Kuypers, 2006, p. 8). Media framing works to give events coherence by organizing them according to principles drawn from "shared cultural narratives" (Gamson, 1989, pp. 158–161). Resulting storylines are simplified along ideological lines and work to shape the direction that future stories will take. Frames "resonate with existing underlying schemas" such as ideologies, and as a result provide communities with "moral judgments" on events (Kuypers, 2006, p. 8; Scheufele, Dietram, & Tewksbury, 2007, p. 12). In symbolic boasting the hero's performances are framed as ideological successes. Over time the hero becomes synonymous with the principles with which she is framed until a mere mention of the hero enthymematically calls up positive associations with communal ideology.

The practice of symbolic boasting, through the framing of communal heroes, raises an important question about the hero's identity. The hero is a "poetic" image, one that can "*stand for* things that never were or never will be*" (Burke, 1969b, p. 84). To achieve that status, she must be framed according to the community's ideology, while the corporate unit must contend with the individual's ongoing identity. Because the symbolically boasted hero is such a potent rhetorical figure, any inconsistency in her identity is easily viewed as inconsistency in the ideology of the group. For example, Butterworth's (2007a) framing of the contentions raised by the Bush administration's use of the Iraqi soccer team highlights problems associated with borrowing others' achievements (p. 199). Burke (1954) termed this phenomenon "cultural lag," which occurs when a communal hero is enacted in "conditions for which it is unfit" (p. 179). However, because the ideology of the corporate unit is significant to the collective identity of the group the lag is most easily taken up through alterations in the communal hero. Hence, for the community to retain its ideological symbol the hero is *rhetorically fossilized*, symbolically frozen as an idealized image, eradicating the organic identity of the individual.

In this project I analyze this problem by examining the role of Jesse Owens in the public sphere. In the build up to World War II Owens was "incorporated into American discourses on national identity" and framed as a refutation against Nazi doctrine (Dyreson, 2008b, p. 225). Repeated use of Owens as a communal hero framed his athletic achievements as the ultimate salvo fired against the Nazi Regime. Eventually, Owens became a rhetorical fossil, frozen in time in Berlin to the point that his individual identity all but vanished. An examination of Owens's rise to communal hero, his use as an ideological enthymeme, and the cultural lag that fossilized him provides insight into the functions and limitations of symbolic boasting as a rhetorical form.

JESSE OWENS AS IDEOLOGICAL ENTHYMEME

The process of symbolic boasting that turns individuals into communal heroes is best demonstrated by examining the role of Jesse Owens at the

1936 Olympics. Before the Games, Owens was a world-class athlete, but certainly not a powerful communal hero. The first national attention he received was in 1934 when he was briefly mentioned as a possible contributor to the 1936 Olympic team in the broad jump (Kelley, 1934, p. S2). He made a name for himself in the athletic world in 1935 when he set world records in the 100-meter, 200-meter, and broad jump all within 1 hour (Dorinson, 1997, p. 121; Roberts, 1940, p. 5). This cemented Owens's celebrity among sporting enthusiasts, but he was hardly a household name. In fact, his inclusion on the Olympic team that year was most notable not for his supposed dominance but because he was only one of "ten colored athletes" on the team (Daley, 1936b, p. 10; "Ten Colored Athletes," 1936, p. 2).

To get a sense of the symbolic boasting of Jesse Owens, I collected dozens of representations of Owens in the public sphere. The media have always been a significant force in framing the Olympics, and in 1936 this meant newspapers that have long played a pivotal role in framing the Games as an ideological struggle (Farrell, 1989, p. 158; Sivek, 2008, pp. 256–257). Taking these principles into consideration, I started with major news sources from which articles were used to spread Owens's story around the country. I concentrated my research on major media outlets such as the *New York Times, Atlanta Journal-Constitution*, and the *Dallas Morning News*, as well as two prominent African -American newspapers, the *Baltimore Afro-American* and the *Atlanta Daily World*, primarily through the magic of Lexis-Nexis. From there I expanded my search to international papers, magazines, and noted biographies on Owens and the 1936 Games in an effort to discover how the initial frames chained out over time. All of these sources, 75 years' worth, coalesced in a consistent escalating image of Owens as a corporate hero. Jesse Owens was framed as a communal hero who functioned to refute Nazi ideology and enthymematically prove Hitler's downfall. I begin by outlining Owens's significance as a communal hero, examine the role the Olympics played as the scene in the Owens drama, demonstrate the importance and unimportance of Owens's race, and take a critical look at the central metaphor of Owens's framing, The Snub.

Jesse Owens as Communal Hero

In the media buildup to the Olympics, Owens's name came up in conjunction with three storylines: how he was expected to perform (quite well), how he forgot his specially designed kangaroo hide shoes (he only brought one pair), and his race (he was one of only 10 black athletes on the American team; Daley, 1936a, p. 11; A. Gould, 1936b, p. 7; "Jesse Owens Wins," 1936, p. 1; "Olympic Games," 1936, p. 4; "Owens, Metcalfe, Draper," 1936, p. 8; Rice, 1936a, p. 3). However, once he started winning medals his performances were quickly framed as something more significant. From August 1936 on, the defining characteristic of Owens was his single-handed defeat of Hitler's theories of Aryan superiority. Over time, descriptions of Owens were amplified to sound more like the exploits of Captain America than a track and field athlete: "At the eleventh Olympiad, Owens... delivered the death blow to Herr Hitler's pet theory of Aryan supremacy" (Brown, 1943, p. 23). Brown's (1943) headline testifies to such: "Owens Scored First Victory Over Hitler at 1936 Olympics" (p. 23). He became the lone challenger to the Nazi regime and "must be chiefly credited with foiling the Fuhrer's purpose, exposing Nazi theories to ridicule and giving satisfaction if not hope to those marked first as inferior, thereafter as victims" (Pitt, 1999, para. 28). Over 75 years, Owens became the one who ruined "the games for Adolf Hitler and his 'master race' theory" ("Jesse Owens Frowns," 1967, p. 9).

Owens's primary function as a communal hero was to refute Nazi ideology. The American media developed Owens into living proof of the absurdity of the Aryan doctrine, and as years passed, his performances became more and more significant. In 1940, only 4 years after the Games, reports emphasized that he didn't go to the Olympics to compete athletically, but "to show Hitler and Goering and all the other Nazi population" a thing or two (Roberts, 1940, p. 5). By 1968 Owens had "stole[n] the spotlight from the attempts of Hitler and the Nazis to convert the Olympiad into a political propaganda show extolling the theory of the Aryan super race" (J. Gould, 1968, p. 67). In 1976 Owens had been convinced of his own significance, commenting that he went to Berlin "because Hitler had declared the dominance of the German Aryan race and we had the impudence to come over and prove him wrong in so many cases" (pp. 89–90). By the 21st century, Owens had single-handedly "showed the world that Hitler's beliefs about Aryan supremacy were wrong," as each medal he won refuted "Hitler's beliefs about racial superiority" (Barnes, 1999, para. 1; "Great Olympic Moments," 2000, pp. 130–131). Hurst (2000) waxed poetic about Owens's achievements in a much more eloquent way than Owens's media contemporaries: "But for athletic grace under pressure, there is no greater symbol than Jesse Owens—destroyer of records, destroyer of the Nazi myth of Aryan supremacy" (p. 41). Through consistent media framing 75 years in the making Owens was transformed into an "instant global symbol refuting the Nazi leader's notions of Aryan racial superiority" (G. Smith, 2001, p. 108).

This is not to say Owens didn't occasionally appear as a representative of American ideology. The ideology he promoted was often vague, equivocal, and increasingly amorphous. In the 1950s he was framed as the "finest representative of our greatest secret weapon," that our athletes can "fight a good fight, run a good race. ...Nothing finer can be excepted from

American Sportsmanship and such sportsmanship will be our greatest secret weapon for world peace" (Eagan, 1955, p. 267). Similarly, in the 1980s Owens's framers took a page from President Reagan, crediting Owens for demonstrating the "continued promise of the American experiment as the 'city on the hill'" (Jefferson, 1988, p. 64). However, the lack of concrete ideological principles in connection with Owens's framing demonstrates that refutation was his primary function. Owens was designed to discredit ideology, not promote it. As I demonstrate later, this lack of ideological promotion stemmed from the fact that the racist ideology Owens supposedly destroyed in Berlin was alive in well in most corners of his own country.

Because Owens functioned to refute Nazi ideology he was consistently framed in superlative-laden terms emphasizing his greatness at their expense. For instance, by the 1970s, Owens had gestated into the "greatest sprinter the world [had] known," and an "immortal name in sports," and his performance was voted as the defining moment of the modern Games, a top feat of the past 100 years (Bowman, 1972, p. 5; "Jesse Owens 1936," 1973, p. 8; A. Jones, 1979, p. XX19; "Owens Returns," 1972, p. 3). He "flawlessly" represented the "unyielding espousal of the Olympic spirit," by proving "that Hitler's Aryan supremacy was a lot of baloney" ("Jesse Owens Honored," 1976, p. 8; Renfroe, 1980, p. 6; Tolchin, 1980, p. A6). Ten years later his achievements had transcended the confines of the stadium: "A child of history Hitler despised and vowed to exterminate, Owens had been fine-tuned by history for the role history asked him to play" (Bennett, 1996, p. 6). Terms like "greatest," "immortal," "flawlessly," and "unyielding" served in Owens's case as indicators of symbolic boasting, establishing his heroic status.

Owens's victories in Berlin also functioned as enthymematic proof of Hitler's eventual downfall. The events were framed concurrently, as if one had always referenced the other. During World War II, when the Roosevelt administration was using Owens as a poster boy by in the Civil Defense and later at a Ford defense plant in Detroit, the media releases always began with Owens's victories over the Fuhrer (Brown, 1943, p. 23; "Still Toiling," 1942, p. 1). This became a consistent pattern, as each mention of Owens was accompanied by a preamble of his victory over the Nazi ideology. Later writers, with the benefit of hindsight, depicted Owens as the one who first brought down Hitler, as if through Owens the nation "anticipated the verdict" (Bennett, 1996, p. 72). He was the first to teach Hitler a lesson: "[Owens] proved something else, a point the Nazi spectators ignored and which had to be proved to them again a few years later at the horrible cost in World War II: It isn't the race that matters, it's the man" ("Remember 'Aryan Power'", 1968, p. 2). Hitler's downfall was "forecast" when "Jesse Owens...won four gold medals which shattered the myth of Aryan racial superiority" (Kass, 1976, p. 223). To paraphrase Burke (1966), the U.S. victory over Hitler became "implicit in the terminology" used to describe Owens in Berlin (p. 47).

It is clear that over time the media framed Owens to serve two specific functions. First Owens was framed to refute Nazi ideology. Each mention of Owens's achievements was accompanied by a degradation of Aryan superiority. Similarly Owens functioned as the first shot in the war that ended the Nazi regime. Owens was temporally framed in such a way that his victories in the Games were concurrent with Hitler's defeat. The superlatives used to describe Owens show a concerted effort to raise him to a heroic level, christening him as the chief representative of American ideology. It is no surprise then that hyperbole followed close on Owens's heels as the more the media praised him the more they celebrated themselves. Thus Owens's form followed from his function: he was framed as the ideal athlete in order to dismantle Nazi ideals.

Jesse Owens in the Olympics

The Berlin Games played the key role in the media's symbolic boasting of Owens. Burke (1969b) noted that a substantial scene demands a magnified act, and a magnified act is only performed by an elevated agent (pp. 3–9). In Owens's case, to make the scene a "fit 'container' for the act" of defying Nazi ideology, the Berlin Games had to be framed to match his status (Burke, 1969a, p. 3). In reality the Berlin Olympics were a poor fit for an ideological showdown. Olympic media coverage 1936 revealed an encouraging Berlin. Although many assumed that because of Owens's race he would be derided in Berlin, the reality was that the German crowds were warm and receptive to the black American athletes (A. Gould, 1936a, p. 4; "Owens, Metcalfe, Woodruff," 1936, p. 1). When Owens broke the world record in the 100 meters the crowd roared with approval, chanting his name ("Olympic Sidelights," 1936, p. 3; Turnbull, 2009, p. 46; von Eckardt, 1980, p. F2). Robert L. Vann, the only African American correspondent at the Games, frequently commented on the friendliness and enthusiasm of the German people for Owens (Stevens, 1997, p. 99). In one interview Owens's wife said that the Nazis arranged special tours and bodyguards for Owens to sightsee around the city when he wasn't competing ("Sports People," 1984, p. S10; "Treat Everybody Courteously," 1939, p. 3). Political strife was also low on the athletes' priority lists. Owens and his compatriots admitted that the political situation was so far in the background that many were completely unaware of any contentions (Anders, 1971, p. 1). As an arena for an ideological death match the accounts of a peaceful, accommodating Berlin just wouldn't do.

To contain Owens's ideological struggle, the city was reframed as a bigoted Berlin abundant with Nazi propaganda, "festooned with swastikas and menaced by swaggering Storm Troopers" (Bennett, 1996, p. 68). Over time the Games became a mechanism designed to "extol the racial superiority of the Aryans" and a "worldwide public platform" to "proclaim their political agendas" (Nyad, 1995, p. S9; "Owens Returns," 1972, p. 3). As the frame took hold, the Games became known as the "Nazi Games," because of their strong portrayal as "a showcase for the Nazi doctrine of Aryan supremacy" (Bowman, 1972, p. 5; Litske, 1980, p. A1). In this now ideologically charged setting "Adolf Hitler hoped to demonstrate the soundness of his belief in the superiority of the Aryan race and the efficacy of the Nazi doctrine" at the expense of other races (J. Y. Smith, 1980, p. B6). The supportive crowds Owens mentioned were recast into "more than 100,000" Nazi supporters "out to cheer for Aryan supremacy" (Bennett, 1996, p. 68; Daley, 1972, p. S2). Nearly 80 years after supportive crowds chanted Owens's name, Berlin and the Games had been shaped as an ideological setting of racial antagonism toward non-Aryans, purposefully designed to enhance Owens's achievements as an ideological vessel.

The Games' reframing was a pivotal part of Owens's symbolic boasting. In order for his victory to carry ideological weight, it had to occur in an ideological environment that would lend it rhetorical power. The media's efforts were so successful in framing the Olympics that the Berlin Games became the standard by which all other attempts to politicize the Games were measured. They are considered the point at which the Olympics moved from the sports page to the editorial page ("Where Hitler Failed," 1972, p. 2). It is argued that the belief that the Olympics are an unofficial "national scoring system" stems directly from Owens's performance at the Berlin Games (Baker, 1976, p. 3). The media's framing of the Games as an ideological battleground seems to have been quite successful.

Jesse Owens and The Snub

Framing Owens as a communal hero required not only a powerful ideological setting but also a central metaphor that defined the essence of the struggle. In Owens's case the symbolic boasting often centered around what came to be known as The Snub. After winning his four gold medals, the tale goes, Hitler snubbed Owens by refusing to invite him up to his box for a handshake and left the Games early. The longer the story was told, the more significant The Snub became. Early reports barely mentioned it, commenting that Hitler's early exit that day was due to bad weather ("Olympic Sidelights, 1936," p. 3). Influential sportswriter Arthur J. Daley (1936c) was the first to attribute Hitler's actions to ideology, pointing out that Hitler had time to greet the German and Finnish winners before ducking out, and other reporters quickly picked up the yarn (p. 19; Birchall, 1936, p. 24; A. Gould, 1936c, p. 4). The equally distinguished Grantland Rice (1936b) speculated that Hitler escaped because he feared he might be "entertaining Jesse Owens" for the rest of the Games (p. 3).

Just as Berlin was reframed into an ideological setting to add octane to Owens's status, so was The Snub. Hitler's dismay became more demonstrative until it was in proportion to Owens's heroism. During World War II, The Snub was elevated to emotional disappointment. Hitler left his box "to keep the colored lads from seeing the tears run down his face" (Brown, 1943, p. 23; Danzig, 1948, p. 17; Rea, 1945, p. 8). By 1968 Hitler could barely control himself: "Adolph Hitler was so outraged that a Negro should do so well he stormed out of the stadium and refused to present Owens with the medals" ("Owens Selected," 1968, p. 5). From there it escalated, becoming a "snub of international repercussions" as writers connected The Snub to Owens's refutative function as a communal hero (Anders, 1971, p. 1). In this frame, Hitler "not only refused" Owens, but "blatantly snubbed" him for "making a wash of Hitlerian theory about Aryan supremacy" (Baker, 1976, p. 3). Eventually Hitler's exit was tied to his disappointment at losing to what he perceived as an inferior race. Vecsey (2006), on a visit to the stadium, recounted that he had "the distinct sensation of Hitler's inner circle, bolting down the stairs, fleeing the medal ceremony, snubbing Owens" (p. G8). The ideological framing resonated with the corporate unit, and The Snub became part of the enthymematic proof of Hitler's defeat, acting as a sort of thesis statement for the Owens canon.

Jesse Owens as an African American

If Owens was the hero, the Olympics his arena, and The Snub his climactic battle, his weapon was his race. When the Berlin Games were reframed as an ideological struggle, Owens's race functioned as proof refuting Hitler's theories of Aryan superiority. For example, Rice (1936b) made much of Owens's race: "The heritage of the cotton fields and cane breaks of the South and the foothills of the Ozark Mountains of Missouri dominated the second day of the Olympic show" (p. 3). Rice wasn't alone: Owens's nicknames names over time show a consistent preoccupation with connecting his race to his performance. He was labeled "Ohio State's coffee-colored speedster," "the Brown Bullet," the "Ohio State Negro," "One of God's chillun with wings," the "Dynamic American Negro," the "Ebony Gazelle," the "Ebony Express," and the "Ebony Antelope" ("The Day Jesse," 1996, para. 3; "Jesse Owens R.I.P.," 1980, p. 456; "Olympic Team," 1936, p. 4; "Owens, Metcalfe, Draper," 1936, p. 1; "Owens, Metcalfe, Woodruff,"

1936, p. 1; "Owens Out," 1936, p. 27; G. Smith, 2001, p. 108). What is significant about these names is that although many of them were introduced in 1936 they continued into the 1990s and 2000s. The community had to be constantly reminded of Owens's race, as that was his primary weapon in refuting Nazi theories of Aryan superiority.

However, one problem raised by references to Owens's race was that they threatened to undermine him as a communal hero. Constant references to the "Brown Bullet" were an ill fit with the racially charged America of the 1960s and 1970s. One could easily spot the irony of an athlete competing in Hitler's Berlin who was not allowed to participate in meets held in the Deep South. In an effort to reconcile these inconsistencies Owens's race became truncated: implied but not discussed. In this manner the reporters were able to maintain Owens's status as a communal hero while preventing any dissonance in the corporate unit. Writers began framing events in Berlin in more generic terms, arguing that the whole thing was about proving the irrelevance of race: "It isn't the race that matters, it's the man" ("Remember 'Aryan Power,'" 1968, p. 2). Another report stated that Owens was responsible for teaching Aryans that it is "how well they can compete as individuals that determines the victor" ("Where Hitler Failed," 1972, p. 2). Owens (1976), in a series of articles he wrote for the *Saturday Evening Post*, commented that he felt "just like any other man" when he ran in America's uniform and argued that the Olympics transcended "all prejudices and national and racial lines" (p. 89). In this way Owens's race was both emphasized and diluted in order to protect his status as a communal hero while symbolically boasting about his accomplishments.

As you can see, the media framing of Jesse Owens resulted in a powerful rhetorical figure that served as a communal hero. Over time, each report on Owens's life and achievements was merged and magnified into a portrait of an ideological figure representing the philosophy of the corporate unit. His achievements at the Games, the Olympic scene, and his race all played compelling parts in the symbolic boasting of the corporate unit. Along the way, Owens was refashioned to better align with the dominant ideology of the American public, eventually emerging as a powerful archetypal figure. Jesse Owens became a communal hero for the corporate unit, an ideological enthymeme on the world's stage, refuting arguments with each stride.

Jesse Owens as Rhetorical Fossil

Burke (1954) argued that any significant communal symbol suffers from cultural lag when it finds itself in circumstances that are an ill fit for its design (p. 179). The corporate unit must maintain its icons, or risk losing its ideology along with them. When those communal symbols are heroes the corporate unit must account for another type of lag. As was previously mentioned, when a communal hero is reframed for use by a corporate unit the community must reconcile the ongoing life of the individual with the idealistic image of their hero. Such was the case with Jesse Owens. As Spivy (1983) commented, Jesse was not an "inert, unthinking object" but because of his superhuman status he was forced to harmonize his persona with the corporate hero (p. 116).

The inconsistencies between the two incarnations of Jesse Owens were startling. Owens the communal hero remained in the Olympic arena a victor, frozen in time as the champion of U.S. ideology. Each mention always referred to him running down Hitler's agenda one graceful stride at a time. In reality, Owens left the American Olympic team's European tour a few weeks after the Games and came home to financial hardships. Because he abandoned the tour the Amateur Athletic Union (AAU) who governed track and field events in the United States at the time ruled him ineligible ("Owens to Doff," 1936, p. 1). So, whereas Owens the symbolic hero ran and jumped his way into the pantheon of Olympic heroes over and over again, in the real world he was resigned to race exhibitions against horses and cars while working as a playground janitor (W. Jones, 1936b, p. 2; Litske, 1980, p. A1). All Owens knew was athletics, and without the support of the AAU there was no access to the financial opportunities available in that arena. By 1938 he was out of track and field completely, and because the 1940 and 1944 Games were canceled he never competed again (Carter, 1938, p. 18). As a result of his financial distress Owens made some questionable decisions, once implicated in a scandal with the Teamsters Union resulting in charges for tax evasion (Farber, 1984, p. C18). Bennett (1996) wrote, "To make ends meet, Hitler's nemesis was forced to race cars, dogs and horses," a comment that aptly sums up the dichotomy between the communal hero and the individual (p. 68).

The primary contributor to Owens's real-world problems was the thing he supposedly outran in Berlin: race. As Dyreson (2008b) argued, "While Owens's runs and jumps supposedly annihilated Nazi racial ideology, they had little impact on American versions of white supremacist philosophy" (p. 224). When Owens arrived in New York, fresh from his great ideological victory, the city threw a ticker tape parade in his honor, though he had to take the freight elevator up to his room because the lobby elevators were reserved for White guests only (Gillon, 2009, p. 15; "Jesse Owens Back," 1936, p. 8). Owens often recounted how frustrated he was that "after all those stories about Hitler and his snub" he returned to an America where, in Litske's (1980) words, he "couldn't ride in the front of the bus" (p. D17). For all the praise heaped on the heroic Owens, few realized that he didn't get to visit the White House until 1976, 40 years after his Olympic victories

(Grill & Jenkins, 1992; "People in Sports," 1976, p. 54). Bennett (1996) summed up his plight well: "He was a hero, but he was a Black hero, and the market for black heroes was limited" (p. 70). Few writers picked up on this element of Owens's identity, but those who did worded their displeasure strongly: "Jesse Owens was America's hero. Yet how we treated him will forever be America's shame" (Edelson, 1999, p. 44). Comments like Edelson's were too few and came too late, after Owens's heroic depictions in Berlin were already ensconced in the American consciousness.

When Owens tried to reframe his role of communal hero on his own, he found that his rhetorical power wasn't his to command. The African American protests at the 1968 Olympics in Mexico City provide a good example. Owens, trying to tap into his rhetorical power, publicly opposed an African American boycott of the Games, arguing the Olympics was one of the few venues where African Americans could be judged on their own merits as opposed to their collective identity (Anders, 1971, p. 1; Bass, 2002, pp. 248–249). Owens felt that participation was necessary because of the social opportunities available, claiming, "Attacking the Olympics is like burning down the building we live in" as they were "a site for promoting interracial harmony and understanding" (Daley, 1968, p. 59; Gent, 1968, p. D29; Hartmann, 2003, p. 234). Owens went so far as to go to the Olympic Village in Mexico City to meet with African American athletes and warn them against overt displays like Tommie Smith and John Carlos's raised-fist protest (Bass, 2002, p. 249). In response, Harry Edwards, the Berkeley sociologist who encouraged Smith and Carlos's protests, argued that Owens was the perfect example of how the United States used Black athletes for broader political purposes, calling him a "bootlicking Uncle Tom," responding more to the communal Owens than the individual (Bass, 2002, p. 94; Beston, 2003, p. 69; Lipsyte, 1998, p. SP13). A few older sportswriters commented that the younger athletes would do well to listen to the man who defied "Aryan power," but their arguments fell on deaf ears with younger frustrated audiences (Remember "Aryan Power," 1968, p. 2). Owens's own rhetorical identity came to be the very thing that kept him from being taken seriously in this aspect of the civil rights movement.

Conversely, Owens was occasionally chided for not using his newfound status to promote a "world wide movement among colored peoples" (Jones, 1936a, p. 4). In 1936 Jones (1936a) argued, "In ten and three-tenths seconds Jesse Owens not only tied the Aryan race superiority myth into a snarl, but sowed the seeds of color-bar liberation in every section of the world" (p. 4). Later, Owens was called upon to alleviate the racial tensions surrounding the immediate post–civil rights era. In 1968 Gent argued that Owens, who had "demolished the myth of Aryan superiority," would know better than anyone about refuting claims of racial superiority (p. D29). Although

Owens tried, his efforts were, for the most part, met with derision. The problem was that writers like Jones and Gent were calling upon the real-world Owens to wield the rhetorical power of the communal hero, something disallowed by the corporate unit that constructed him. As Dyreson (2008a) argued, "Owens became a symbol to a variety of groups seeking to alter or defend American ideas about race" (p. 252). Owens was a hero designed for their purposes, though as far as they were concerned he had served his purpose. In the end he was left, as Dorinson (1997) noted, in a position common to Black sports heroes: "Hailed by one group, alienated by another" (p. 116). Owens became an example of the dichotomous identity of high-profile athletes, such as Joe Louis, Muhammad Ali, and particularly Jackie Robinson, whose apotheosis often runs parallel with Owens's (Alpert, 2008; Grano, 2009; Hartmann, 2003, p. 62; Pope, 1997, pp. 281–285). In each case the athlete was hailed as a communal hero, until his message ran contrary to the dominant ideology. Aside from Ali, the others struggled to reconcile their heroic and personal identities, much like Owens.

Over time, the corporate unit was able to reconcile the inconsistencies between the two Owens by eradicating the real-world Owens from the equation, leaving only the ideological hero as the "over-all form" (Burke, 1969b, p. 23). The inconsistencies between "Hitler-bane" Owens and the financially struggling victim of racism were agonistic. But for the purpose of symbolic boasting, Owens's individuality was subsumed to the greater ideological goals of the corporate unit. Reducing Owens to a singular ideological moment alleviated the agonistic tension. In doing so, the two Owens were denied coexistence. Jesse Owens demonstrated that ideological icons are fossilized in a simplistic form, a rhetorical loop that continually trumpets a moment of ideological victory.

CONCLUSION

The case of Jesse Owens reveals the power of symbolic boasting. By framing an individual as a communal hero, the community is able to imbue the hero's activities with ideological significance. The hero becomes the representative for the community's ideals, and with each appearance functions to reinforce ideology and/or refute opposition. This creates a strong sense of consubstantiality as the community is now able to participate in the hero's achievements. In a sense the communal hero becomes an ideological enthymeme, implicitly reinforcing communal ideals through shared actions. The media functions as the primary caretakers in the creation and framing of the communal hero. Thus, the media become some of the foremost outlets for symbolic boasting, the celebration of a community's ideology via a focus on its most august representatives.

Owens provides a good example of the power of media framing in symbolic boasting. The sports media were responsible for taking Owens from a world-class athlete to a national icon. By framing Owens as a champion wielding the power of race in the grand Olympic ideological arena, they were able to dismantle the Hitler's pro-Aryan doctrine. Owens became a refutative enthymeme, challenging Hitler with each stride. Thus, Owens was reduced to an ideological singularity, his life captured and frozen in time. The consubstantiality created by the strong ideological connection made Owens's achievements our own and ever after ran as a monument to our ideological greatness.

Owens's case also demonstrates one of the side effects of symbolic boasting. In an effort to create a communal hero large enough for the community, the hero must be framed in such a way that consubstantiality is possible, primarily by relying on dominant ideology. Any inconsistency must be pruned, resulting in a caricature, an object playing the part of the subject. In Owens's case, this meant his personal identity; individuals can change their minds, principles do not. In this manner a communal hero becomes rhetorically fossilized, a frozen relic of conditions past. For Owens that meant a stark delineation between the man who ran (and is still running) in Berlin and the one who faced racism at home nearly as sinister as the one he challenged. Owens's dichotomy has served to generate dialogue on the social construction of race. Writers like Schaap (2007) and Dyreson (2008b), among others, have taken up the case for a less heroic but more complete Owens in an effort to "construct a more inclusive model of American nationhood while at the same time ... deconstruct[ing] doctrines of white racial superiority" (Dyreson, 2008a, p. 249). One could argue that writers like Schaap and Dyreson are decalcifying these communal heroes, engaging in rhetorical maintenance so that the community's heroes reflect a new set of values.

The symbolic boasting of Owens also draws attention to the rhetorical power of the Olympics. As Farrell (1989), Rothenbuhler (1989), Bernstein (2000), Thomas (2005), and others have convincingly argued, the Games' close ties with nationalism make the Olympics a forum not just for athletic competition but political strategy as well. The competitive appeal of sport mixed with international politics in the Games generates significant rhetorical power (C. Young, 2008, p. 85). With this in mind, one can't help but note that Owens's legend grew during the Cold War, which dominated Olympic scorecards for decades. Although it is possible that the Olympics *can* be used, as Goldberg (2000) advocated, to reduce international tensions, the more likely result is that the Games *will* be (are, and have been) used as an ideological scorecard (p. 63). When this nationalism is combined with other ideological issues (like state-sponsored racism for example) the significance of the Games is off the charts. Combined with the power of the media to frame societal symbols the Olympics achieve a heightened state of rhetorical meaning. Owens could not have been heroically framed at the Goodwill Games or the World Championships; it took the ideological octane of the Olympics to set the scene. From this perspective, the intersection of sport, media, and ideology that occurs every 4 years is staggering.

As for the dichotomy of the Olympian versus the struggling Owens, one reporter summed it up nicely. There was a dispute over the locale of the Jesse Owens memorial in his hometown of Danville, Alabama (Schmidt, 1984, p. A1). Apparently a few citizens were upset at the idea of a monument to an African American in their town. One writer wryly pointed out, "This is ironic because the name of Jesse Owens is hammered deep in bronze, embedded in the stone Marathon Gate of the Berlin Stadium, and it appears there more often even than that of Hitler" ("Black Olympians," 1984, p. 6). This case sums up the symbolic boasting of Jesse Owens. The man was never a match for the hero: One lives on as an ideological icon and the other is forgotten.

REFERENCES

Alpert, R. (2008). Jackie Robinson, Jewish icon. *Shofar: An Interdisciplinary Journal of Jewish Studies, 26,* 42–58.

Anders, J. (1971, July 20). Olympic flames still burns. *The Dallas Morning News,* p. 1. Retrieved from http://www.dallasnews.com

Baker, R. (1976, February 2). On being a good bad sport. *The Dallas Morning News,* p. 3. Retrieved from http://www.dallasnews.com

Barnes, S. (1999, December 11). Bad day for Great Britain. *The London Times.* Retrieved from http://www.timesonline.co.uk

Bass, A. (2002). *Not the triumph, but the struggle.* Minneapolis, MN: University of Minnesota Press.

Bennett, Jr., L. (1996). Jesse Owens' Olympic triumph over time and Hitlerism. *Ebony, 51,* 68–72.

Bernstein, A. (2000). Things you can see from there you can't see from here: Globalization, media, and the Olympics. *Journal of Sport and Social Issues, 24,* 351–369.

Beston, P. (2003, August 1). Betrayers and betrayed. *American Spectator, 36,* 69–71. Retrieved from http://spectator.org

Birchall, F. T. (1936, August 6). Luck of Nazis with the weather failing during the Olympic games. *The New York Times,* p. 24. Retrieved from http://www.nytimes.com

Black Olympians in history—Part I. (1984, February 12). *The Atlanta Daily World,* p. 6. Retrieved from http://www.atlantadailyworld.com

Bowman, H. (1972, August 5). Jesse Owens special Sunday. *The Dallas Morning News,* p. 5. Retrieved from http://www.dallasnews.com

Brown, L. (1943, January 9). Owens scored first victory over Hitler at 1936 Olympics. *Baltimore Afro-American,* p. 23.

Burke, K. (1931). *Counter-statement.* Berkeley, CA: University of California Press.

Burke, K. (1937). *Attitudes toward history* (3rd ed.). Berkeley, CA: University of California Press.

Burke, K. (1947). Ideology and myth. *Accent, 7,* 195–205.

Burke, K. (1954). *Permanence and change* (3rd ed.). Berkeley, CA: University of California Press.

Burke, K. (1966). *Language as symbolic action.* Berkeley, CA: University of California Press.

Burke, K. (1969a). *A grammar of motives.* Berkeley, CA: University of California Press.

Burke, K. (1969b). *A rhetoric of motives.* Berkeley, CA: University of California Press.

Butterworth, M. L. (2007a). The politics of the pitch: Claiming and contesting democracy through the Iraqi national soccer team. *Communication and Critical/Cultural Studies, 4,* 184–203. doi: 10.1080/14791420701296554

Butterworth, M. L. (2007b). Race in "The Race": Mark McGuire, Sammy Sosa, and heroic constructions of whiteness. *Critical Studies in Media Communication, 24,* 228–244. doi: 10.1080/07393180701520926

Carpenter, R. H. (1972). A stylistic basis of Burkeian identification. *Today's Speech,* pp. 19–24.

Carter, A. (1938, November 12). Jesse pays DC businesses visit. *Baltimore Afro-American,* p. 18.

Daley, A. J. (1936a, July 27). American athletes engage in best workout since reaching Olympic village. *The New York Times,* p. 11. Retrieved from http://www.nytimes.com

Daley, A. J. (1936b, January 25). Brundage expects complete U.S. representation in Berlin Olympic events. *The New York Times,* p. 10. Retrieved from http://www.nytimes.com

Daley, A. J. (1936c, August 3). 110,000 see Owens set world record at Olympic games. *The New York Times,* pp. 1, 19. Retrieved from http://www.nytimes.com

Daley, A. (1968, April 9). Sports of the Times. *The New York Times,* p. 59. Retrieved from http://www.nytimes.com

Daley, A. (1972, August 20). Return visit to Berlin. *The New York Times,* p. S2. Retrieved from http://www.nytimes.com

Danzig, A. (1948, July 20). Denies Hitler story. *The New York Times,* p. 17. Retrieved from http://www.nytimes.com

The day Jesse beat the Reich. (1996, June 5). *The Sydney Daily Telegraph.* Retrieved from http://www.dailytelegraph.com.au

Dorinson, J. (1997). Black heroes in sport: From Jack Johnson to Muhammad Ali. *Journal of Popular Culture, 31,* 115–135.

Dyreson, M. (2008a). American ideas about race and Olympic races in the era of Jesse Owens: Shattering myths or reinforcing scientific racism? *The International Journal of the History of Sport, 25,* 247–267. doi:10.1080/09523360701740364

Dyreson, M. (2008b). Prolegomena to Jesse Owens; American ideas about race and Olympic races from the 1890s to the 1920s. *The International Journal of the History of Sport, 25,* 224–246. doi: 10.1080/09523360701740349

Eagan, E. P. (1955). Athletics—Medium for international good-will. *Journal of Educational Sociology, 28,* 266–267.

Edelson, M. (1999). Jesse Owens. *Sport, 90,* 44–46.

Entman, R. M. (1993). Framing: Toward clarification of a fractured paradigm. *Journal of Communication, 43,* 51–58.

Farber, S. (1984, June 26). The making of "Jesse Owens." *The New York Times,* p. C18. Retrieved from http://www.nytimes.com

Farrell, T. B. (1989). Media rhetoric as social drama: The Winter Olympics of 1984. *Critical Studies in Mass Communication, 6,* 158–182.

Gaines, R. N. (1979). Identification and redemption in Lysias' *Against Eratosthenes. Central States Speech Journal, 30,* 199–210.

Gamson, W. A. (1989). News as framing. *American Behavioral Scientist, 33,* 157–161.

Gent, G. (1968, March 24). Hitler scowled. *The New York Times,* p. D29. Retrieved from http://www.nytimes.com

Gillon, D. (2009, February 16). Jesse Owens: Olympic icon. *Glasgow Herald*, p. 15. Retrieved from http://www.heraldscotland.com

Goldberg, J. (2000). Sporting diplomacy: Boosting the size of the diplomatic corps. *The Washington Quarterly, 23*, 63–70. Retrieved from http://www.twq.com

Gould, A. (1936a, August 6). Earle Meadows of Fort Worth establishes new Games record to capture pole vault event. *The Dallas Morning News*, p. 4. Retrieved from http://www.dallasnews.com

Gould, A. (1936b, August 2). U.S. Athletes do not give Nazi salute, dip flag. *The Dallas Morning News*, p. 7. Retrieved from http://www.dallasnews.com

Gould, A. (1936c, August 3). U.S., Germany and Finland share day's track honors. *The Dallas Morning News*, pp. 4, 8. Retrieved from http://www.dallasnews.com

Gould, J. (1968, March 30). TV: At long last, "Jesse Owens returns to Berlin". *The New York Times*, p. 67. Retrieved from http://www.nytimes.com

Grano, D. (2009). Muhammad Ali versus the "modern athlete": On voice in mediated sports culture. *Critical Studies in Media Communication, 26*, 191–211.

Great Olympic moments. (2000). *Ebony, 55*, 130–134.

Grill, J. H., & Jenkins, R. L. (1992). The Nazis and the American South in the 1930s: A mirror image? *The Journal of Southern History, 58*, 667–694.

Hartmann, D. (2003). *Race, culture, and the revolt of the Black athlete*. Chicago, IL: University of Chicago Press.

Heath, R. L. (1986). *Realism and Relativism: A Perspective on Kenneth Burke*. Macon, GA: Mercer University Press.

Hochmuth, M. (1952). Kenneth Burke and the "New Rhetoric." *Quarterly Journal of Speech, 38*, 3–19.

Hurst, M. (2000, May 25). The day Owens ran into history. *The Queensland Courier Mail*, p. 41. Retrieved from http://www.couriermail.com.au/

Jefferson, A. P. (1988). "No where to run and no where to hide": Black workers on the farms, in the mills, on the playing fields, and at arms: A review essay. *Journal of American Ethnic History, 8*, 63–73.

Jesse Owens 1936 Olympics voted top feat of 100 years. (1973, July 7). *The Baltimore Afro-American*, p. 8.

Jesse Owens back home. (1936, August 29). *The Baltimore Afro-American*, pp. 1, 16.

Jesse Owens frowns on Olympic boycott idea. (1967, October 28). *The Baltimore Afro-American*, p. 9.

Jesse Owens honored on "Jesse Owens Day" in Phoenix, Arizona. (1976, March 11). *The Atlanta Daily World*, p. 8. Retrieved from http://www.atlantadailyworld.com

Jesse Owens, R. I. P. (1980, April 18). *National Review, 32*, 456–457.

Jesse Owens wins fourth Olympic gold medal. (1936, August 10). *The Atlanta Daily World*, p. 1. Retrieved from http://www.atlantadailyworld.com

Jones, A. (1979, May 13). Olympia: Echoes of the ancient Games. *The New York Times*, p. 19. Retrieved from http://www.nytimes.com

Jones, W. (1936a, October 31). Day by day. *The Baltimore Afro-American*, p. 4.

Jones, W. (1936b, August 15). Jesse likely to turn "pro." *The Baltimore Afro-American*, p. 2.

Kass, D. A. (1976). The issue of racism at the 1936 Olympics. *Journal of Sport History, 3*, 223–235.

Kelley, R. F. (1934, December 16). Sports of the times. *The New York Times*, p. S2. Retrieved from http://www.nytimes.com

Kraft, R., & Brummett, B. (2009). Why sport and games matter. In B. Brummett & R. Kraft (Eds.), *Sporting rhetoric* (pp. 9–25). New York., NY: Peter Lang.

Kuypers, J. A. (2006). *Bush's war: Media Bias and justifications for war in a terrorist age.* New York, NY: Rowan & Littlefield.

Large, D. C. (2007). *Nazi games: The Olympics of 1936.* New York, NY: Norton.

Lipsyte, R. (1998, June 21). Now and then, Us. vs. Them. *The New York Times,* p. SP13. Retrieved from http://www.nytimes.com

Litske, F. (1980). Jesse Owens dies of cancer at 66. *The New York Times,* pp. A1, D17. Retrieved from http://www.nytimes.com

McGee, M. C. (2000). The "ideograph": A link between rhetoric and ideology. In C. R. Burgchardt (Ed.), *Readings in rhetorical criticism* (2nd ed., pp. 456–470). State College, PA: Strata.

Nyad, D. (1995, July 2). Special athletes play up the true Olympic ideals. *The New York Times,* p. S9. Retrieved from http://www.nytimes.com

Olympic Games at a glance. (1936, August 6). *The Dallas Morning News,* p. 4. Retrieved from http://www.dallasnews.com

Olympic sidelights. (1936, August 3). *The Dallas Morning News,* p. 3. Retrieved from http://www.dallasnews.com

Olympic team, 334 strong, embarks for Olympic Contest. (1936, July 15). *The Dallas Morning News,* p. 4. Retrieved from http://www.dallasnews.com

Owens, J. (1976, March). Golden moment of Triumph. *The Saturday Evening Post, 248,* 1, 48, 89–90.

Owens, Metcalfe, Draper, Wykoff star in 400. (1936, August 9). *The Atlanta Daily World,* pp. 1, 8. Retrieved from http://www.atlantadailyworld.com

Owens, Metcalfe, Woodruff star in second day of Olympics: Register thirty points. (1936, August 4). *The Atlanta Daily World,* pp. 1, 6. Retrieved from http://www.atlantadailyworld.com

Owens out of relay. (1936, August 5). *The New York Times,* p. 27. Retrieved from http://www.nytimes.com

Owens returns to Berlin Monday night special on TV. (1972, July 25). *The Atlanta Daily World,* p. 3. Retrieved from http://www.atlantadailyworld.com

Owens selected to baseball post. (1968, July 3). *The Dallas Morning News,* p. 5. Retrieved from http://www.dallasnews.com

Owens to doff track togs. (1936, August 5). *The Atlanta Daily World,* p. 1. Retrieved from http://www.atlantadailyworld.com

People in sports. (1976, August 26). *The New York Times,* p. 54. Retrieved from http://www.nytimes.com

Pitt, N. (1999, March 7). Black day for Hitler. *The Sunday London Times,* Sport. Retrieved from http://www.timesonline.co.uk

Pope, S. W. (1993). Negotiating the "Folk Highway" of the nation: Sport, public culture, and American identity, 1870–1940. *Journal of Social History, 27,* 327–340.

Pope, S. W. (1997). *Patriotic games: Sporting traditions in the American imagination, 1876–1926.* New York, NY: Oxford University Press.

Rea, E. B. (1945, May 19). Encores and echoes. *The Baltimore Afro-American,* p. 8.

Remember "Aryan Power." (1968, July 4). *The Dallas Morning News,* p. 2. Retrieved from http://www.dallasnews.com

Renfroe, C. (1980, May 11). Let's go down memory lane. *The Atlanta Daily World,* p. 6. Retrieved from http://www.atlantadailyworld.com

Rice, G. (1936a, August 2). The sportlight. *The Dallas Morning News,* p. 3. Retrieved from http://www.dallasnews.com

Rice, G. (1936b, August 3). The sportlight. *The Dallas Morning News,* p. 3. Retrieved from http://www.dallasnews.com

Riggs, K. E., Eastman, S. T., & Golobic, T. S. (1993). Manufactured conflict in the 1992 Olympics: The discourse of television and politics. *Critical Studies in Mass Communication, 10*, 253–272.

Roberts, R. (1940, April 18). When you look at Jesse Owens, you're looking at hero. *The Atlanta Daily World*, p. 5. Retrieved from http://www.atlantadailyworld.com

Rothenbuhler, E. W. (1989). Values and symbols in orientations to the Olympics. *Critical Studies in Mass Communication, 2*, 138–157.

Schaap, J. (2007). *Triumph*. Boston, MA: Houghton Mifflin.

Scheufele, D. A., & Tewksbury, D. (2007). Framing, agenda setting, and priming: The evolution of three media effects models. *Journal of Communication, 57*, 9–20.

Schmidt, W. E. (1984, August 10). Jesse Owens: A monument stirs regret. *The New York Times*, pp. A1, A12. Retrieved from http://www.nytimes.com

Schultz, B., & Sheffer, M. L. (2008). Left behind: Local television and the community of sport. *Western Journal of Communication, 72*, 180–195.

Sivek, S. C. (2008). Editing conservatism: How *National Review* magazine framed and mobilized a political movement. *Mass Communication and Society, 11*, 248–274. doi: 10.1080/15205430701791030

Smith, G. (2001, August 24). How Hitler was humbled. *The Sydney Daily Telegraph*, Features, p. 108. Retrieved from http://www.dailytelegraph.com.au/

Smith, J. Y. (1980, April 1). Olympic track great Jesse Owens is dead at 66. *The Washington Post*, Metro, p. B6. Retrieved from http://www.wasthingtonpost.com

Spivy, D. (1983). The black athlete in big-time intercollegiate sports, 1941–1968. *Phylon, 44*, 116–125.

Sports people. (1984, March 11). *The New York Times*, p. S10. Retrieved from http://www.nytimes.com

Spyropoulos, E. (2004). Sports and politics: Goodbye Sydney 2000—Hallo Athens 2004. *East European Quarterly, 38*, 65–84.

Stevens, J. (1997). The black press and the 1936 Olympics. *American Journalism, 14*, 97–102.

Still toiling for Uncle Sam. (1942, March 12). *The Atlanta Daily World*, p. 1. Retrieved from http://www.atlantadailyworld.com

Ten colored athletes with Olympic team. (1936, July 24). *The Atlanta Daily World*, p. 2. Retrieved from http://www.atlantadailyworld.com

Thomas, D. (2005). Is it really ever just a game? *Journal of Sport and Social Issues, 29*, 358–363.

Tolchin, M. (1980, January 24). House unit backs Carter's call for Olympics boycott. *The New York Times*, p. A6. Retrieved from http://www.nytimes.com

Treat everybody courteously. (1939, September 9). *The Baltimore Afro-American*, p. 3.

Turnbull, S. (2009, August 11). Hitler was there. But Jesse Owens had gone to fulfill a dream. *The London Independent*, Sport, p. 46. Retrieved from http://www.independent.co.uk

Vecsey, G. (2006, July 9). Sports of the times. *The New York Times*, pp. G1, G8. Retrieved from http://www.nytimes.com

von Eckardt, W. (1980, April 13). Another side of the Berlin Olympics. *The Washington Post*, Outlook, p. F2. Retrieved from http://www.washingtonpost.com

Walsh, J. F. (1986). An approach to dyadic communication in historical social movements: dyadic communication in a Maoist insurgent mobilization. *Communication Monographs, 53*, 1–15.

Where Hitler failed. (1972, August 24). *The Dallas Morning News*, p. 2. Retrieved from http://www.dallasnews.com

Wolin, R. (2001). *The rhetorical imagination of Kenneth Burke*. Columbia, SC: University of South Carolina Press.

Young, C. (2008). In praise of Jesse Owens: Technical beauty at the Berlin Olympics 1936. *Sport in History, 28*, 83–103. doi: 10.1080/17460260801889269

Young, D. C. (1984). *The Olympic myth of Greek amateur athletics*. Chicago, IL: Ares.

Fans, Nonfans, and the Olympics: Predictors of Audience's Multiplatform Experience with the 2008 Beijing Games

Roger Cooper
School of Media Arts and Studies
Ohio University

Tang Tang
School of Communication
University of Akron

The 2008 Beijing Olympics was the most watched television event in U.S. television history and represented a broad expansion and emphasis on online sports content. This study examined audience's multiplatform experience with the 2008 Beijing Games, particularly differences and commonalities between sports "fans" and "nonfans." Results indicate key distinctions between sports fans and nonfans in terms of overall behaviors, motivations, and preferences. Although sports fans watched the 2008 Olympics significantly more than nonfans, use of online platforms were not significantly different between fans and nonfans. Explanations of why fans and nonfans watched were notably similar. Findings highlight the dynamic interplay between choice, habit, and structure in newer media environments, particularly for big-event sports programming.

INTRODUCTION

For decades, the Olympics has been an important television event for a broad range of viewers (e.g., Billings & Angelini, 2007). The 2008 Beijing Olympic Games drew 217 million American viewers and became the most watched television event in U.S. television history (Hiestand, 2008). Moreover, the 2008 Games represented the first wide-scale expansion to online and digital environments (Tang & Cooper, 2011). NBCOlympics.com offered more than 3,500 hours of online coverage from Beijing, including 2,200 hours of live video coverage (http://NBCOlympics.com; Steinberg, 2008). More than 50 million unique users watched 75 million video streams. Eighteen percent of viewers consumed content on both television and the Internet (J. Cooper, 2008). Such large viewership via traditional broadcast and newer online platforms implies that both sports fans and those less interested in sports (i.e., "nonfans") watched the Olympics, which drew significantly more women and older viewers than typically watch sporting events (Nielsen, 2008). This broad viewership for the Olympics, combined with expansion of coverage to the Internet and mobile devices, highlights the need to determine the interactions between sports fanship and "big-event" sports viewing in convergent environments. However, scant attention has been given to the reasons why sports fans and nonfans watched the Olympics on both traditional and online platforms. This study examines the differences and similarities between sports "fans" and "nonfans" and the predictors of their multiplatform experience during the 2008 Beijing Olympics.

THEORETICAL CONCEPTUALIZATION AND RELATED STUDIES

Sports Fanship and Media Use

Sports fanship has attracted considerable attention within media scholarship. The term "fan" generally applies to those who follow sports, although the term could also be linked with those interested in particular performers, personalities, and programs (see Gantz, Wang, Paul, & Potter, 2006). However, sports fans appear to be a different type of "fan" when compared to other types of content, particularly in terms of time and emotional investment. Sports fans are more likely than nonfans to seek information before and after a game/event, are more motivated to watch, are more emotionally involved while viewing, care more about the outcome, and are more likely to stay in a good mood after a victory (and vice versa after a defeat; see Dietz-Uhler, Harrick, End, & Jacquemotte, 2000; Eastman & Land, 1997;

Gantz et al., 2006; Gantz & Wenner, 1991, 1995). By contrast, nonfans watch TV sports less often, with less interest, less involvement, and with less responsiveness. However, the classification of an individual as a "nonfan" does not necessarily imply a *dislike* of sports but may reflect an individual who has less personal commitment and emotional involvement than a sports fan of major U.S. team sports (i.e., the "Big Four" of baseball, basketball, football, and hockey) that receive extensive media exposure (Hu & Tang, 2010; Milne & McDonald, 1999).

At a minimum, fans refer to active audiences with more experience, knowledge, and affective attachments to their favorite personalities/ programs than nonfans (Gantz et al., 2006). Abercrombie and Longhurst (1998) noted that fans are "those people who become particularly attached to certain programmes or stars within the context of a relatively heavy media use" (p. 138). Studies found a significant association between the level of fan identification and the level of self-reported emotional reaction one has to the sports content (e.g., Gantz et al., 2006; Hillman, Cuthbert, Bradley, & Lang, 2004; Hillman et al., 2000; Potter, Sparks, Cummins, & Lee, 2004). Researchers suggest that the operational definitions of sports fanship should look beyond self-identification, carving up the concepts to include knowledge about sports, interest in viewing televised sports, and the amount of televised sports viewed (Gantz et al., 2006; Gantz & Wenner, 1995). In other words, when compared to nonfans, fans are those who enjoy viewing televised sports, are knowledgeable about sports, and spend a lot of time seeking sports content on TV and via the Internet (see Gantz & Wenner, 1995). Thus, although studies indicate meaningful differences in the ways fans and nonfans approach TV sports (see Gantz & Wenner, 1995), scholarship has typically focused specifically on the "fan" of a team, a sport, or a specific game rather than broader engagement (or lack thereof) with sports-related content to explain overall behaviors and preferences. Simply put, we have little knowledge of the differences and similarities that might exist between fans and nonfans across the broader spectrum of sports content.

The Olympic Games provide a unique context through which to consider both the sports fan and the nonfan. During its two-plus week run, the Olympics presents a broad array of sports, offers spectacle (e.g., opening and closing ceremonies), stories of personal achievement, and avenues to express national pride. Moreover, Olympic coverage devotes relatively more time to individual sports and personalities than team sports. Because sports are a male preserve (Frank & Greenberg, 1980; Gantz, Wenner, Carrico, & Knorr, 1995), most sports coverage includes the major male-dominant sports (e.g., football, baseball, basketball, and hockey). The Olympics pro- vides exposure to nonmale, individual sports (e.g., tennis, track and field, gymnastics) that receive much less exposure at times other than the Olympics (Dietz-Uhler et al., 2000). The Olympics also prompts sharp structural changes in content and promotion. Rights holders for Olympic telecasts (e.g., NBC in 2008) heavily promote the Olympics before and during the Games and devote most of their programming time toward Olympic coverage, preempting regularly scheduled programming or embedding Olympics content in regular programming (e.g., the show *Today*). Competing networks offer less original content to avoid competing against high ratings expected by Olympic telecasts. These factors would appear to "encourage" both sports fans and nonfans to watch a disproportionate amount of sports during this concentrated period of "big-event" programming. Thus, the Olympics, unlike any other event, generate a broader audience by combining spectacle with concentrated exposure to a variety of heavily promoted sports and personalities.

Uses and Gratifications, Technology Adoption, and Sports Viewing

In addition to the sports viewing literature, a wealth of uses and gratifications and technology adoption studies have provided important insights in understanding audience exposure to sports content and their uses of new technologies (e.g., Gantz & Wenner, 1995; Lin, 2006). Uses and gratifications researchers have identified two orientations toward media use—instrumental use and ritualistic use (Rubin, 1984). Instrumental media use, such as information and entertainment seeking, is generally linked to watching specific program types, especially sports. Ritualistic media use reflects a habitual use with a medium and is less connected to specific types of content (Cooper & Tang, 2009; Katz, Blumler, & Gurevitch, 1974). These orientations imply that sports fans are more likely to specifically seek out this type of content, whereas those less interested in sports would not only watch less sports overall but also partake in sports viewing as a function of habits that develop for a medium. However, instrumental and ritualistic orientations to media use are not exclusive concepts, and individuals appear to use a medium such as television both purposefully *and* out of habit (Cooper & Tang, 2009). Because so much programming time and promotion are devoted to the Olympics throughout the event (with less competition from other networks), both fans and nonfans of sports likely watch the Olympics both purposefully and out of habit.

Studies employing the uses and gratifications approach have also suggested specific motivations for sports viewing. Sloan (1989) identified six reasons for fans to watch sports: sense of belonging, routine, stimulation, relief of tension and aggression, entertainment, and achievement. Wann (1995) demonstrated that positive arousal, self-esteem, escape, entertainment, economic, aesthetic, group affiliation, and family needs were the motivations that people watched sports. Gantz and Wenner (1995) also employed the uses and gratifications framework to examine audience experience with televised sports and found that sports fans watched sports events to follow their favorite teams, relax, and enjoy the uncertainty of sports.

In terms of Internet-based uses and gratifications research, Hong and Raney (2007) found that entertainment, information, and perceived interactivity explained why fans visited sports sites. Farquhar and Meeds (2007) suggested that surveillance and arousal were the primary motives for people to play fantasy sports. In general, social interaction, surveillance, escape, arousal, and entertainment were the most frequently mentioned motivations in uses and gratifications research on sports viewing and new media use. Researchers also suggest that sports fans should share similar motivations for watching sports, regardless of gender. Their motives should be able to explain their attitudes and behaviors toward mediated sports (Gantz & Wenner, 1995; Hu & Tang, 2010).

Technology adoption theories further suggest that perceived usefulness, perceived ease of use, attitude, social norms, and perceived behavior control have an impact on the adoption and actual use of new technologies (e.g., Lederer, Maupin, Sena, & Zhuang, 2000; Porter & Donthus, 2006). Although there is no available work on perceived benefits of online Olympics viewing, it would be useful to review previous new technology adoption studies related to sports. Lam (2001) suggested that people adopt streaming videos because they would like to access national sports highlights. Dupagne (1999) also found that the viewing of sports programs was positively related to HDTV purchase intent. Sandomir (2008) demonstrated that compared to nonfans, sports fans are more likely to adopt new media technologies. End (2001) suggested that social norms and social identity impact sports fans' use of sports teams' websites and message boards.

However, uses of newer and traditional media for sports may not neatly fit a zero sum game, whereby use of one medium or platform simply replaces another. Recent studies seek to provide nuance to the relationship between abundant media choice and structures that might influence these choices. Lin (2006) suggested that the amount of time people spent online significantly predicted webcast viewing interest. Cooper and Tang (2009) found that Internet use was a significant positive predictor of audience exposure to television. When facing an expanded media menu, media users increasingly use two or more media simultaneously, or use one medium to encourage or enhance other media use. In addition, individuals may not be "functionally available" to use all media platforms at all times (Cooper & Tang, 2009). Moreover, because the 2008 Beijing Games was considered to be the first "online Olympics" (Tang & Cooper, 2011), most of the previous Olympic studies have solely focused on television. As the media industry continues to expand Olympic coverage to the Internet and mobile devices, there is clearly a need to determine the interactions between and among sports fanship, viewing of the Olympics, and uses of new media.

This study addresses this gap by (a) examining the differences between sports fans and nonfans watching the Beijing Olympics on various media platforms, (b) providing a profile of both sports fans and nonfans across a range of motivations and behaviors, and (c) analyzing the predictors of Olympics viewing on an NBC broadcast platform and online Olympics viewing for fans and nonfans. In this study, "online Olympics viewing" refers to seeking Olympic content on NBCOlympics.com and other Web sites (e.g., YouTube, Hulu, etc.). Thus, the following research questions are proposed:

RQ1: What are the differences between sports fans and nonfans in watching the Olympics?

RQ2: What factors are significantly related to Olympics viewing on an NBC broadcast platform among sports fans and nonfans?

RQ3: What factors are significantly related to online Olympics viewing among sports fans and nonfans?

METHODOLOGY

Sampling and Procedure

This study examined the similarities and differences between sports fans and nonfans in Olympics viewing by conducting a Web survey at a large Midwestern university. The university's computer network service sent e-mail messages to the university's students, faculty, and staff. The e-mail message included a link to the Web survey and invited recipients to take part in "a study of sports viewing." In all, 458 respondents completed the survey. Among the respondents, 363 watched the Beijing Olympics, whereas 95 did not watch the Games. Respondents that did not watch the 2008 Olympics were not included in the analyses. Independent t tests found no statistically significant differences between Olympics viewers and nonviewers in terms of gender, age, and ethnicity.

Among the 363 respondents who watched the 2008 Olympics, 52.9% (192) were female and 47.1% (171) were male (53.7% female and 46.3% male for those who did *not* watch the Olympics). Overall, 55.9% were students and 44.1% were nonstudent adults. Respondent ages ranged from 18 to

71 with a mean age of 28 ($SD = 13.36$). In terms of ethnicity, 93.1% were Caucasian, 2.2% were African or African American, and 1.9% were Asian or Pacific Islander. Thirty-eight percent of the sample had average household incomes less than $50,000, whereas the remaining 62% had incomes greater than $50,000. In addition, 93.7% of the respondents self reported having access to the Internet at their current residence. Seventy-five percent of them subscribed to cable, and 22% had satellite TV. On average, they could access 126 television channels at an average cost of $49.02. No statistically significant relationships were found between household income and access to technologies.

Measures

Measures used in this study could be clustered into three main categories: sports fanship, Olympics viewing, and sports viewing in general. These measures are detailed next.

Sports fanship. To measure sports media fanship, respondents were first asked to indicate how much they enjoy watching sports programming in general on a 0 to 10 scale (i.e., 0 indicating "do not enjoy watching it at all"; 10 indicating "enjoy watching it a great deal"). In addition, respondents were asked to report respectively the estimated time they spend watching sports news on television and following sports news on the Web on a typical day. Based on previous research, sports fans were operationally defined as the respondents who scored 8 or above on the enjoyment scale, and spent at least 1 hour a day watching sports news on television and at least 1 hour following sports news online (see Gantz et al., 2006). As such, among the 363 respondents in this study, 199 (54.8%) were sports fans, and 164 (45.2%) were nonfans. Among 171 men that responded to the survey, 114 (66.7%) were considered "fans," whereas 85 of the 192 female respondents (44.3%) were considered "fans" ($\chi^2 = 18.32$, $p < .001$). This operationalized distinction between fans and nonfans was used to test the differences among Olympics viewers for the measures described next.

Olympics viewing. Respondents were asked whether they watched the Beijing Olympic Games. Respondents who watched the Games were subsequently asked to report the estimated number of hours/minutes that they spent on the following activities on a typical day during the Games: watching the Olympics on an NBC broadcast platform, watching the Olympics on cable channels (e.g., MSNBC, USA, etc.), and watching the Olympics on NBCOlympics.com and other websites (e.g., YouTube, Hulu, etc.).

Participant responses to each of these activities were summed to create a measure of total time spent viewing the Olympics on various platforms.

In addition, preference for various Olympic sports was measured with a 7-point scale, from 1 (*do not enjoy watching it at all*) to 7 (*enjoy watching it a great deal*). Respondents were asked to indicate how much they enjoy watching each of 28 sports[1] on television. These sports were the 28 summer sports currently on the Olympic program (http://en.beijing2008.cn). Respondents also rated the quality, variety, and timeliness of NBC's telecast on the 2008 Beijing Games respectively on a 7-point scale with a range from *extremely unsatisfied* to *extremely satisfied*.

Perceived benefits of online Olympics viewing were measured with eight Likert-type items[2] drawn from previous technology adoption research (Lederer et al., 2000; Lin, 2006). The Cronbach's alpha coefficient for the perceived benefits of online Olympics viewing was .895 ($M = 2.52$, $SD = 1.36$). Furthermore, on a 5-point scale from 1 (*very negative*) to 5 (*very positive*), respondents were asked to identify their general attitude toward online Olympics viewing.

Sports viewing. A 7-point Likert scale was employed to measure motivations for sports viewing. Respondents were asked to rate each of the 10 statements[3] according to their level of agreement, ranging 1 (*strongly disagree*) to 7 (*strongly agree*). All the statements were drawn from previous sports fanship studies (Gantz et al., 2006; Wann, 1995). The Cronbach's alpha coefficient for motivations for sports viewing was .909 ($M = 4.03$, $SD = 1.39$).

---

[1]The 28 sports types used in this study were archery, badminton, baseball, basketball, beach volleyball, boxing, cycling, diving, equestrian, fencing, field hockey, gymnastics, judo, mountain biking, rowing, sailing, shooting, soccer, softball, swimming, synchronized swimming, table tennis, tennis, track and field, volleyball, water polo, weightlifting, and wrestling.

[2]The eight statements used to measure perceived benefits of online Olympics viewing were "I watched the Olympics on the Web because it was more convenient"; "because it provided a wide variety of programming"; "because it was a quicker way to get information"; "because it fit my schedule better"; "because it enhanced the quality of the Olympics coverage"; and "because it brought me more entertainment"; "It was easy for me to figure out how to watch the Olympics on the web"; and "It was too much trouble when watching the Olympics on the web (reversed)."

[3]The 10 statements used to measure motivations for sports viewing were: "I watch sports to see who does well/who wins"; "because I care about the players or teams"; "to follow a specific player or team"; "because I like the unpredictability of the shows/games"; "to put aside responsibilities, including studying, for a while"; "because I don't want to miss a thing on the show or game"; "to relieve stress and escape from pressures of the day"; "to feel connected with the players or teams"; "to be in the know"; and "to add some excitement to my life."

A 7-point Likert scale was also employed to measure concomitant behaviors and postviewing behaviors. Respondents were asked to rate each of the five concomitant behavior statements (e.g., "When watching sports, I feel happy if my favorite player or team does well.")[4] ($\alpha = .808$; $M = 4.85$, $SD = 1.57$). In addition, participants responded to each of the five postviewing behavior statements (e.g., "After watching sports, I will watch more about it on TV.")[5] ($\alpha = .907$; $M = 4.10$, $SD = 1.69$). All statements were drawn from previous sports fanship literature (Gantz et al., 2006; Gantz & Wesson, 1991).

Moreover, on a 7-point scale from 1 (*do not enjoy watching it at all*) to 7 (*enjoy watching it a great deal*), respondents indicated how much they enjoy watching televised live sporting events and watching recorded sporting events, respectively. They also reported the estimated time they spend on watching sporting events/games on television and watching/listening to sports events/games on the Web on a typical day.

Finally, respondents were asked to report their general media use, including the estimated number of hours/minutes on a typical day that they use the Internet, watch live television, and watch television on the Web. They also provided demographic variables, including age, gender, ethnicity, and household income.

Data Screening and Analysis

Independent t tests were used to examine the differences between sports fans and nonfans in Olympics viewing. Stepwise multiple regression analyses were conducted to analyze the predictors of Olympics viewing on an NBC broadcast platform and online Olympics viewing for sports fans and nonfans, respectively.

RESULTS

The 363 respondents reported spending a total of 3 hours 45 minutes on an average day watching the Beijing Olympics on various media platforms. Specifically, they watched the Olympics on an NBC broadcast platform

---

[4]The five statements used to measure concomitant behaviors were "When watching sports, I feel happy if my favorite player or team does well"; "I feel sad or depressed if my favorite player or team does poorly"; "I yell out at the players, teams, or action"; "I hope (or pray) for an outcome I want"; and "I talk with others about the show/game."

[5]The five statements used to measure postviewing behaviors were "After watching sports, I will watch more about it on TV"; "I will stay in a good mood for a while if my favorite player or team did well"; "I will read about the players, teams, or games in the newspaper"; "I will talk with my friends about it"; and "I will check the Web to read more about it."

for 2 hours 32 minutes a day, spent about 57 minutes watching the Olympics on cable channels (e.g., MSNBC, USA, etc.), and 15 minutes (range = 0–3 hours 15 minutes a day) watching the Games on NBCOlympics.com and other websites. Overall, 92 respondents (25.3%) watched the Olympics on the web, and these web Olympics users spent 1 hour 2 minutes a day watching the Games online during the 2008 Beijing Olympics.

Results indicate that sports fans and nonfans spent a significantly different amount of total time watching the 2008 Beijing Olympics through different media. Overall, sports fans spent 4 hours 22 minutes, whereas nonfans spent 3 hours watching the Games on various media platforms ($t = 4.69$, $p < .001$; see Table 1). In addition, sports fans spent significantly more time watching the Olympics on an NBC broadcast platform ($t = 3.91$, $p < .001$) and on cable channels than nonfans ($t = 4.25$, $p < .001$). However, there was no significant difference in online Olympics viewing ($t = 1.37$, $p = .172$). Sports fans and nonfans spent a similar amount of time watching the Beijing Games on NBCOlympics.com and other websites.

Consistent with the previous sports fanship literature, this study found several significant differences between sports fans and nonfans in general sports viewing as shown in Table 2. Compared to nonfans, sports fans spent significantly more time watching sporting events on television ($t = 9.96$, $p < .001$) and following sporting events on the web ($t = 3.92$, $p < .001$). Significant differences were also found between sports fans and nonfans in postviewing behaviors ($t = 14.91$, $p < .001$), preference for watching live sporting events ($t = 13.63$, $p < .001$), motivations for sports viewing ($t = 13.03$, $p < .001$), concomitant behaviors ($t = 10.66$, $p < .001$), and preference for recorded sporting events ($t = 7.61$, p .001). Nonfans were significantly older ($t = -3.61$, $p < .001$) and more likely to be female ($t = -4.40$, $p < .001$) than fans. However, fewer differences were found in factors related

TABLE 1
Differences in Olympic Viewing During the Beijing Games Between Sports Fans and Nonfans

Variables	Fans M (SD)	Nonfans M (SD)	t
Total time spent watching the Olympics on various platforms	261.9 (180)	179.5 (149)	4.69***
Time spent watching the Olympics on cable channels	72.4 (65)	39.0 (31)	4.25***
Time spent watching the Olympics on an NBC broadcast platform	171.2 (110)	127.7 (100)	3.91***
Time spent watching the Olympics on the Web	18.3 (9)	12.8 (8)	1.37

Note. $N = 363$ (199 fans; 164 nonfans). Means are reported in minutes spent watching.
***$p \leq .001$.

TABLE 2
Profile of Sports Fans and Nonfans

Variables	Fans M (SD)	Nonfans M (SD)	t
Postviewing behaviors	5.0 (1.3)	3.0 (1.4)	14.91***
Preference for live sporting events	6.7 (.6)	4.6 (2.0)	13.63***
Motivations for sports viewing	4.8 (1.0)	3.2 (1.3)	13.03***
Concomitant behaviors	5.6 (1.2)	4.0 (1.6)	10.66***
Watch sporting events on TV	143.1 (103)	51.6 (51)	9.96***
Preference for recorded sporting events	4.2 (1.8)	2.8 (1.8)	7.61***
Time spent watching TV in general	196.4 (122)	135.7 (114)	4.81***
Gender	1.4 (.5)	1.7 (.5)	−4.40***
Watch sporting events on the Web	16.6 (11)	4.2 (3.9)	3.92***
Age	30.3 (13)	35.5 (14)	−3.61***
Preference for various Olympic sports	73.1 (25)	64.4 (24)	3.40***
Quality of NBC's Olympic telecast	5.7 (1.2)	5.3 (1.4)	3.13**
Overall use of the Internet	216.2 (147)	249.7 (197)	−1.80
Variety of NBC's Olympic telecast	5.0 (1.5)	4.7 (1.6)	1.78
Timeliness of NBC's Olympic telecast	5.1 (1.6)	5.0 (1.5)	1.01
Perceived benefits of online Olympics viewing	2.6 (1.4)	2.4 (1.4)	1.01
Attitude towards online Olympics viewing	2.9 (.9)	2.9 (.9)	.14

Note. $N = 363$ (199 fans; 164 nonfans). Scales for which means are reported can be referenced in the methods section of the article.
$**p \leq .01$. $***p \leq .001$.

to Olympics viewing between sports fans and nonfans. For example, sports fans and nonfans had similar ratings on the variety ($t = 1.78$, $p = .077$) and timeliness of NBC's Olympic telecast ($t = 1.01$, $p = .314$). In addition, there were no significant differences in perceived benefits of online Olympics viewing ($t = 1.01$, $p = .313$) and attitude toward online Olympics viewing ($t = .14$, $p = .887$), although sports fans and nonfans were different in their rating on quality of NBC's Olympic telecast ($t = 3.13$, $p = .002$) and their preferences for various Olympic sports ($t = 3.40$, $p = .001$).

Stepwise multiple regression analyses were conducted to examine the factors that predicted time spent watching the Beijing Olympics on an NBC broadcast platform for sports fans and nonfans, respectively. For sports fans, four factors—time spent watching television in general, preference for various Olympic sports, variety of NBC's Olympic telecast, and time spent watching sporting events on television—significantly predicted time spent watching the Beijing Olympics on NBC. Together, these four variables explained 28.9% of the variance in sports fans' Olympics viewing on an NBC broadcast platform ($p < .001$). Table 3 indicates the partial correlations for each variable, plus the explanatory value for a variable when all other

TABLE 3
Significant Factors That Explain Watching the Beijing Olympics on an
NBC Broadcast Platform for Sports Fans

Predictors	Partial correlation	β	All variables controlled R^2	Sig. F change
Time spent watching TV in general	.319***	.327***	.080***	.000
Preference for various Olympic sports	.248***	.217***	.047***	.001
Variety of NBC's Olympic telecast	.241***	.211***	.044***	.001
Time spent watching sporting events on TV	.176*	.173*	.023*	.018

Note. $R^2 = .289$. Adjusted $R^2 = .273$, $p < .001$.
*$p \leq .05$. ***$p \leq .001$.

variables were controlled. Time spent watching television in general provided a unique explanation of 8% when all other variables were controlled. Preference for various Olympic sports added 4.7%, variety of NBC's Olympic telecast 4.4%, and time spent watching sporting events on television provided another 2.3% of unique explanation when all other variables were controlled.

For nonfans, three factors significantly predicted time they spent watching the Beijing Games on an NBC broadcast platform. Similar to sports fans, time spent watching television in general was the strongest predictor, which provided a unique explanation of 10.2% when all other variables were controlled. Quality of NBC's Olympic telecast added 6.7%, whereas preference for various Olympic sports provided 6.1% of unique explanation when all other variables were controlled. Altogether, these three variables explained 26.9% of the variance in nonfans' Olympics viewing on an NBC broadcast platform ($p < .001$; see Table 4).

Finally, this study used stepwise multiple regression to examine online Olympics viewing for both sports fans and nonfans. For sports fans, four

TABLE 4
Significant Factors That Explain Watching the Beijing Olympics on an
NBC Broadcast Platform for Nonfans

Predictors	Partial correlation	β	All variables controlled R^2	Sig. F change
Time spent watching TV in general	.351***	.324***	.102***	.000
Quality of NBC's Olympic telecast	.290***	.268***	.067***	.000
Preference for various Olympic sports	.276***	.255***	.061***	.001

Note. $R^2 = .269$. Adjusted $R^2 = .254$, $p < .001$.
***$p \leq .001$.

TABLE 5
Significant Factors that Explain Online Olympics Viewing for Sports Fans

Predictors	Partial correlation	β	All variables controlled R^2	Sig. F change
Perceived benefits of online Olympics viewing	.365***	.329***	.104***	.000
Time spent watching TV on the Web	.299***	.268***	.066***	.000
Preference for various Olympic sports	.266***	.230***	.051***	.000
Time spent using the Internet	.156*	.135*	.017*	.036

Note. $R^2 = .329$. Adjusted $R^2 = .314$, $p < .001$.
*$p \leq .05$. ***$p \leq .001$.

factors—perceived benefits of online Olympic viewing, time spent watching television on the Web, preference for various Olympic sports, and time spent using the Internet—were significant predictors of watching the Beijing Olympics online (see Table 5). Together, these four variables explained 32.9% of the variance in fans' online Olympics viewing ($p < .001$). As the model indicates, perceived benefits of online Olympics viewing provided a unique explanation of 10.4% when all other variables were controlled. Time spent watching television on the Web added 6.6%, preference for various Olympic sports 5.1%, and time spent using the Internet provided 1.7% of unique explanation when all other variables were controlled.

For nonfans, five factors significantly predicted their online Olympics viewing. Time spent watching television online was the strongest predictor, providing 11.2% of unique explanation when all other variables were controlled, followed by perceived benefits of online Olympics viewing (which added 8.6% of unique explanation), time spent using the Internet (4.2%), age (3.4%), and preference for recorded sporting events (3.2%). Together,

TABLE 6
Significant Factors That Explain Online Olympics Viewing for Nonfans

Predictors	Partial correlation	β	All variables controlled R^2	Sig. F change
Time spent watching TV on the Web	.387***	.353***	.112***	.000
Perceived benefits of online Olympics viewing	.344***	.307***	.086***	.000
Time spent using the Internet	.247**	.208**	.042**	.003
Age	.223**	.192**	.034**	.007
Preference for recorded sporting events	.218**	.181**	.032**	.009

Note. $R^2 = .360$. Adjusted $R^2 = .338$, $p < .001$.
**$p \leq .01$. ***$p \leq .001$.

these factors explained 36.0% of the variance in time spent watching the Beijing Olympics online for nonfans ($p < .001$; see Table 6).

DISCUSSION

This study's focus on fans and nonfans in the context of the Olympic Games provides a unique lens through which to examine broader engagement with sports content through both traditional and newer media. Most studies have focused on the "fan" of a team, sport, or specific game/event while not fully considering what might influence sports media uses among both fans and those less typically engaged with sports content. Results indicate that respondents identified as sports "fans" were quite different in their overall behaviors, motivations, and preferences for mediated sports than were "nonfans." Sports fans also watched the 2008 Beijing Olympics significantly more than non–sports fans. However, uses of online sources for Olympic content were very similar between fans and nonfans, and fewer differences existed between fans and nonfans with respect to assessments of Olympic telecasts. Explanations for why fans and nonfans watched the Olympics on traditional broadcast or via newer online platforms were notably similar between the two groups.

As a worldwide event that transcends sports, the Olympics attract both sports fans and non-sports fans. As Billings, Angelini, and Duke (2010) demonstrated, "At the Olympics, national flags trump all other forms of identity" (p. 9). The Olympics also seems to transcend many differences that exist between sports fans and nonfans through its sheer spectacle and relevance, its focus on individuals and personalities, its ubiquitous presence, its broad range of competitions (e.g., rowing, gymnastics, track and field, cycling), and its relative deemphasis on the Big Four U.S. team sports that may drive concepts of "sports fandom." Preference for various Olympic sports was a common significant predictor among both fans and nonfans. However, among sports fans, the variety of NBC's Olympic telecast and overall time spent watching sports events on television were also significant predictors, whereas respondent ratings for the quality of NBC's Olympic telecast significantly predicted viewing for nonfans. Being a "nonfan" did not imply that she or he does not like sports but rather that the respondent does not self-identify as a sports fan and does not exhibit behaviors under the operational definition. This is underscored by the stated purpose of the survey, which sought individuals for a "study of sports viewing." Nearly half (45%) of respondents that completed the survey on "sports viewing" were operationally defined as "nonfans." Although this study offers clear distinctions between the fan and nonfan in terms of behaviors, motivations, and preferences, it is clear that many nonfans also like sports and are perhaps more motivated to watch the variety of sports offered through the Olympics. Fans benefit to an even greater degree because they have opportunity to use both traditional and online sources to access a variety of sports.

These findings highlight the dynamic interplay between choice, habit, and structure in newer media environments. Theoretical conceptualizations of the sports viewer as "active" in choice or "instrumental" in orientation would seem to hold true for specific teams and sports and would certainly seem to play a role in watching the 2008 Olympics. For example, the perceived benefits of viewing online (e.g., wider range of sports, anytime/ anywhere access, viewing live sports not available on Olympic broadcasts) were significantly related to watching the Olympics online for both fans and nonfans. Likewise, preferences for various Olympic sports were significantly related to viewing on NBC for both fans and nonfans. This indicates that more media users have greater access to content when, where, and how they want it and are more likely—at least more of the time—to select content rather than the medium that delivers it.

However, habit also appears to play a key role in exposure to Olympic content. For both sports fans and nonfans, the time spent watching TV in general was most strongly related to watching the Olympics on NBC, and time spent watching TV on the Web also explained Olympic viewing on the Web. This suggests that individuals already in the "general mode" of watching video content on television and the Web were more likely to watch more Olympic content. Likewise, structural influences appear to play a role in exposure to Olympic content. NBC structured its schedule and promotion toward this big-event programming. The massive amount of content and promotion of the Olympics by NBC "funneled" viewers to the Olympics. Although nonfans did not watch the Olympics as much as sports fans, they nevertheless watched an average of 3 hours each day, including more than 2 hours a day on a traditional broadcast network. Competing networks "aided" NBC by scheduling less first-run programming to compete against this high-profile event. Moreover, Olympic viewing remained governed, if to a lesser degree than before, by availability and access to Olympic content because viewers cannot access all content at any point of any day (e.g., work, sleep, lack of access to media), even for a 2-week event like the Olympics. Thus, structural factors continue to play a role in media choice among all viewers.

Cooper and Tang (2009) conceptualized today's media user as "active within structures." This perspective highlights the role of active choice in convergent media environments while also acknowledging the continuing influences of habit and structure. Under this conceptualization, media uses and choices are both active *and* passive because converging media serve a variety of needs within/across communication processes. As Cooper and Tang proposed,

> With hundreds of television channels and millions of websites currently available to many media users, individuals may even *seek structure* as a way to deal with the vast multitude of content and media options available. This may be manifest in decisions to pay for one type of content or delivery system over another, or to self-impose limits on media use. Thus, structure should not be viewed as a "passive" characteristic of media use, but rather as one of several valid influences on media use. (p. 416)

The results of this study reinforce the need for both uses and gratifications and media choice theories to put both individual cognitive and media structural factors into consideration when explaining media choice and use in convergent environments.

The Olympics also provides an interesting venue for analyses of online viewing, because the unique nature of the Olympic Games itself changes sports media habits among fans and nonfans. Those who watched the Olympics online did so because of their overall use of the Internet and being in the mode of watching television online but also perceived strong benefits for watching the Olympics online. This would seem to indicate that the "anytime" access of content is appealing to online viewers, and sports fans further gravitated to online content because of preference for a variety of Olympic sports. As more viewers become accustomed to watching content online, especially younger users (age was significantly related to online viewing among nonfans), content providers have an opportunity to offer a wide variety of sports content to both the fan and nonfan. For example, NBC could show a greater range of sports online, including competitions leading up to the Olympics (or in non-Olympic years) to drive traffic online and to get more people in the mode to use online platforms to access the Olympics and other sports content. This will further encourage viewers to watch the Olympics across platforms. As people use online platforms more, media outlets can direct them online or to broadcast thus enhancing the value of each. The Internet provides a relatively inexpensive means to "sell" less traditional sports for media consumption, thereby broadening its potential audience and engaging those classified as the "nonfan" when the Olympics are not shown. In this way, the Olympics offers insight for media outlets to align themselves more effectively with users more likely to access certain types of content on preferred platforms.

This study was based on self-reports using a Web survey, which cannot provide precise information beyond correlations. Future Olympics research should attempt to gain more in-depth insights into the causal relation between Olympic content and audience experience. For example, select open-ended questions for sports fans and nonfans will yield greater nuance and understanding about the similarities and differences between these two groups. It is conceivable, for example, that sports fans are relatively less involved in Olympic sporting events than other team sports (or their favorite teams), whereas nonfans are relatively more engaged because of the "big-event status" of the Olympics, the wider variety of sports offered, and greater focus on personalities and personal stories. This study does not answer this question specifically, and future research should include experimental designs that allow greater statistical sophistication to address these issues.

Despite the limitations, this study demonstrates commonalities and differences that highlight why and how sports fans and nonfans seek Olympic content across media platforms. Simply put, both fans and nonfans gravitated to various sources (both traditional and newer) for the Beijing Games. The Olympics is less of a "sporting" event and more of a large media and societal event. In addition, since the 2008 Beijing Olympics, the media industry has brought smart phones, tablets, and other mobile devices to carry big sporting events. Large increases in use of the web and mobile devices for Olympics viewing are expected for the 2012 London Games. As sports communication continues to undergo dramatic changes, scholars need to increasingly consider sports fanship, content, and effects across media forms rather than to isolate concepts to a single medium. This study expands our theoretical understanding of fanship, new media, and big-event sports viewing while encouraging future inquiry.

REFERENCES

Abercrombie, N., & Longhurst, B. (1998). *Audiences: A sociological theory of performance and imagination*. London, UK: Sage.

Billings, A. C., & Angelini, J. R. (2007). Packing the games for viewer consumption: Gender, ethnicity, and nationality in NBC's coverage of the 2004 summer Olympics. *Communication Quarterly*, *55*, 95–111.

Billings, A. C., Angelini, J. R., & Duke, A. H. (2010). Gendered profiles of Olympic history: Sportscaster dialogue in the 2008 Beijing Olympics. *Journal of Broadcasting & Electronic Media*, *54*, 9–23.

Cooper, J. (2008). Let the Web games begin. *MediaWeek*, *18*(28), 12.

Cooper, R., & Tang, T. (2009). Predicting audience exposure to television in today's media environment: An empirical integration of active-audience and structural theories. *Journal of Broadcasting & Electronic Media*, *53*, 400–418.

Dietz-Uhler, B., Harrick, E. A., End, C., & Jacquemotte, L. (2000). Sex difference in sport fan behavior and reasons for being a sport fan. *Journal of Sport Behavior*, *23*, 219–231.

Dupagne, M. (1999). Exploring the characteristics of potential high-definition television adopters. *Journal of Media Economics*, *12*, 35–50.

Eastman, S. T., & Land, A. (1997). The best of both worlds: Sport fans find good seats at the bar. *Journal of Sport and Social Issues, 21*, 156–178.

End, C. M. (2001). An examination of NFL fans' computer mediated BIRGing. *Journal of Sports Behavior, 24*, 162–182.

Farquhar, L. K., & Meeds, R. (2007). Types of fantasy sports users and their motivations. *Journal of Computer-Mediated Communication, 12*, 1208–1228.

Frank, R. E., & Greenberg, M. G. (1980). *The public's use of television.* Beverly Hills, CA: Sage.

Gantz, W., Wang, Z., Paul, B., & Potter, R. F. (2006). Sports versus all comers: Comparing TV sports fans with fans of other programming genres. *Journal of Broadcasting & Electronic Media, 50*, 95–118.

Gantz, W., & Wenner, L. A. (1991). Men, women, and sports: Audience experiences and effects. *Journal of Broadcasting & Electronic Media, 35*, 233–243.

Gantz, W., & Wenner, L. A. (1995). Fanship and the television sports viewing experience. *Sociology of Sports Journal, 12*, 56–74.

Gantz, W., Wenner, L. A., Carrico, C., & Knorr, M. (1995). Televised sports and marital relationship. *Sociology of Sports Journal, 12*, 306–323.

Hiestand, M. (2008, August 25). NBC scores mixed bag of pros, cons. *USA Today*, 3C.

Hillman, C. H., Cuthbert, B. N., Bradley, M. M., & Lang, P. J. (2004). Motivated engagement to appetitive and aversive fanship cues: Psychophysiological responses of rival sport fans. *Journal of Sport Exercise Psychology, 26*, 338–351.

Hillman, C. H., Cuthbert, B. N., Cauraugh, J., Schupp, H. T., Bradley, M. M., & Lang, P. J. (2000). Psychophysiological responses of sports fans. *Motivation and Emotion, 24*, 13–28.

Hong, M., & Raney, A. (2007, November). *Online sports fans' motive research: Does interactivity lead motives or follow them.* Paper presented at the 2007 National Communication Association Annual Convention, Chicago, IL.

Hu, A. W., & Tang, L. (2010). Factors motivating sports broadcast viewership with fan identification as a mediator. *Social Behavior and Personality, 38*, 681–690.

Katz, E., Blumler, J. G., & Gurevitch, M. (1974). Utilization of mass communication by the individual. In J. G. Blumler & E. Katz (Eds.), *The uses of mass communication: Current perspectives on gratifications research* (pp. 19–32). Beverly Hill, CA: Sage.

Lam, K. (2001). Stream dreams: Broadband and rich media may force TV to take a backseat. *American Demographics, 1*, 12–14.

Lederer, A. L., Maupin, D. J., Sena, M. P., & Zhuang, Y. (2000). The technology acceptance model and the World Wide Web. *Decision Support Systems, 29*, 269–282.

Lin, C. A. (2006). Technology fluidity and on-demand webcasting adoption. *Telematics & Informatics, 25*, 84–98.

Milne, G. R., & McDonald, M. A. (1999). *Sport marketing: Managing the exchange process.* Sudbury, MA: Jones and Bartlett.

Nielsen. (2008). *Beijing Olympics draw largest ever global TV audience.* Retrieved from http://blog.nielsen.com/nielsenwire/media entertainment/beigjing-olympics-draw-largest-ever-global-tv-audience/

Porter, C. E., & Donthus, N. (2006). Using the technology acceptance model to explain how attitudes determine Internet usage: The role of perceived access barriers and demographics. *Journal of Business Research, 59*, 999–1007.

Potter, R. F., Sparks, J. V., Cummins, R. G., & Lee, S. (2004). "I bleed Crimson!": The impact of fan identification level on viewers' attention and emotional response during sports news. *Psychophysiology, 41*(51), 62.

Rubin, A. M. (1984). Ritualized and instrumental television viewing. *Journal of Communication, 34*, 67–77.

Sandomir, R. (2008, August 18). New web site aims to be Facebook for sports fans. *The New York Times*, 4.

Sloan, L. R. (1989). The motives of sports fans. In J. H. Goldstein (Ed.), *Sports, games, and play: Social and psychological viewpoints* 2nd ed., (pp. 175–240). Hillsdale, NJ: Erlbaum.

Steinberg, B. (2008). NBC tracks Olympic viewers wherever they're watching. *Advertising Age*, 79(32), 3–21.

Tang, T., & Cooper, R. (2011). The first online Olympics: The interactions between Internet use and sports viewing. *Journal of Sports Media*, 6, 1–22.

Wann, D. L. (1995). Preliminary validation of the sport fan motivation scale. *Journal of Sport and Social Issues*, 19, 377–396.

The Expediency of Hybridity: Beijing 2008

Robert Moses Peaslee
College of Mass Communications
Texas Tech University

Shu-Ling Chen Berggreen
Department of Journalism and Mass Communication
University of Colorado

In this article, we examine the Opening Ceremonies of the Beijing Olympiad as an opportunity for the Chinese government to "speak" using a highly expedient discourse of hybridity (Pieterse, 2004). Moreover, we ask how Beijing 2008 may be representative of a larger trend whereby Olympic events serve to chill free speech. We suggest that it is important to see how the apolitical discourse adopted by the International Olympic Committee and its corporate partners can serve to minimize conflicts for the sake of entertainment value. Building on previous work engaging the Chinese television show *Super Girl* (Peaslee, Berggreen, & Kwak, 2010), in which the authors suggested that the show's disruption of gender conservatism (hybridity) was "expedient," we apply the same theoretical construct to the 2008 Opening Ceremonies, where overt political control and abnegation of personal and press freedoms are obscured by a celebration of Sino-Olympic diversity. Using discourse and textual analysis, we examine the discursive context within China prior to the

Games, the artistic program, and the cultural-linguistic packaging of that program by the American broadcaster NBC. We suggest that engaging these texts in close proximity allows the clearest view of the problematic relationship between states, artists, and corporations that background any Olympiad.

INTRODUCTION

Relations of power and hegemony are inscribed and reproduced *within* hybridity, for wherever we look closely enough we find the traces of asymmetry in culture, place, descent. Hence, hybridity raises the question of the *terms* of mixture, the conditions of mixing. At the same time, it's important to note the ways in which hegemony is not merely reproduced but *refigured* in the process of hybridization. (Pieterse, 2004, p. 74)

Jacques deLisle (2008) pointed out that the biennial spectacle that is the Olympiad provides occasion for diverse discourses of humanity, globality, and nationhood to be played out against the backdrop of a "semiotic battleground," and recent Olympic history has given us no better example of this than the 2008 Beijing Games. Focusing on Beijing in the run-up to the games, deLisle positioned the pre-Olympic cleanup of the city (in aesthetic and socioeconomic terms) as a dimension of the Chinese government's desire to promote the city as a modern metropole (navigable, beautiful, functional). At the same time, however, deLisle suggested that this story of Beijing is couched squarely in context of a robust Chinese nationalism. DeLisle captured quite succinctly the Janus-faced nature of China's approach to the Games: the paradoxical duality of being both traditionally, explicitly Chinese and (post)modernly, openly global. In this article, we examine the Opening Ceremonies of the Beijing Olympiad as an opportunity for the Chinese government to "speak" more or less directly to a global community of television viewers using a highly expedient discourse of hybridity (Pieterse, 2004), a term used in both popular and academic parlance to describe the changes, challenges, and opportunities presented by "globalization." This article analyzes the deployment of this term (and its variants) as a framing device and attempts to deconstruct, through discourse analysis, the packaging of China as, rather than an autocratic state, a modern society engaged in a productive process of change. Moreover, we ask how Beijing 2008 may be representative of larger trend whereby Olympic events serve to chill free speech. Although it is crucial to understand what the Olympiad is being mobilized to represent on behalf of the host country, we suggest that it is equally important is to see how the apolitical discourse adopted by the International Olympic Committee (IOC) and its corporate partners can serve to quell protest, sanctify inaction, and minimize conflicts for the sake of entertainment value.

THE EXPEDIENCY OF HYBRIDITY

In *The Expediency of Culture*, George Yúdice (2003) suggested that

> a key premise of modernity is that tradition (safeguarded in the domestic sphere) is eroded by the constant changes of industrialization, new divisions of labor, and concomitant effects such as migration and consumer capitalism. ...Disorganized capitalism thrives on this erosion, assisted by new technologies that enable, for example, time compression in financial markets, the internationalization of advanced producer services, the dissemination of risk, greater mobility of people, commodities, sounds, and images, the proliferation of styles, and...a new international division of cultural labor. Both these changes and the attempts to recuperate tradition feed the system. *Consequently, the failure to repeat normative behavior as the constitutive feature of subversive performativity may actually enhance the system rather than threaten it. The system feeds off of "disorder."* [emphasis added] (p. 33)

Culture, Yúdice offered, is increasingly used as a resource in managing systems of power through the "expediency" of its apparently oppositional quality, "such that management, conservation, access, distribution, and investment—in 'culture' and the outcomes thereof—take priority" (p. 1). In such cases, "culture" is made to perform any number of tasks for which states are decreasingly equipped or predisposed. Thus, the emancipatory dialogue of diversity is often confederate in obscuring social inequality even as the forms of which it is composed react to disempowerment. Culture, as a concept and as a collection of practices, thus becomes expedient. Pieterse (2004), meanwhile, theorized the concept of "hybridity" in the context of previous work on globalization, problematizing earlier correlations of the latter with modernity and homogenization (pp. 59–64). Building on the work of Robertson (1995) and joining him in seeing globalization (or "globality") as a much older historical phenomenon, and utilizing Appadurai's (1990) notion of "scapes" to aid his construction of "structural hybridization" as an analytic, Pieterse asks us to consider the complexity and increased empirical richness afforded by careful attention to "global mélange." The latter is characterized by other regionalized terms for difference (creolization, mestizage, orientalization) mindful of the multidirectionality or counterflow of influence. Such formulations present welcome palliatives to the overdetermined power relationships assumed by preceding approaches following a cultural imperialism paradigm. Pieterse was careful to point out, however, that mélange as a term and as an empirical strategy is incomplete without careful attention to "the actual unevenness, asymmetry, and inequality in global relations" (p. 71). "What," Pieterse asked, "is the political portée of the celebration of hybridity?" (p. 72). It is strange, then, that Pieterse concluded his development of hybridity as a theoretical concept without considering how the appearance of hybridity could be mobilized. "Hybridity," he suggested,

> unsettles the introverted concept of culture that underlies romantic nationalism, racism, ethnicism, religious revivalism, civilizational chauvinism, and cultural essentialism. Hybridization, then, is a perspective that is meaningful as a counterweight to introverted notions of culture; at the same time, the very process of hybridization unsettles the introverted gaze, and accordingly, hybridization eventually ushers in post-hybridity, or transcultural cut-and-paste. (pp. 82–83)

It is unclear exactly what Pieterse meant to suggest by "post-hybridity"; who, exactly, is cutting and pasting here? What if the introverted gaze and external impression are overtly controlled, thereby utilizing hybridity as a tool to destabilize the rather assumed "ushering in" of difference (at least as difference is relative to power relations)? This is a question relevant to Wang (2008), who built on the work of Pieterse (2004) and Kraidy (2005) and recuperated a critical space within which to examine the notion of media hybridity. She suggested that "investigating the real face and influence of media hybridity is crucial because it can help us better understand the actual process that generates cultural globalization, as well as the process that produces hegemonic cultural relations" (p. 47).

Our contention, following Wang, is that "hybridity" is a concept as expedient for power-holders as is "culture" in Yúdice's writings. Building on previous work engaging the performative space of the Chinese television show *Super Girl* (Peaslee, Berggreen, & Kwak, 2010), we apply the "expediency of hybridity" lens to the Opening Ceremonies of the Beijing Games and, using discourse and textual analysis, examine the discursive context within China in the run-up to the 2008 Games, the artistic program executed by the Beijing Organizing Committee for the Games of the XXIX-Olympiad (BOCOG), and the cultural-linguistic packaging of that text by the American broadcaster NBC. We suggest that engaging these three texts in close proximity, and that doing so particularly in the case of Beijing 2008, allows the clearest view of the problematic relationship between states, artists and corporations that background any Olympiad.

BEIJING 2008 AS DISCURSIVE ENVIRONMENT

The Beijing Olympiad is not unique in its status as a particularly fecund political arena. New Zealand's rugby tour of South Africa and subsequent participation in the 1976 Montreal games led many countries to sit out in protest. Cold War tensions, of course, led to boycotts by the United States, among others (Moscow, 1980), and the Soviet Union (Los Angeles, 1984). That an explicitly authoritarian state played host to the Games amidst controversy is therefore not without precedent, but what is perhaps most notable in the 2008 case is the *lack* of boycotts.

Our interest here is in the Games not so much within the context of other Olympic events but rather against the backdrop of China's general ascendancy in the 21st century. In this context, the lack of boycotts is highly significant; with preceding Olympic boycotts, a hegemonic discourse operative at either a national or international level allowed for direct action to be taken, while either the lack of power on the part of the "offender" (New Zealand) or the political-economic inapproachability of the offender in any case (the United States or USSR, depending on one's positionality vis-à-vis the "Iron Curtain") assured limited consequences and attendant benefits for boycotters. That China was and remains simultaneously a major player in the world economy, a patron for many client states internationally, *and* an autocratic state necessitated in 2008 a discourse that would allow nations politically opposed to autocracy and censorship an avenue for saving face among their constituents (specifically because a boycott was presumably deemed politically and economically *inexpedient*).[1] There is in this case an opportunity to examine the 2008 Games as both a dimension and outcome of China's attempt to appear hybridized: both ancient and contemporary, both East and West, both closed and open.[2]

In this sense, Beijing 2008 can be seen as the most recent in a long line of Asian Olympics that have attempted to capitalize on such dualities (Collins, 2008), and China's success in doing so, even before the Games were under way, is a prominent feature of understanding the importance of the Opening Ceremonies. Narrating the video package he produced as a contributor to

---

[1]Quite on the contrary, then U.S. president George W. Bush attended the opening ceremonies, making him, according to NBC commentator Bob Costas, the first sitting U.S. head of state to attend an Olympics outside the borders of his home country. He did so, according to the broadcast, in part "to show respect for China's accomplishments." Coincidentally, perhaps, Bush also wore a red tie.

[2]Other aspects of this pre-Games positioning include the architectural reconfiguration of Beijing (Marvin, 2008) and a host of domestic and international promotional materials (Haugen, 2008).

NBC's first-night coverage, Tom Brokaw characterized the Opening Ceremonies as the conclusion to a "long, long march" and a night that "may be the most significant in modern Chinese history."[3] As both a culmination (of the effort to attract the Games and, thus, symbolically join the world order into which China was already well imbricated in political and economic terms) and a beginning (of the century in which, many have suggested, China is poised to again become a/the world power), the Opening Ceremonies provided the Chinese government an opportunity to narrate the past, explain the present, and perhaps shape the future.

METHODOLOGY

Embracing the principles of the discourse analysis and following the steps of thematic networks analysis, our goal is to explore the meanings and implications of the 2008 Opening Ceremonies. Although the term "discourse" has been used in different ways by various disciplines, it is generally agreed upon that "discourse" describes a system of representation. By choosing a particular system, it excludes and restricts alternative depictions (van Dijk, 1993). However, this doesn't imply a singular or universal decoding scheme from the audience (Hall, 1997). Therefore, discourse analysis views texts as complex cultural and psychological products. Contextual information surrounding the texts is as crucial as the texts themselves (Wetherell, 2001).

It follows, then, that when considering the Beijing 2008 Opening Ceremonies, it is important to make distinctions of context. The most important of these relates to audience: Although the events that constituted the Ceremonies were in many ways the same regardless of who broadcast them, broadcasters play an important role in explaining those events to a viewing public. In the broadest of senses, the Ceremonies had distinct domestic and international audiences, roughly coterminous with the China Central Television (CCTV) broadcast and those of other media outlets. Within this binary, there are further audience divisions: the Chinese-language broadcast was likely to have been received differently by mainland Chinese than by Mandarin speakers in Taiwan, Hong Kong, or the greater Chinese diaspora, whereas international audiences, and the meanings attached to the broadcast by them, were as diverse as the linguistic and cultural variations inherent in local media coverage. The NBC broadcast, delayed 12 hours in the United States in order to maximize prime-time

---

[3]We are limited in our analysis to the broadcast of the Opening Ceremony as packaged and sold by NBC and the United States Olympic Committee in DVD form. This study leaves aside, thus, the CCTV broadcast of the Opening Ceremonies, an text equally worthy of investigation.

advertising rates, attracted nearly 70 million American viewers, a record audience for an Olympics held outside the United States (Folkenfink, 2008).

Also, it is important to understand that, for the domestic Chinese audience, the Opening Ceremonies were part of a much longer text that began with Beijing's selection as an Olympic Host City. On July 13, 2001, residents in Beijing cheered the news of the selection, which to them meant much more than sports competitions. It signified the recognition of Beijing as a world-class city, the acknowledgment of China as a world-class country, and the redemption of a people whose various social and economic developments were seen as lagging behind the rest of the world. Nationalism and cultural pride undoubtedly intertwine with such an event, which is not unexpected for Olympic host countries. China, however, set a new standard. Although the international audience was largely not privy to many of these developments within China, the latter are nonetheless an important dimension of and context for the Opening Ceremonies as domestic propaganda.

We have thus chosen in this study to examine three discrete dimensions of the larger textual package that is the 2008 Opening Ceremonies. There is, first and foremost, the imagery produced by the choreography and technology placed within the stadium itself. Connected to this is the prominence given, in both domestic and international media, to the Chinese government's selection of film director Zhang Yimou as the Ceremonies' creative director, which we discuss. Then, because it is outside the scope of a single article to account for each linguistically differentiated broadcast of the event, we analyze the particular visual and discursive frame within which NBC chose to broadcast the Ceremonies to its record audience (an audience to which, we would argue, much of the artistic program was addressed). Finally, because one of the authors is a native Mandarin speaker, we also examine the discourse around the games as it was produced for domestic audiences in China, particularly during the preceding 100 days. For Chinese audiences, particularly urban Chinese, this preliminary coverage of the event provides important context for what follows. It also provides a clearer picture of how the Ceremonies were engineered as discursive texts.

Our approach was to engage in repeated readings of the texts with the focus of a discourse analysis: how the discourse is constructed and performed to fulfill a certain function (Wood & Kroger, 2000). To comprehend it as a system of representation, our repeated reading of the Ceremony itself was also examined through the thematic networks analysis, "a robust and highly sensitive tool for the systematization and presentation of qualitative analyses" (Attride-Stirling, 2001, p. 385). Through this technique, we deconstructed the texts in search of their "explicit rationalization(s)" and "implicit signification(s)" (Attride-Stirling, 2001, p. 388). Although we see these three elements as distinct texts, we have chosen not to approach them in such a way as to rigorously divide them from one another and analyze each in turn. Rather, our contention is that these three texts coalesce in important ways, and that it is only through seeing the artistic program within the context of the government-controlled propaganda that preceded it, and only through seeing the NBC broadcast in close relation to the discursive moves made in the artistic program, that the fullest understanding can be achieved. Moreover, the interrelational approach we have taken here brings into clearest focus the larger import of the article, especially as part of this special issue on the Olympics, which is its interrogation of the depoliticization of the Games by the host city/country, the IOC, and the broadcaster alike.

FINDINGS: DECONSTRUCTING THE BEIJING 2008 OPENING CEREMONIES DISCOURSE

Zhang Yimou as Both Author and Text

The Opening Ceremonies in Beijing actually began in the summer of 2004— perhaps quite ironically—in Athens, the seat of modern democratic thought and practice. It was here that China first presented its Olympic self to the viewing public under the direction of world-renown film and theater director Zhang Yimou, who produced an 8-minute program emphasizing traditional—demonstrably Orientalist, many suggested—images of Chinese culture.[4] These were, to the West, familiar representations, comforting even, in their framing of China as an innocuous, ancient civilization emerging into modernity. Although Zhang was criticized at home and abroad for his Athens production (Yang, 2008), it clearly pleased the Chinese government, who invited him back to produce the Opening and Closing Ceremonies in 2008.

Zhang was at once a safe bet and a provocative choice to helm the Ceremonies, and it is in this sense that we see him (or more particularly his selection) as a discursive text. In addition to his film work, the director had overseen the outdoor productions of spectacular, site-specific events, including the Puccini opera *Turandot* (first in Florence in 1998 and then in Beijing's Forbidden City in 1999) and the *Impression* series of theater performances, staged in a variety of dramatic rural locations around China. Experience managing personnel, material, narrative, and occasion on such a scale surely contributed to Zhang's selection. At the same time, however, his filmography as a cinematographer and director (and the literature critiquing it) shows an artist with, at best, an ambivalent attitude toward

---

[4]See Kennett and de Morages (2008) for a more detailed analysis of the Athens closing ceremonies that pays explicit attention to the role of Western broadcasters.

China's past, present, and future. As a member of the so-called Fifth Generation of Chinese filmmakers, Zhang began his career with a series of films—characteristic of this group, emerging into public consciousness in the mid-1980s—showing a "renewed desire for an enlightenment modernity" coupled with a desire to "excavate some hitherto suppressed Chinese Zeitgeist" (Li, 2007, p. 295) left unexamined (and effectively *unexaminable*) during the Cultural Revolution (roughly 1966–1973). Continuing from his first film, *Red Sorghum* (1987), until roughly the mid-1990s, Zhang prosecuted a veiled critique of Communist authority and a narrative exploration of personal (capitalistic) fulfillment often obscured as the fulfillment of sexual or other desires (Li, 2007). During the 1990s, however,

> the economic logic of the market had indeed begun to determine if not monopolize other kinds of cultural logics [in China]. Against this transformation of the social landscape, Zhang Yimou's cinema evinces a sudden shift of focus...it turns with fondness toward the masses, the ordinary and homely Chinese who are deprived of their capabilities of self-sufficiency in the nation's unprecedented saturation of transnational capital. (Li, 2007, pp. 301–302)

Landa (2007) suggested that this shift is symbolized by Zhang's approach to patriarchy (standing in for the Communist state), which often played the role of overt villain prior to the late 1990s and, beginning with *Not One Less* in 1999, simply disappears from view. In Landa's view, these later films "focus on daily life and its essential struggles...bring[ing] to the fore the perspective of the social losers, so to speak, of market liberalization and accelerated industrialization" (p. 232) who have been left behind by the absent patriarch of socialist government.

Zhang's early personal history is also defined by a difficult—if not oppositional—relationship with the Chinese government (Barboza, 2008; Cardullo, 2011, p. 186; Yau, 1999, p. 702). Although contemporaries and Zhang himself maintain that he has consistently had "no interest in politics"—the disavowal that has served as his defense in the face of international criticism of his decision to produce the Ceremonies and cultivate a closer relationship with the government bodies that censor him—it is clear that his work is defined by eminently historical mediations on Chinese history and culture. In particular, Zhang's later work has shown special interest in the concept and process of hybridization. As a director, much of his work found its primary audience overseas (largely due to government interference), an arena in which he has been very successful, at least in critical terms (Yau, 1999, p. 702). *Hero*, Zhang's 2002 film about feudal China that some critics have suggested implicitly supports authoritarian rule (Barboza, 2008; Chan, 2009), alongside *House of Flying*

Daggers (2004), finds the director using bold color palettes, heavily stylized action sequences, and big budgets (in a word, spectacle) to appeal, successfully, to an international audience. "China has stepped into a new era, an era of consumption and entertainment," Zhang stated in 2007. "You can condemn it if you like, but it is a trend of globalization" (as cited in Barboza, 2008).

Although Zhang himself demures when asked if he considers foreign tastes in his work (Cardullo, 2011, p. 192), it is clear that the Opening and Closing Ceremonies provide another outlet for production oriented toward both internal and external audiences. In a 2008 interview with *China Today* (a public relations mouthpiece aimed at "explaining China" to an international readership), Zhang stated of the ceremony project, "If the audience can't read the visual performance immediately, it means we have wasted an opportunity." In the same piece, Zhang collaborator Wang Chaoge suggested that "a good host should prepare dishes that are to the guests' taste. ... We will offer 'Chinese cuisine' which suits foreigners' palates" (Tang, 2008, p. 52).

Given his family's social position early in his life and his subsequent early international success as an auteur working against the grain of a censoring government (he was once banned for 5 years from making films in China with foreign support; Barboza, 2008), it is perhaps difficult to understand the cozy position Zhang has come to adopt with regard to the Chinese Communist Party. In an interview given in 2007, however, he again asserted his complete lack of interest in "politics," suggesting that his project is in service of the Chinese people and the Chinese homeland, regardless of who is power (Cardullo, 2011, p. 187). This reasoning, alongside the work of the Ceremonies themselves, has led some to see Zhang as a kind of Leni Riefenstahl figure, "creating beautiful backdrops for iron-fisted rulers" (Barboza, 2008). In the end, it was Zhang's reputation internationally that secured him this position, as in hiring him the Chinese Communist Party has presented itself as open to the leadership of a "gritty renegade" (Barboza, 2008) who has not always walked in step with Party doctrine.

Zhang's politics aside, there can be little argument about the grandeur of the piece he oversaw. Considering the nature and size of the audience to which it was addressed, the text's propagandistic power was perhaps incomparable in modern history. The 91,000 in attendance were clearly spellbound and amazed by the show and undoubtedly persuaded to various degrees by the show's intended message. This representational prowess was compounded during the Ceremony's NBC broadcast by the hosts' repeated assertions that comparisons to previous artistic programs were exercises in futility. Zhang's (and China's) was simply the greatest accomplishment in the history of the genre. It was also, as Brokaw reminded us at the outset, the culmination of a long journey.

The Discourse of Hybridity: Tradition and Modernity

In preparing for Olympics 2008, BOCOG consistently demonstrated its understanding of hybridity as an expedient concept by promoting Beijing's modernity while showcasing China's traditions and ancient civilization. This was especially evident in the discourse of the Olympics Release Party and the employment of the so-called Olympic Misses.[5]

Although Olympic preparation began in 2001, the public blitz exploded on April 17, 2008. This was the day of the Olympics Release Party, showcasing Olympic songs, mascots, and costumes to pave the way for the upcoming 100-day countdown to the opening ceremony (Yang, 2008). "Beijing Welcomes You" (2008a), a ballad extolling the hospitality of the Chinese people, debuted in Beijing on April 17 in a spectacular gala hosted by a renowned CCTV male anchor and a famous female model/entertainer from Taiwan. Exactly 100 Chinese singers, stars, and entertainers (from China, Taiwan, Hong Kong, Japan, and Korea) took part in performing the song. This song was also produced into a music video and released on April 30, exactly 100 days before the opening ceremony ("Beijing Welcomes You," 2008b). Each singer in the video is presented in scenes where modern skyscrapers and traditional Chinese architectural elements are juxtaposed. Within the "Beijing Welcomes You" text, political differences are put aside. Famous Chinese entertainers across Asia come together to make this happen.

Our analysis further revealed that the visual imagery of "Beijing Welcomes You" is compounded by its lyrics, which also attempt to balance old and new. The song opens with the phrase, "Let's embrace another morning, which brings completely new and ever fresh air." This is a clear symbolization of a new and modern China (though the "fresh air" reference could be scene as ironic, considering Beijing's notorious air pollution problem). This is followed immediately by the line, "Let's form friendship in a place full of the fragrance of tea." The tea here obviously signifies an essential Chinese tradition. This harmonious arrangement of dichotomies can be heard throughout the song with phrases such as "in the soil rich in traditions, we are planting new, great memories for you," and "5,000-year-old China is blossoming a youthful smile."

This self-portrait of modernity compounded with ancient pride also characterizes the presentation of nonathlete young Chinese women recruited as Olympic ambassadors. The selection of the so-called Olympic Misses received intensive press coverage leading up to and during the Olympics. The Olympic Misses were a group of carefully selected and heavily trained Chinese women, performing various duties: medal presenters at each competition event, country placard presenters at the opening ceremony, and the

---

[5]This translation is provided by one of the authors, a native speaker of Mandarin Chinese.

cheerleaders to entertain Olympics spectators. In many ways, their true function was to display the image of China BOCOG wished to convey: a modern, global power with a proud ancient civilization. After many rounds of fierce auditions with the strictest criteria, roughly 400 women were chosen. They were between 17 and 25 years old. Their average height was 5 feet 8 inches. They could converse in English. Their body had "the right proportions."[6] During the audition, the standard of proportions was judged according to the ability to fit in the costumes to be designed and provided later ("The High Standard," 2007). In the end, these tall, properly proportioned women fluent in English were presented as the faces of China. Statistically speaking, they were the ultimate outliers of average Chinese womanhood.

After the selection, intensive daily training with male coaches began. For the noncheerleaders, they were trained to project a reserved smile (showing no more than five teeth), wear high heels, and walk in a straight line with small steps and perfect postures ("The Reuters," 2008). With each reserved step, they also practiced carrying (a medal tray, a flower tray, or a placard, depending on their assigned functions) and following submissively behind authority figures, such as the men who would actually put the medals on the Olympic winners. This reservation and submissiveness was intended to represent and showcase the "Oriental beauty" lacking in the West (Du, 2008). A total of 15 sets of costumes in five colors were released in July 2008 at a center known for contemporary art in Beijing. All costumes integrated both Chinese and Western fashion elements. Almost all were floor-length gowns able to display those proper proportions and were by no means revealing ("Chinese Qipao," 2010).

Cheerleaders' costumes were quite the opposite. The "uniform" for beach volleyball cheerleaders was the bikini, so small that even the cheerleaders themselves were said to feel too embarrassed to wear them in the beginning. These cheerleaders also had a male coach, training them to have big smiles (presumably showing all the teeth one is able to), sexy and inviting postures, loud voices, big gestures, and overt movements. They were brought in to show the Westernized, modernized, and globalized side of China (Barrett, 2008); however, it is no stretch to see them as self-objectified symbols of a sexualized Orient.

This top-down construction of femininity in the Beijing Olympiad illustrates a significant early example of what we are calling the expediency of hybridity. Although the Olympic Misses program could be seen as

---

[6]This criterion is reminiscent of how Prince Charming found Cinderella: the shoe size was never specified, but the princess must be able to fit in the shoe provided. In the Olympics Misses' recruitment process, ideal weight and measurements were not specified.

empowering women—they play a crucial role in showcasing "the faces of China" to the world—it is not difficult to argue that BOCOG reinforces women's subordination and naturalizes the gender inequality that characterizes one of China's thousand-year-old traditions. It is a tradition the official cultural gatekeepers of China aim to safeguard, especially in the face of encroaching Westernization and globalization. The Olympic Misses program, much like the televisual text *Super Girl* referenced earlier (Peaslee et al., 2010), exemplifies the complexities and tensions in incorporating women into China's modernization project, tensions that played out similarly in NBC's introductory video package opening their 2008 Olympic broadcast schedule.

NBC and the Discourse of Juxtaposition

As a part of the discourse analysis, we specifically applied formal analysis to deconstruct the production cues of NBC's video packages. Both the ancient/modern dichotomy and the hyperbolic tone of the broadcast are established from the first frame, as NBC's preproduced content pastes familiar images of China (the Great Wall, Beijing landmarks) behind a deep-throated male voice-over:

> The footprints in their history stretch back 5,000 years, but for the world's greatest wall builders, makers of a Forbidden City, what happens tonight is not merely a small step, but a great leap. (Ten Mayflower, 2008)

This is of course a direct reference to the Great Leap Forward, an ultimately ironically named program of mandatory rural development implemented by Mao in the late 1950s and ending in widespread death and disaster.[7] The words are uttered against images of brand-new Olympic architecture, commissioned as part of a mandatory program of urban development in response to the impending Olympiad, and one is left to consider the ideological weight of this juxtaposition. The voice-over continues:

> China is welcoming the world. Who will they be when this is over? (Ten Mayflower, 2008)

---

[7]The "great leap" comment, as a discursive maneuver, may also be read by American audiences ignorant of Chinese political history as an intertextual reference to the 1969 moon landing and Neil Armstrong's "small step, giant leap" quote. In the latter scenario, a past American supremacy in the space race is invoked even as a new Chinese ascendancy is displayed. Our thanks to our reviewers for pointing out this possibility.

At this point in the package, the imagery shifts to clips of Olympic athletes, allowing the pronoun "they" in the previous quote to slip in its connotation from the Chinese to the competitors and back. Thus a corollary is established between the evolution of China as a modern, open state and that of a competitive athlete achieving excellence through perseverance. The narrator continues, with a string of mixed metaphors:

> The clock of their lives has been beating with a scream of urgency. They have pushed themselves to be as sharp as a razor's edge, for this summer, to be here, now and nowhere else. Beijing. The first ever Olympics for the world's most populist nation, 1.3 billion, to frame the front-page story of the 21st century. A China both outside time and bursting every which way in a bewildering rush of transformation. (Ten Mayflower, 2008)

Again, at this point, the supporting video switches from images of contemporary Beijing to images of training athletes.

> They have made themselves anew, relentlessly, devotedly, so they might, on these days, step in to history. They have submitted to an uncompromising search for mastery. Repetitive motion, technique polished toward an impossible ideal. Fall, fail, get up. (Ten Mayflower, 2008)

We are then presented with a series of American Olympic athletes, facing the camera, suggesting that "It's not the triumph, but the struggle," concluding with American swimmer Michael Phelps.

The next vignette pursues the question of why the athletes "begin" and "endure" the rigors of training, and it features two Chinese athletes (a female diver and a male hurdler) who provide answers related to winning on one's own "turf" and being the "first" and "remembered by history." The section is concluded by the ominous beating of a drum against a backdrop of marching, uniformed Chinese soldiers saluting one another, Mao gazing over their shoulder from a nearby mural. Again, we might consider the ideological import of this juxtaposition, given the established American discourse of athletic training regimens in Communist countries and their relationship to authoritarian rule.

The remainder of the opening previews a number of personal narratives the broadcaster plans to pursue in the coming days, and as the package concludes with a restatement of several key phrases from the beginning of the piece, it becomes clear that the comparison between an Olympics-hosting China and the finely tuned bodies of Olympic athletes has been quite intentional. As these individuals have transformed themselves, so has this country. And yet, as the prerecorded opening concludes, NBC chooses to transition to its studio segment not with an image of new China but rather the Forbidden City. Like the aforementioned usage of the term "great leap" and juxtaposition of militaristic imagery with discussion of Chinese athletes, this decision reflects a preoccupation on the part of NBC to always keep old and new discourses of China within easy reach. Their audience, NBC seems to presume, will not accept one without the other.

Discourses of Ancient and Modern in the Artistic Program

NBC clearly sees this duality as one of this Olympics' central novelties and one of its central sources of story-generating tension; the broadcast, not surprisingly, seeks from the outset to exploit it fully. But the suggestion that China is both traditional and modern is also fully imbricated into the program itself. In terms of both form and content, Zhang's production is an effective marriage between advanced engineering, architecture, and media technology, on one hand, and images of the most ancient traditions, on the other. The formation of 2008 Fou drummers, which mark the start of the welcoming ceremony, for example, use one of the most ancient percussive instruments known to humankind rigged with high-tech LED lights. The countdown they produce is echoed by the setting off of 29 firework "footprints" across Beijing, marking the number of the Olympiad and timed in such a way as to form an approach to the Bird's Nest. (Deemed too risky for producing good televisual images, the footprints were according to CNN and other sources reproduced using CGI for the broadcast and stadium audiences, another juxtaposition of China's ancient gunpowder innovation and its ability to create three-dimensional, live-action special effects.) The explosions reflect ancient history, their timing and placement reinforce the proficiency and potency of a modern techno-state.

Focusing on another ancient Chinese invention, Zhang later produces the world's largest-ever LED screen in the shape of a paper scroll. The screen is used to dramatic effect for much of the remainder of the artistic section, providing images (largely of ancient China) that cascade across the stadium floor and frame a white canvas. The latter will, over the course of the evening, be painted in traditional brushstrokes by dancers and then filled in by the colored footprints of marching athletes. The scroll is then moved to make room for an homage to the host country's invention of movable type, wherein the relationship between ancient and modern (or perhaps analog and digital) is cleverly inverted: following a series of numbers featuring the synchronized movement of individual type blocks, the segment concludes with a reveal of the 897 performers who were inside the blocks and in so doing belies the expectation that the squares were controlled electronically. This is an interesting moment for an American viewer, who is here forced to contend with the dissonance of having their expectations simultaneously met and unmet. China, represented by the synecdoche of the Opening Ceremonies, is represented as ancient and powerful enough to make the technological prowess one assumes they possess seem quaint by comparison with collective human action.

Gender, so crucial in the Olympic Misses preparation, remains in Zhang's program a primary channel through which the complimentary images of tradition and modernity are transmitted. In the Ceremony it is male soldiers who are doing the drumming and handling the Olympic and Chinese flags. They are shown as disciplined, solemn, dignified, and important. The female country plaque holders, on the other hand, personify grace and beauty. Their costumes provide a material realization of the East/West, Old/New dichotomy: The top is Chinese Qipao (a traditional female gown evolved from China's last dynasty), and from the waist down the gown is reminiscent of that worn by Cinderella in the classic Disney film. The outfit pairs the grandiosity of a Western design with the understated elegance of the East, another combination no doubt realized through a great deal of careful contemplation. And yet the functional appearance of females remains, with the exception of the Chinese Olympic athletes themselves, traditionally passive. To paraphrase Berger (1972, p. 45), the men act while the women appear.

Our analysis thus demonstrates that past and present, ancient and modern present the most fruitful polarities through which BOCOG produces the expedient discourse of hybridity. One is likely to be convinced by the performance: China clearly *is* both ancient and modern. A careful examination, however, would then ask whether this necessarily means that China *is* hybridized (or hybridizing) in such a way as to promote dialogue and diversity of ideas.

One World, One Dream: Hybridity and the Discourse of Harmony

The tensions inherent in a situation where a globalized media event (Dayan & Katz, 1994) is broadcast under conditions of both implicit and explicit oversight on the part of the host government are rearticulated in two further discourses constructed during the Opening Ceremonies. The motto of the 2008 Games, echoed repeatedly by NBC broadcasters Matt Lauer and Bob Costas during the Opening Ceremonies—"One World, One Dream"—is a slippery bit of discourse. It breaks down national boundaries, dissolving state concerns in favor of global aspirations, and appears to clear a space for a hybridized, diverse conception of global citizenship. *China Today* is explicit about this dimension of Zhang's intent:

> In an effort to expand the ceremony's universal "visual language," Zhang Yimou spent a year collecting photographs of children's smiles from all over

the world. . . . For Zhang, a child's smile transcends the boundaries of race and national borders, representing a common human emotion to people the world over. (Tang, 2008, p. 54)

Indeed, this effort pays off dramatically as one of the more poignant vignettes of the artistic portion of the Opening Ceremonies. But we would suggest that the assumption that the "dream" referred to in BOCOG's motto corresponds to a functional global diversity of people, ideas, and cultures is an unexamined one. Rather, such an assumption amounts to a pouring of standard Olympic discourse into the empty vessel provided at the outset by BOCOG.

What Zhang offers as a "dream," in fact, is not a great diversity of anything, but rather the conformist concept of "harmony." We may look again to *China Today* for an explicit articulation of this intention:

As a central part of any Olympiad, the opening ceremony reflects the Olympic spirit of peace, unity and friendship. This spirit is particularly evoked in the slogan of the Beijing Olympiad: "One World, One Dream." . . . Zhang Yimou sought advice on this point from 97-year-old Professor Ji Xianlin, a master of Chinese national culture and a BOCOG art consultant. Ji enigmatically suggested Zhang "invite" Confucius to the opening ceremony. . . . "I hope the whole world can accept the concept of harmony," says Professor Ji, "the world will be more peaceful." (Tang, 2008, p. 54)

Zhang seemingly took Ji's advice to heart, as "harmony" emerges clearly as the central theme of the artistic program. During the welcome portion of the event, the Chinese flag is marched in by 56 children, each wearing costumes reflecting the 56 ethnic groups of China. This turns out to be only a superficial visual representation of hybridity, however, as all 56 children are actually of the dominant Han Chinese ethnicity (Spencer, 2008). The drumming and movable type set pieces, meanwhile, perhaps the two most breathtaking in terms of their choreographical complexity, are possible only through the careful attention of each individual performer to the needs of the group of which he or she is a part. This collectivist sentiment is made even more explicit in the latter number, as the undulating "woodblocks" of type are made to form three variations on the Chinese character for "harmony." When the audience discovers the blocks to be operated by people rather than computerized machinery, this serves to further reinforce the beneficial results of harmonious action. As Macartney (2008) pointed out in her review of the performance, the latter concept acts throughout the program as a palliative to the potentially disturbing message of a robust, dominant China:

The film director left his audience in no doubt of his intention to intertwine the show of Chinese cultural achievements with a message that China wanted to be friends with the world. . . . As if to emphasise China's hope that the world would not see its growing might as a threat, the deep-throated cries of another Confucius saying echoed out: "We are all brothers in this world."

Over and over again, great masses of undifferentiated individual performers provide audiences with novel aesthetic configurations, the military might and discipline of Riefenstahl deemphasized in favor of Zhang's discourse of harmony and smiling faces.

CONCLUSION

It is not only to the advantage of the Chinese government that it appear hybridized in such away as to suggest a benign presence. As President Bush's attendance to the Opening Ceremonies suggests, it is to the advantage of an American government deeply indebted to Chinese patronage, as well as that of a wider, international corporate citizenry eager to take advantage of China's great market possibilities without the bad publicity likely to be generated through doing business with an authoritarian regime. It is also to the advantage of NBC and the IOC, both of whom have substantial investment in the Games being, above all, entertaining and sponsor-friendly (i.e., more or less apolitical). As Wang (2008), referencing Boyd-Barrett (1998), reminded us, "Transnational and local businesses are the main actors in producing hybrid products and promoting media hybridization" (p. 48).

It is both fair and germane to ask if the discourse was ultimately "successful." Just before the artistic portion transition to the so-called modern era (the NBC broadcasters mentioned "around the time of 1978"), the segment conveyed the ancient glories of China with a parade of female performers wearing costumes from various dynasties and male performers on top of columns, playing instruments. Oddly, the NBC broadcasters had nothing to say about this, except, "Watch these women . . . how they move their hands." They then linked this comment to a musing about how elegantly food would be likely to be served to them in a Beijing McDonald's. While they watched the whole show with amazement, Lauer and Costas couldn't help but fall back to the old habits of "othering" by making light of something potentially meaningful but unfamiliar to them. This slippage on the part of the broadcast team echoes the aforementioned moments in the opening NBC package that provided reminders of the Cultural Revolution, and—perhaps unintentionally—cast a suspicious eye on its Olympic hosts.

Also, the staying power of Zhang's powerful message may be difficult to demonstrate. Three years after the ceremony, as the United States and most of the world struggle with the economic crisis and the role China plays in it, however indirectly, how many people remember the "One World, One Dream" theme positively, and how many people recall the respect they had for China in August 2008? These questions could perhaps be asked of any Olympic host country, and in any case would necessitate some sustained engagement with audiences, a worthy project for which we obviously have no space here. But there can be little doubt, from our perspective, that China utilized these games to "speak" to the world in a way few previous host nations have, and that their strategy in doing so has been one of omission and misdirection. Absent from the history lesson Zhang presents are references to horrors of mid-20th-century Maoist doctrine; missing is any reference to the events of Tiananmen Square (from an external perspective, at least, perhaps the defining moment of modern Chinese history up to 2008). Chinese involvement in Darfur was papered over with allusions to global harmony, even as creative consultant Steven Spielberg dropped out of the planning committee in protest of this involvement and, hours before the start of the Opening Ceremonies, American speed skater Joey Check was refused a visa in response to his public support for Team Darfur (Chase, 2008). Such discursive maneuvers on the part of BOCOG—and the IOC and NBC are confederate in this, focused as they are on "not politicizing" the Olympics—show that what amounts to hybridity in the Chinese context is indeed harmony and not dissent. The latter is far less expedient.

REFERENCES

Appadurai, A. (1990). Disjuncture and difference in the global culture economy. *Theory, Culture, and Society, 7*, 295–310.

Attride-Stiriling, J. (2001). Thematic networks: An analytic tool for qualitative research. *Qualitative Research, 1*, 385–405.

Barboza, D. (2008, August 7). Gritty renegade now directs China's close-up. *The New York Times*. August 7. Retrieved from http://www.nytimes.com/

Barrett, J. (2008, August 6). Chinese cheerleaders join in the fun. *Reuters*. Retrieved from http://www.reuters.com/

Beijing Welcomes You [Video]. (2008a, April 17). Release gala. Retrieved from http://www.youtube.com/watch?v=HHYzDqMJnqQ

Beijing Welcomes You [Music video]. (2008b, April 30). Retrieved from http://www.youtube.com/watch?v=hvSRkY4eEfM

Berger, J. (1972). *Ways of seeing*. New York, NY: Penguin.

Boyd-Barrett, O. (1998). Media imperialism reformulated. In D. K. Thussu (Ed.), *Electronic empires: Global media and local resistance* (pp. 157–176). London, UK: Arnold.

Cardullo, B. (2011). *World directors in dialogue*. Lanham, MD: Scarecrow Press.

Chan, E. (2009). Zhang Yimou's *Hero*: The temptations of fascism. In S. Tan, P. Feng & G. Marchetti (Eds.), *Chinese connections: Critical perspectives on film, identity, and diaspora* (pp. 263–277). Philadelphia, PA: Temple University Press.

Chase, C. (2008). China revokes visa of gold medalist, Darfur activist Cheek. *Yahoo Sports*. Retrieved from http://sports.yahoo.com/

Chinese Qipao on Beijing 2008 Olympics [Video]. (2010, August 14). Retrieved from http://www.youtube.com/watch?v=zqy0OVbRvrY

Collins, S. (2008). The fragility of Asian identity in the Olympic Games. In M. Price & D. Dayan (Eds.), *Owning the Olympics: Narratives of the new China* (pp. 185–209). Ann Arbor, MI: University of Michigan Press.

Dayan, D., & Katz, E. (1994). *Media events: The live broadcasting of history*. Cambridge, MA: Harvard University Press.

deLisle, J. (2008). "One world, different dreams": The contest to define the Beijing Olympics. In M. Price & D. Dayan (Eds.), *Owning the Olympics: Narratives of the new China* (pp. 17–66). Ann Arbor, MI: University of Michigan Press.

Du, Y. (2008, June 13). The Olympic Medal presenters: Beautifully-shaped body and elegant posture demonstrating the Oriental Beauty. *The Chinese News Net*. Retrieved rrom http://2008.163.com/08/0613/08/4EA8PBKM00742K6N.html

Folkenfilk, D. (2008, August 12). Live From Beijing: Computer-enhanced fireworks. *National Public Radio*. Retrieved from http://www.npr.org/templates/story/story.php?storyId=93522548

Hall, S. (1997). *Representation: Cultural representations and signifying practices*. London, UK: Sage.

Haugen, H. Ø. (2008). "A very natural choice": The construction of Beijing as an Olympic City during the bid period. In M. Price & D. Dayan (Eds.), *Owning the Olympics: Narratives of the new China* (pp. 145–162). Ann Arbor, MI: University of Michigan Press.

Kennett, C., & de Morages, M. (2008). From Athens to Beijing: The Closing Ceremony and Olympic television broadcast narratives. In M. Price & D. Dayan (Eds.), *Owning the Olympics: Narratives of the new China* (pp. 260–283). Ann Arbor, MI: University of Michigan Press.

Kong, W. (Producer), & Yimou, Z. (Director). (2002). *Hero*. [Motion Picture]. China: Beijing New Picture Film Co.

Kong, W. (Producer), & Yimou, Z. (Director). (2004). *House of Flying Daggers*. [Motion Picture]. China: Beijing New Picture Film Co.

Kraidy, M. (2005). *Hybridity or the cultural logic of globalization*. Philadelphia, PA: Temple UP.

Landa, I. (2007). The absent father: Patriarchy and social order in the films of Zhang Yimou. *Nature, Society, and Thought*, 20, 228–234.

Li, D. L. (2007). Capturing China in globalization: The dialectic of autonomy and dependency in Zhang Yimou's cinema. *Texas Studies in Language and Literature*, 49(3), 293–317.

Macartney, J. (2008, August 9). Olympics: The power and the glory—China leaves world awestruck. *Times of London*. Retrieved from http://www.timesonline.co.uk/

Marvin, C. (2008). "All Under Heaven"—Megaspace in Beijing. In M. Price & D. Dayan (Eds.), *Owning the Olympics: Narratives of the new China* (pp. 229–259). Ann Arbor, MI: University of Michigan Press.

Peaslee, R. M., Berggreen, S. L., & Kwak, S. (2010). Idol-izing the past, present and future: *Super Girl*, democracy and the expediency of hybridity in contemporary China. *Mass Communicator: A Journal of Communication Studies*, 4(3), 14–22.

Pieterse, J. N. (2004). *Globalization and culture: Global mélange*. Lanham, MD: Rowman & Littlefield.

Robertson, R. (1995). Glocalization: Time space and homogeneity–heterogeneity. In M. Featherstone, S. Lash & R. Robertson (Eds.), *Global modernities* (pp. 25–43). London, UK: Sage.

Spencer, R. (2008, August 15). Beijing Olympics: "Ethnic" children exposed as fakes in opening ceremony. *London Telegraph*. Retrieved from http://www.telegraph.co.uk/

Tang, Y. (2008, March). Beijing Olympics Opening Ceremony: Zhang Yimou keeps everyone guessing. *China Today*, 3, 52–55.

Ten Mayflower (Producer). (2008). *2008 Olympics: Beijing 2008 Complete Opening Ceremony.* [DVD]. United States: National Broadcasting Company.

The high standard of the three measurements of the Olympic Medal Presenters and the Opening Ceremony will demonstrate multi-ethnicity. (2007, November 21). *XinJing Daily.* Retrieved from http://sports.sina.com.cn/o/2007-11-21/10043308415.shtml

The Reuters: The Olympic Misses won praises. (2008, August 19). *Xinhua Net.* Retrieved from http://news.xinhuanet.com/world/2008-08/19/content_9496639.htm

van Dijk, T. A. (1993). Principles of critical discourse analysis. *Discourse & Society, 4*, 249–283.

Wang, W. C. (2008). A critical interrogation of cultural globalisation and hybridity: Considering Chinese martial arts films as an example. *Journal of International Communication, 14*, 46–64.

Wetherell, M. (2001). Themes in discourse research: The case of Diana. In M. Wetherell, S. Yates & S. Taylor (Eds.), *Discourse theory and practice: A reader* (pp. 14–28). London, UK: Sage.

Wood, L. A., & Kroger, R. O. (2000). *Doing discourse analysis: Methods for studying action in talk and text.* Thousand Oaks, CA: Sage.

Wu, T. -M.(Producer), & Yimou, Z. (Director). (1987). *Red Sorghum.* [Motion Picture]. China: Xi'an Film Studio.

Yang, Y. (2008, April 18). Beijing welcomes you. *CRIENGLISH.com.* Retrieved from http://english.cri.cn/7146/2009/01/08/1361s441371_2.htm

Yau, E. (1999). China after the revolution. In G. Nowell-Smith (Ed.), *The Oxford history of world cinema* (pp. 693–704). Oxford, UK: Oxford University Press.

Yúdice, G. (2003). *The expediency of culture: Uses of culture in the global era.* Durham, NC: Duke University Press.

Zhao, Y. (Producer), & Yimou, Z. (Director). (1999). *Not One Less.* [Motion Picture]. China: Guangxi Film Studio.

Media Reports of Olympic Success by Chinese and American Gold Medalists: Cultural Differences in Causal Attribution

Mei Hua and Alexis Tan
The Edward R. Murrow College of Communication
Washington State University

Our study examines media reports of attribution of success by American and Chinese gold medalists at the 2008 Beijing Summer Olympics. Broadcast interviews were selected from official websites of NBC from the United States and CCTV from China. In addition, news reports from Chinese and American print media were selected through the Access World News database between August 8, 2008 (start of the Olympics) and August 31, 2008 (1 week after the closing ceremony). Results show that Chinese athletes, as reported by both Chinese broadcast and print media, attributed success to situational factors such as support and encouragement from socially important others, societal motivation, and national pride. American athletes were reported by American media to attribute success to dispositional factors such as personal characteristics and self-motivation. These results suggest that individual accounts of success as reported in the media are consistent with cultural norms and values.

INTRODUCTION

Cultural differences between the United States and East Asian countries such as China are well documented in cross-cultural research (e.g., Choi, Nisbett, & Norenzayan, 1999; Hofstede, 1991; Kim, 1994; Ting-Toomey, 2003). Although numerous studies show differences at the individual level, few have looked at societal institutions as possibly reflecting cultural values and beliefs. This study examines how the press—broadcast and print media—reported attributions of success by Chinese and American gold medalists at the 2008 Beijing Summer Olympics. We ask whether these reports reflect cultural differences between the United States and China in individualism and collectivism, a cultural dimension in which each country has been identified at opposite ends of the continuum (Hofstede, 1991).

Most studies of individualism and collectivism use surveys of large samples of individuals from different countries to map out possible differences. Our study provides an alternative methodology. We look at how this specific cultural dimension might be evident in an artifact (news reports) of an international event (the 2008 Olympics). We test the proposition that Olympic news reports reflect the prevailing cultural values of the reporters and the athletes interviewed, a premise suggested by theories of cultural influence on media framing (e.g., Carpenter, 2007; Pew Research Center, 1998). Although other studies have analyzed sports and sportswriting as reflections of a country's (mostly American) values (e.g., Trujillo & Ekdom, 1985), our study provides a cross-cultural comparison and is focused on a specific cultural dimension in the context of an international sporting event as reported in the media. We propose that media contents are influenced by both the journalists and the subjects of the stories, in this case the athletes themselves. Our analysis focuses on the resulting media representations of cultural values.

Journalistic Values and Culture

The influence of culture on journalistic values and performance has been documented in a number of studies. Sylvie and Huang (2008) identified "social values" as a distinct component of the value systems of U.S. newspaper editors. Social values included influence from peers, personal ties, and tradition and were found to influence decision making. In a cross-cultural study (17 countries) of journalists' perceptions of influences on their work, Hanitzch et al. (2010) identified "reference groups" as a distinct dimension along with political, economic, organizational, procedural, and professional influences. Influence from reference groups included friends, family, and acquaintances, commonly referred to in the socialization literature as conduits of culture (Blau, 1960). Blau (1960) noted that individuals within cultures behave according to prevailing values. Reinforcing this view, Brislin (1997) suggested that clusters of values unique to a culture influence journalistic performance and may be an obstacle toward establishing universal journalistic values (or an "ethic") across cultures. In a comparison of value hierarchies, he found that Chinese journalists ranked "humility" and "loyalty" more important than "aggressiveness" and "inquisitiveness," whereas the reverse was true for American journalists.

Because some journalistic values may be influenced by cultural and social factors, researchers have asked whether these values influence performance. Sylvie and Huang (2008) found that certain values affect decision-making styles of U.S. editors. Organizational and journalistic value systems were associated with "rational" decision making, defined as reliance on the "right facts," double-checking information sources, logic, and careful thought. Social values predicted an intuitive and spontaneous decision-making style that relied on instincts, intuition, decisions that "feel right," and "inner feelings." Carpenter (2007) used framing theory to explain differences in coverage of the Iraq war by U.S. elite and nonelite newspapers. She suggests that news reporters exert influence in the framing of stories by selective focus on information that will be attractive to news consumers. Although this process may be subconscious, the influence of culture and values on the reporter's frame is suggested by theory (e.g., Blau, 1960) and previous research on mechanisms by which media framing is accomplished in television interviews (e.g., Huls & Varwijk, 2011) and newspaper reports (e.g., Pew Research Center, 1998).

In an analysis of political bias in television interviews, Huls and Varwijk (2011) concluded that Dutch television reporters, allegedly with a "left-wing" bias, were less adversarial in their interviews with left-wing politicians compared to right-wing politicians. They found significant differences in three dimensions of "adversarialness"—assertiveness, opposition, and persistence—as well as in question design. They concluded that the reporters shaped the public presentation of politicians by managing the interviews, which was accomplished by setting the topic, asking the questions, determining who speaks, and deciding when a question has been answered sufficiently (Clayman, Elliott, Heritage, & McDonald, 2007).

Studies of message framing in newspaper reports have identified a number of narrative frames journalists use to interpret the news, including conflict, consensus, horse race, and personality (e.g., Pew Research Center, 1998). An underlying assumption is that journalists can influence the focus of news reports by using one or more of these devices (Iyengar & Kinder, 1987) and that underlying cultural values and broad beliefs may be implicit in the news (Pew Research Center, 1998). Consistent with this analysis,

Tuchman (1978), Gans (1979), and Schrag (1977) suggested that journalists' values subtly influence news judgments and the construction of news stories. According to Schrag, every journalist "operates with certain assumptions about what constitutes normative behavior, if not the good society" (p. 41).

In the current study, we expect American and Chinese reporters to be influenced by their cultures in reporting about Olympic gold medalists from their respective countries, resulting in stories and interviews that highlight cultural values, specifically attributions for success by the athletes.

Sportswriting and Cultural Values

Real (1977) suggested that media reports of sports reflect the values and ideals of a given culture. In the American context, sports have been analyzed as an instrument by which American values are disseminated and reinforced (Edwards, 1973) and as the "symbolic expression of the values of the larger political and social milieu" (Lipsky, 1978, p. 351).

As journalists, sportswriters are bound by the same code of ethics adhered to by journalists in general. They also are susceptible to the same influences that may detract from this code. As Gans (1979) asserted, both newswriting and sportswriting are ideological; they "assume a consensus about values" (p. 40), and "continuously present and affirm social consensus on a broad set of cultural values" (Trujillo & Ekdom, 1985).

In an analysis of sportswriting about baseball (the 1984 Chicago Cubs) Trujillo and Ekdom (1985) identified several themes linked to American values, among them winning, tradition, work and play, youth, logic and rationality, teamwork, and individualism. Individualism was evident in reports of statistics and awards for individual players, supporting Warshay's (1982) analysis that the focus on individualism "helps to relate the longtime popularity of baseball to the individualistic ideology that has long been emphasized in American culture" (p. 233).

Individualism and Collectivism

A basic premise of this study is that differences between Chinese and American cultures will influence how Olympic success is reported in the media and how the participants themselves, when interviewed by reporters, will explain their success. As suggested by previous research, a major difference between the two cultures is placement on the individualism-collectivism continuum.

Hofstede (1991) defined individualistic societies as those in which "ties between individuals are loose; everyone is expected to look after himself or herself and his or her immediate family" (p. 51). Collectivism, on the other hand, "pertains to societies in which people from birth onwards are integrated into strong, cohesive ingroups, which throughout people's life-times continue to protect them in exchange for unquestioning loyalty" (p. 51). In a survey of IBM employees from 66 countries, Hofstede (1980) found that employees from the United States, Canada, and western European countries scored high on individualism, whereas employees from Asian, Latin American, and African countries scored high on collectivism. Interpreting these data, Hofstede (1980) described Americans as being encouraged to be autonomous, self-sufficient, unique, and respectful of the privacy and freedom of others. The Chinese, on the other hand, are "we"-focused. They value social relationships, depend on their in-groups for protection and resources, and are loyal to their group in order to maintain group cohesiveness (Kim, 1994). Although recent studies have identified some variations between groups (e.g., young and old) in Chinese and other East Asian countries, the basic distinctions between the United States and these countries continue to be found (Nonini, 2008; Oyserman, Coon, & Kemmelmeier, 2002).

Individualistic and collective values lead to differences in causal attribution of behaviors. Ting-Toomey (2003), for example, found that individualists explain success in terms of internal factors like personal attributes, whereas collectivists cite external factors such as help from others and motivation from the community. In sum, individualistic societies emphasize dispositional attributes embodied in the "self" as causes for behaviors, whereas collectivist societies emphasize situational and contextual attributes embodied in the group.

In the context of sports journalism, the 2008 Beijing Olympics provides a cross-cultural setting to analyze how cultural values might affect reporting and the resultant stories. Based on the potential dual influence of culture on the journalist and the subject interviewed for the story, and given cultural differences between China and the United States on the individualist/collectivist value dimension, we test the following hypotheses:

H1: U.S. television interviews of U.S. gold medalists are more likely than Chinese television interviews of Chinese gold medalists to emphasize dispositional factors such as personal characteristics, self-motivation, and the desire to win.

H2: Chinese television interviews of Chinese gold medalists are more likely than U.S. television interviews of U.S. gold medalists to emphasize situational factors such contributions of socially important others, societal motivation, and national pride.

H3: U.S. print media coverage of U.S. gold medalists is more likely than Chinese print media coverage of Chinese gold medalists to emphasize dispositional factors such as personal characteristics, self-motivation, and the desire to win.

H4: Chinese print media coverage of Chinese gold medalists is more likely than U.S. print media coverage of U.S. gold medalists to emphasize situational factors such as contributions of socially important others, societal motivation, and national pride.

METHOD

This study analyzed U.S. and Chinese television interviews and newspaper stories about gold medalists at the 2008 Beijing Summer Olympic Games.

Samples

The broadcast interviews were selected from official websites of NBC from the United States and from CCTV from China. The NBC website provides exclusive records of interviews of U.S. Olympic athletes, and CCTV is the only national media outlet in China with broadcast interviews of Chinese Olympic athletes. The sample included only in-depth interviews of individual gold medalists, resulting in 21 Chinese and 18 U.S. interviews.

Newspaper reports were selected through the Access World news database between August 8, 2008 (start of the Olympics) and August 31, 2008 (1 week after the closing ceremony). National and local newspapers were included in the U.S. sample. Local papers were included because they were expected to be more likely than national media to cover local athletes competing in low profile sports. Chinese news reports were selected from *China Daily* and *Xinhua News Agency*, the two major English print news sources in China.

A two-step process was used to select news reports from both U.S. and Chinese sources. First, we used the keywords "Beijing," "Olympics," "gold," and "medalist," resulting in 4,489 U.S. and 339 Chinese stories. Next, we selected personal in-depth stories about gold medalists, excluding stories about groups of athletes (e.g., team sports), daily summaries of the games, and other Olympic-related reports. The resulting sample included 28 Chinese and 31 U.S. news stories.

A graduate student at a large public university on the U.S. West Coast selected the American sample; a graduate student at a large public university in Beijing selected the Chinese sample. Neither knew the purpose or hypotheses of the study.

Our purposive samples of broadcast and news reports met one criterion: They were personalized in-depth stories and interviews about individual gold medalists. The sample sizes are consistent with the number of gold medalists from China (51) and the United States (36), considering that stories and interviews of medalists from team sports were excluded from the analysis (http://Beijing 2008.com).

Measures

Four major categories including a total of 10 specific themes were used to measure dispositional and situational factors, adapted from Markus and Kitayama (1991) and Markus, Yukido, Omoregie, Townsend, and Kitayama (2006). The four major categories are personal characteristics (themes = athletic abilities, personality, to win or to do one's best in competition, and individual style), training (themes = difficulties encountered, stress, hardship), social support (themes = advice, support and encouragement from family, friends, coach, team/teammates, fans), and social motivation (themes = meeting or exceeding expectations of others; national pride). Following Markus et al. (2006), we created two variables: dispositional (personal characteristics) and situational (training, social support and social motivation) to reflect individualistic American and collectivist Chinese societies.

Coding

The units of analysis were the video segments of broadcast interviews and the newspaper articles. Two male graduate students, one at a large public university in the United States and another at a large public university in China, did the coding. One of the authors trained the coders to familiarize them with the operational definitions of the categories and themes.

Coding was accomplished in two stages. First, the coders rated whether a particular theme was present in a television interview or newspaper story, resulting in a nominal variable (Yes/No). Second, the coders rated the frequency of mention of each of the 10 themes on a 4-point scale: 1 (*vaguely referred to with a few words*), 2 (*one or two clear references*), 3 (*theme repeated more than 2 times*), and 4 (*theme clearly central and repeatedly mentioned*). This coding scheme yielded an interval measure of the emphasis of a specific theme. The intent was to capture the overall focus of broadcast interviews and newspaper articles because the themes could be reflected in different words and phrases.

After training, each coder independently coded the same random sample of 10 broadcast and newspaper items from China and the United States, representing 10% of the total sample (Wimmer & Dominick, 2002.) Following Hayes and Krippendorff (2007), intercoder agreement for the

TABLE 1
Intercoder Reliability Coefficients

Theme	Holsti's coefficient	Krippendorff's α
Personal characteristics (athletic ability, personality, individual style, desire to win)	.90	.883
Training (difficulties, stress, hardships)	.90	.727
Social support		
Family	1.00	.888
Friends	.80	.726
Coach	.70	.834
Teammates	1.00	1.00
Fans	.70	.732
Motivation		
Expectations of others	.80	.737
National pride	.70	.698

nominal variable was computed with Holsti's Coefficient (Saris-Gallhofer, Saris, & Morton, 1978), resulting in a range of 1.00 to .70. Intercoder agreement for the 4-point interval scale for each of the ten themes over the broadcast and newspaper samples was computed using Krippendorf's alpha, resulting in a range of 1.00 to .69. Table 1 shows the intercoder agreement coefficients for the 10 themes. After coding the random sample, each coder analyzed 50% of the remaining sample. Therefore, the rest of the sample was coded by only one person given the acceptable intercoder reliability coefficients.

RESULTS, DISCUSSION, AND CONCLUSIONS

Themes in Broadcast Interviews

Table 2 shows that U.S. broadcast interviews of American athletes focused more on composite dispositional attributions for success compared to Chinese broadcast interviews of Chinese athletes ($p = .02$). Conversely, Chinese broadcasts emphasized situational attributions more than did U.S. broadcasts ($p = .000$; Table 2). A comparison of themes shows that American television interviews of U.S. gold medalists were more likely than Chinese television interviews of Chinese gold medalists to attribute success to athletic abilities, personality, individual style, and desire to win. Chinese television interviews, on the other hand, were more likely than American television interviews to attribute success to rigorous training, the expectations of others and national pride (Table 2). Contrary to expectations, there were no differences between American and Chinese gold medalists in success

TABLE 2
Themes in Television Interviews

Theme	U.S.	China	t	p
Personal characteristics (athletic ability, personality, individual style, desire to win)	2.22 (1.22)	1.33 (1.02)	2.49	.02
Training (difficulties, stress, hardships)	.33 (.49)	1.14 (1.01)	−3.09	.004
Social Support				
Family	.22 (.43)	.33 (.66)	−.61	.54
Friends	.06 (.24)	.14 (.36)	−.88	.38
Coach	.22 (.55)	.76 (.77)	−2.49	.02
Teammates	.28 (.57)	.24 (.44)	.25	.81
Fans	.17 (.51)	.19 (.40)	−.16	.87
Motivation				
Expectations of others	.33 (.59)	1.29 (1.42)	−2.65	.01
National pride	.67 (.59)	1.86 (1.46)	−2.85	.007
Dispositional composite (personal characteristics)	2.22	1.33	2.49	.02
Situational composite (training, social support, motivation)	1.61	4.71	−5.35	.000

Note. Cell entries for themes are means on a 4–point scale, where 4 is the most emphasis. Standard deviations are in parentheses. Composite scores are sums of individual themes.

attributions to family, friends, teammates, and fans. The only difference in social support was that the Chinese were more likely than Americans to acknowledge contributions of the coach ($p = .02$.)

Themes emphasized in American and U.S. newspaper articles are similar to the themes emphasized in broadcast interviews. As Table 3 shows, American newspaper articles were more likely to emphasize dispositional attributions for success of American athletes ($p = .005$), whereas Chinese newspaper articles were more likely to focus on situational attributions ($p = .000$). U.S. articles were more likely than Chinese articles to attribute success to athletic abilities, personality, individual style, and desire to win. On the other hand, Chinese articles were more likely than American articles to focus on training, expectations of others, and national pride (Table 3). In the social support category, Chinese newspaper articles were more likely than U.S. newspaper articles to emphasize influence of the coach ($p = .001$) and teammates ($p = .001$). Consistent with theoretical expectations, media reports of Olympic success reflected Chinese and American cultural values, suggesting that culture-based media framing by journalists operated in both countries and for both print and broadcast media. These results validate theories of cultural influence on the news (e.g., Gans, 1979) and, more recently, theories of journalists' values and media framing (Carpenter, 2007; Pew Research Center, 1998).

TABLE 3
Themes in Newspaper Articles

Theme	U.S.	China	t	p
Personal characteristics (athletic ability, personality, style, desire to win)	2.55 (1.43)	1.46 (1.37)	2.96	.005
Training (difficulties, stress, hardship)	.84 (1.04)	1.57 (1.29)	−2.42	.02
Social support				
Family	.55 (1.03)	.21 (.63)	1.49	.14
Friends	.39 (.80)	.11 (.42)	1.65	.10
Coach	.29 (.59)	1.32 (1.47)	−3.61	.001
Teammates	.35 (.55)	1.21 (1.29)	−3.39	.001
Fans	.39 (.92)	.57 (.96)	− .75	.45
Motivation				
Expectations of others	.52 (.63)	1.68 (1.52)	−3.92	.000
National pride	1.90 (1.89)	3.18 (2.25)	−2.37	.02
Dispositional composite (personal characteristics)	2.55	1.46	3.71	.005
Situational composite (training, social support, motivation)	2.13	7.18	5.01	.000

Note. Cell entries for themes are means on a 4-point scale, where 4 is the highest emphasis. Standard deviations are in parentheses. Composite scores are sums of individual themes.

In sum, these results provide support for H1, H2, H3, and H4, confirming theoretical expectations that a society's individualist and collectivist values will be reflected in media reports of success, in this case, success in Olympic games. According to Hofstede (1991), individualist societies are influenced by dispositional factors, valuing individual traits, and actions, whereas collectivist societies are influenced by situational factors, valuing group affiliations, and support. Although generalizations in characterizations of societies and cultures should generally be accepted with caution, the individualist/collectivist analysis has been shown to be quite robust (Oyserman et al., 2002). The evidence for classifications of societies in the individualist–collectivist continuum is generally provided by large-scale surveys of individuals (e.g., Fiske, 2002). Our study shows that similar results are obtained when the unit of analysis is an artifact or record (i.e., television interviews; newspaper articles) of a significant international event. A theoretical implication is that cultural values, in this case individualism/collectivism, are indeed strongly embedded even in modern-day societies (e.g., Hofstede, 1991; Oyserman et al., 2002). These values take on many forms. They are, for example, articulated by individuals in surveys; they are also represented in the media.

With regards to media framing, our study provides indirect evidence that cultural values of journalists may influence some reporting, in this case, attributions of success of athletes. Previous studies have shown that journalistic, ideological, and personal values can influence reporting (Brislin, 1997; Sylvie & Huang, 2008). The most likely mechanism of influence in our study would be in the questions asked by reporters and in the resulting emphasis in news reports and interviews (Huls & Varwijk, 2011; Pew Research Center, 1998). It is also quite likely that the athletes themselves are influenced by their cultures in their answers to reporters' queries. Thus, our results can be explained by the potential influence of culture on both the journalist/interviewer and gold medalists in the 2008 Beijing Summer Olympics, confirming similar results from Trujillo and Ekdom's (1985) analysis of sportswriting and American cultural values in reporting about baseball (the Chicago Cubs). Our study provides this confirmation in two cultures and across several sports in arguably the most significant worldwide athletic event.

Given the constraints of our content analysis, we were not able to separate out the effects of journalists' and athletes' values on media reports, a limitation of the study. Also, our findings should be tempered by the possibility that a universal journalistic ethic operating across cultures (e.g., Wu & Weaver, 1998) might influence the reporting of American and Chinese journalists, particularly Chinese journalists who have trained or been educated in the United States. However, previous research has shown that international journalists in general, and Chinese journalists in particular, are selective in their acceptance of western journalistic ethics (Brislin, 1997). For example, Lin (2010) concluded that among Chinese journalists, "liberal values co-exist with both modern professionalism and Party journalism values" (p. 421), resulting in journalists who tend to be "inactively liberal." In addition, some cultural values are deeply embedded, particularly individualistic and collectivist values (e.g., Triandis, 1995), which are not likely to change even with direct and vicarious contact with another culture (Tan et al., 2010.) Our results showing cultural differences support the basic premise that Chinese and American sports journalists were influenced by individualistic-cultural values in reporting about 2008 Olympic gold medalists from their respective countries.

Future research could test whether our results are replicable in other individualist and collective societies, and for media reports of success in other spheres such as business, entertainment, and politics.

REFERENCES

Blau, P. (1960). Structural effects. *American Sociological Review, 25*, 178–193.
Brislin, T. (1997, March). *An update on journalism ethics in Asia: Values and practices as context for meaning in Japan, China and Korea.* Paper presented to the Association for Practical and Professional Ethics annual meeting, Washington, DC.

Carpenter, S. (2007). U.S. elite and non-elite newspapers' portrayal of the Iraq war: A comparison of frames and source use. *Journalism & Mass Communication Quarterly, 84*, 761–776.

Choi, I., Nisbett, R. E., & Norenzayan, A. (1999). Causal attribution across cultures: Variation and universality. *Psychological Bulletin, 125*, 47–63.

Clayman, S. E., Elliott, M. N., Heritage, J., & McDonald, L. L. (2007). When does the watchdog bark? Conditions of aggressive questioning in presidential news conferences. *American Sociological Review, 72*, 23–41.

Edwards, H. (1973). *The sociology of sport.* Homewood, IL: Dorsey.

Fiske, A. P. (2002). Using individualism and collectivism to compare cultures—A critique of the validity and measurement of the constructs: Comment on Oyserman et al. (2002). *Psychological Bulletin, 128*, 78–88.

Gans, H. J. (1979). *Deciding what's news: A study of "CBS Evening News," "NBC Nightly News," "Newsweek," and "Time."* New York, NY: Pantheon.

Hanitzsch, T., Anikina, M., Berganza, R., Cangoz, I., Coman, M., Hamada, B., ... Yuen, K. W. (2010). Modeling perceived influences on journalism: Evidence from a cross-cultural survey of journalists, *Journalism & Mass Communication Quarterly, 87*, 5–22.

Hayes, A., & Krippenforff, K. (2007). Answering the call for a standard reliability measure for coding data. *Communication Methods and Measures, 1*, 77–89.

Hofstede, G. (1980). *Culture's consequences.* Beverly Hills, CA: Sage.

Hofstede, G. (1991). *Cultures and organizations: Software of the mind.* London, UK: McGraw-Hill.

Huls, E., & Varwijk, J. (2011). Political bias in TV interviews. *Discourse & Society, 22*, 48–65.

Iyengar, S., & Kinder, D. (1987). *News that matters.* Chicago, IL: University of Chicago Press

Kim, U. (1994). Individualism and collectivism: Conceptual clarification and elaboration. In U. Kim, H. C. Triandis, Ç. Kâğitçibaşi, S-C. Choi & G. Yoon (Eds.), *Individualism and collectivism: Theory, method and applications* (pp. 19–40). Thousand Oaks, CA: Sage.

Lin, F. (2010). A survey report on Chinese journalists in China. *The China Quarterly, 202*, 421–434.

Lipsky, R. (1978). *Sports world: An American dreamland.* New York, NY: Quadrangle.

Markus, H., & Kitayama, S. (1991). Culture and self: Implications for cognition, emotion, and motivation. *Psychological Review, 98*, 224–253.

Markus, H. R., Yukiko, U., Omoregie, H., Townsend, S. S. M., & Kitayama, S. (2006). Going for the gold: Models of agency in Japanese and American contexts. *Psychological Science, 17*, 103–112.

Nonini, D. M. (2008). Is China becoming neoliberal? *Critique of Anthropology, 28*, 145–178.

Oyserman, D., Coon, H. M., & Kemmelmeier, M. (2002). Rethinking individualism and collectivism: Evaluation of theoretical assumptions and meta-analysis. *Psychological Bulletin, 128*, 3–72.

Pew Research Center. (1998, July 13). *Framing the news: The triggers, frames, and messages in newspaper coverage.* Retrieved from www.journalism.org/node/445

Real, M. (1977). *Mass-mediated culture.* Englewood Cliffs, NJ: Prentice-Hall.

Saris-Gallhofer, I. N., Saris, W. E., & Morton, E. L. (1978). A validation study of Holsti's content analysis procedure. *Quality and Quantity, 12*, 131–145.

Schrag, P. (1977, March 23). An earlier point in time. *Saturday Review/World*, pp. 40–41.

Sylvie, G., & Huang, S. J. (2008). Value systems and decision-making styles of newspaper front-line editors. *Journalism & Mass Communication Quarterly, 85*, 61–82.

Tan, A., Han, E. J., Dalisay, F., Zhang, Y., Merchant, M., & Radanielina-Hita, M. L. (2010, November). *Information source use and cultural values in South Korea.* Paper presented to the National Communication Association, San Francisco, CA.

Ting-Toomey, S. (2003). The matrix of face: An updated face-negotiation theory. In W. B. Gudykunst (Ed.), *Theorizing about intercultural communication* (pp. 71–92). Thousand Oaks, CA: Sage.

Triandis, H. (1995). *Individualism and collectivism.* Boulder, CO: Westview.

Trujillo, N., & Ekdom, L. (1985). Sportswriting and American cultural values: The 1984 Chicago Cubs. *Critical Studies in Mass Communication, 2,* 262–281.

Tuchman, G. (1978). *Making news: A study in the construction of reality.* New York, NY: The Free Press.

Warshay, L. H. (1982). Baseball in its social context: In R. M. Pankin (Ed.), *Social approaches to sport* (pp. 225–282). East Brunswick, NJ: Associated University Presses.

Wimmer, R. D., & Dominick, J. R. (2002). *Mass media research: An introduction* (7th ed.). Belmont, CA: Wadsworth.

Wu, W., & Weaver, D. (1998). Chinese journalists for the next millennium—The professionalization of Chinese journalism students. *International Communication Gazette, 60,* 513–529.

"Under the Weather": The Weather Effects on U.S. Newspaper Coverage of the 2008 Beijing Olympics

Bu Zhong
Department of Journalism
The Pennsylvania State University

Yong Zhou
School of Journalism and Mass Communication
Renmin University of China

By using computer-aided content analysis, this study examined how Beijing's weather, which was measured by the Air Pollution Index (API), temperature, and cloudiness (sunny or cloudy), might influence the coverage of the 2008 Beijing Olympics by 4 U.S. newspapers. The results demonstrated that the API and temperature were significantly related to the negativity of the news reports that were filed from Beijing. Specifically, as Beijing's temperature rose or air pollution level increased, U.S. journalists used more negative words in reporting on the Olympics. The temperature was also correlated with the negativity of China-related reports. The findings provided evidence that journalists' news decision making might be influenced by a greater variety of factors than we previously thought. To better understand how journalists make news decisions, it is necessary to explore not only known patterns of journalistic practices but also some exogenous factors, such as weather.

INTRODUCTION

Weather holds a central place in human experience. It has affected harvest yields as long as agriculture started. A stream of research found that weather also influences people's daily mood (e.g., Denissen, Butalid, Penke, & van Aken, 2008; Keller et al., 2005; Watson, 2000). Tromp (1980) observed that people generally reported that they felt happier on sunny days than cloudy days. Other studies found that many people (as high as 70%) believed that air quality, an important part of weather, influenced their well-being, including the mood (Brandstatter, Fruhwirth, & Krichler, 1988; Faust, 1977). But does weather affect news reporting, specifically the positivity or negativity of news coverage? An impromptu answer might be "no," especially for those who believe in the norms of good journalism (e.g., objectivity). To them, any exogenous influence, no matter from weather or advertisers' pressure, is antithetical to the canons of journalism that prize news reports conveying "just the facts."

An alternative view is that weather may influence people's mood, as mood colors judgment and eventually alters behavior (Mayer, Gaschke, Braverman, & Evans, 1992). Hence there is a possibility that weather may affect the way journalists frame events in news reporting by first altering their mood. To investigate if weather might affect news reporting, this research analyzed the influence of Beijing's weather on the tone of four U.S. newspapers' coverage of the 2008 Beijing Olympic Games—the *New York Times, Washington Post, Wall Street Journal,* and *USA Today.*

LITERATURE REVIEW

Mood contains valuable information about the environment in which people live and work (Hirshleifer & Shumway, 2003; Watson, 2000). Mood, however, is something that doesn't get talked about much in the profession of news production. This may be due to the fact that most journalists uphold objectivity and balanced reporting as their professional canons (Weaver & Wu, 1998). Or simply, "we do not often think of news in emotional terms" (Sundar, 2003, p. 275). But journalists could experience mood just like everyone else. Perhaps even more so for overseas correspondents due to the nature of international news reporting, constantly involving pressure of deadlines; difficulty of working with local sources; and anxiety of dealing with different legal, social, and cultural milieus surrounding news creation.

Examining the influence of weather on the tone of news stories provides an appealing means of testing whether psychological biases may influence journalists' news decision making. Any such relationship is not subject to the criticism of data snooping (Hirshleifer & Shumway, 2003). Assessing the pattern of weather effects on news production was stimulated by psychological hypotheses, which may not match a known pattern of journalistic practices. These patterns include various potential levels of influences on news reporting such as organizational constraints, professional orientation, the nature of the news events journalists cover, and the features of a given media system (Berkowitz & TerKeurst, 1986; Seib, 2002; Shoemaker & Reese, 1996). However, a relationship between weather and news decision making, if it exists, may have a more convincing psychological explanation but hardly a conceivable explanation in the literature of journalism studies. Quite possibly, these findings may contrast with some well-known patterns of news decision making for which psychological and journalistic explanations are currently competing (see Hirshleifer & Shumway, 2003).

Previous literature in journalism studies emphasizes the dynamics of social, cultural and psychological influences on news decision making (see Zhong & Newhagen, 2009). This study sidestepped the complexities of the process of social and organizational influences on news production by focusing on an exogenous influence—weather—in the context of its interactions with mood and news decision making, in particular, choices of positive and negative words in the Olympic reports. The rationale is that weather might influence the tone of news reporting by first affecting journalists' mood, and then altering their choice of positive or negative words in news reporting from one weather condition to another (e.g., from a sunny to a cloudy day).

Weather Influences Mood and Cognition

The weather effect on mood and judgment has been systematically documented since the 1970s. The hours of sunshine were found to correlate inversely with self-reports of negative mood (Cunningham, 1979; Persinger, 1975). Barton (1988) discovered that weather had an effect on young people's mood and productivity. Other studies reported that people's positive mood was associated with low levels of humidity (Sanders & Brizzolara, 1982), high levels of sunlight (Parrott & Sabini, 1990; Schwarz & Clore, 1983), and high temperature (Howarth & Hoffman, 1984). However, high temperature was also found to result in negative mood (Goldstein, 1972). Harmatz and colleagues found that mood changed as a function of season and there were strong seasonal effects of weather on normal people's mood and depression (Hartmatz et al., 2000). Cunningham (1979) observed that the hours of sunshine were the most significant predictor of "helping behavior."

Research has also discovered some associations between weather and cognitive activities in various situations. In a study of the relations between mood and manipulating temperature, Allen and Fischer (1978) had college students learn a nine-item paired association list (e.g., box/chair) in thermally controlled rooms at temperatures of 52°, 62°, 72°, 82°, or 92° F. They found that male students' performance on a paired-association memory tasks peaked at 72°F and declined with warmer or cooler temperature. Sinclair, Mark, and Clore (1994) found that both sunny and warm days were associated with more heuristic and less systematic information processing than cloudy and cool days.

A number of studies also reported mixed results regarding the relationships between weather and mood. Some found little or no relationship between mood and any weather variables (e.g., Clark & Watson, 1988). Watson (2000) reported that he found no consistent weather effect on people's daily mood variables based on his analyses of the relations between mood and the amount of sunshine and rain. Keller and colleagues investigated the effect of temperature and air pressure on mood and cognition in three different samples of participants (Keller et al., 2005). In the study, no consistent main effects of weather on mood was found, though a moderate effect of both the season and time people spent outside on their mood. People's mood was positively related to with air temperature when they spent more time outside on spring days, whereas decreased mood was more likely developed when people spent more time outside on warm summer days (Keller et al., 2005). In sum, the literature of psychology demonstrated mixed results of the relationships between weather and mood. No study was found to investigate weather effects on news decision making.

Weather as a Secondary Variable

Prior literature indicates that the tone of news reports could be influenced by seemingly secondary variables. For instance, the geographical location of a newspaper, or in essence the economic influence on the communities served by the newspaper, could accurately predict the positivity and negativity of its coverage of the first U.S. mad cow outbreak (Haigh, Bruce, & Craig, 2008). Specifically, the study found that the Midwest newspapers were more positive in tone than coastal papers in covering the outbreak. Reporters' gender was also found to be a consistent secondary variable that affects news reporting such as story tone, content, and use of a greater diversity of sources (Len-Rios, Park, Cameron, Duke, & Kreuter, 2008). Possibly, weather could be one of such secondary variables that influence the tone of news stories in one way or another.

An entire stream of research had been devoted to investigating how weather might influence people's judgment and behavior. Cohn (1990) found that weather could significantly influence crime rate and crime behavior. Inclement weather, especially extreme heat or cold, reduces assaults and other disorderly conduct (Rotton, 2000). After studying the weather data in New York City from 1927 to 1989, Saunders (1993) found that the weather (cloudy or rainy days vs. bright, sunny days) had an effect on stock prices. Later Hirshleifer and Shumway (2003) found that when people were in a positive mood elicited by, say, sunny weather in New York City, they tended to have more positive judgments in trading stocks. Accordingly, they were more likely to take bolder steps to sell or buy stocks, eventually making greater profits than on cloudy or rainy days. In this vein, weather might also influence the positivity or negativity of the news coverage as a secondary variable.

Positivity and Negativity

Human functions of positive and negative affect have been one of the most systematically researched areas in the literature of psychology (Taylor, 1991). According to psychologists, the most fundamental inference from human beings' language can be classified into positive, negative, and neutral (Osgood, 1959, 1963). Kumata and Schramm (1956) found that even for groups as divergent in language and culture as Americans, Japanese, and Koreans, positive and negative evaluation was still the first and biggest factor. Scheier and Carver (1993) had proposed that positivity and negativity had "an enduring personality characteristic that changes little with the vagaries of life" (p. 27). In studying social interaction, positivity/negativity was one of the three dimensions that accounted for a substantial amount of the variance in individual difference (Bales, 1970; Bales & Cohen, 1979).

Osgood (1959) contended that positive and negative evaluation was the first and the biggest universal dimension of the various ways people use language. Traditionally, the technique social scientists developed to study language characteristics was the semantic differential, where a concept was measured by a number of adjective words related to the specific objects (e.g., Osgood, 1963). Those scale judgments collected from a number of researchers were then factor analyzed. Those factor analyses repeatedly produced roughly the same result: The positive-negative evaluation was first in magnitude and order of appearance.

In social interaction, "positive" refers to "friendly and equalitarian," whereas "negative" is related to "unfriendly and negativistic." The General

Inquirer (GI), a computer-aided content analysis tool, was developed based on the following definition of positivity and negativity (Stone, Dunphy, Smith, & Ogilvie, 1966):

> *Positivity:* words reflecting a positive outlook, that is, friendly, virtue, optimistic.
> *Negativity:* words reflection a negative outlook, that is, angry, passive, weak.

The GI, which was developed by Philip J. Stone and his students at the Massachusetts Institute of Technology in the 1960s (Oglivie, Stone, & Kelly, 1982), has been one of the earliest and most widely used tools for computer-aided content analysis. Past studies have demonstrated that the GI is a valuable methodological tool for content analysis research with high internal and external validity. Nowadays as a program that can be used on any operating systems with a Java Virtual Machine, the GI produces a systematic, reliable, and replicable analysis of news stories on the 2008 Beijing Olympics.

Computer-Aided Content Analysis

Content analysis is a research method that "uses a set of procedures to make valid inferences from text" (Weber, 1990, p. 9). To Stone and his associates (1966), "Content analysis is any research technique for making inferences systematically and objectively identifying specific characteristics within text" (p. 5). Thanks to the diffusion of computer science and the growing capacities of computers since the 1950s, the computer-aided content analysis has offered several distinct advantages over manual content analysis procedures featured by a series of time-consuming and tedious human-coded methods (see Hai, 2003). First, the stability and comparability of coding rules lead to more accuracy of the research findings. Second, once the rules for coding are programmed into a computer, the computer provides perfect coder reliability in applying the rules to texts, eliminating individual differences, human errors, and fatigue factors associated with manual coding. Third, computers can process huge quantities of text data with exceptional speed.

Perhaps the earliest and the most representative computer-aided content analysis application is the GI (Oglivie et al., 1982; Stone et al., 1966), which "was strongly informed by both need-based and psychoanalytic traditions" (Pennebaker, Mehl, & Niederhoffer, 2003, p. 550). As the "mother" of computerized text analysis (Pennebaker et al., 2003), the GI can systematically identify, within texts, instances of words and phrases that belong to categories specified by a researcher and count occurrences and specified co-occurrences of these categories. In sum, the GI is a multipurpose text analysis tool that can be used for making classifications of words, combinations of words (idioms), or sentences (Psathas, 1969).

The classification system is an important part of the GI system, which is often called the "dictionary." The GI employs the Harvard Psychosociological Dictionary, specifically the Harvard-IV-4 TagNeg (H4N) file for the classification of the semantic meaning of words in a content analysis. The present study uses the most recent versions of categories in the GI's H4N. The latest Harvard dictionary is also featured in many other computer-aided content analysis systems, including Protan, TextQuest, and WordStat. For the present research, the GI converted each news report into numeric values, counting the number of words in the news stories and then classifying them into various word categories. The word categories are neither mutually exclusive nor exhaustive, meaning that one word may fall into multiple categories depending on, if any, its various connotations (Tetlock, 2007).

Furthermore, the GI is able to differentiate among the different meanings that a particular word might have prior to assigning it to relevant categories. With a compilation of a set of rather complex word count routines, the GI goes beyond counting words. In a two-step process, it first identifies homographs—ambiguous words that have different meanings depending on the context. It then applies a series of preprogrammed disambiguation rules aimed at clarifying their meaning in the text (Pennebaker et al., 2003). For example, the statement "That's a lofty goal" may mean that it was viewed as "a respectable goal," or the goal was "too ambitious to achieve." When the GI analyzes the statement, it first identifies the word "lofty" as an ambiguous word and will code it as positive or negative only when its connotation was analyzed in a given context. Currently there are 182 predefined word categories in the GI dictionary, among which positive and negative word categories are the latest and largest, reaching 10,827 words (Loughran & McDonald, 2011).

One of the first studies employing the GI is a study by Ogilvie, Stone, and Shneidman (1966). They used the software to compare genuine suicide notes and simulated suicide notes. They found that genuine notes referred to specific things, persons, and places more frequently and used the word "love" more often, whereas simulated notes gained a higher percentage of cognitive process tags. As a result, they successfully identified 17 of 18 pairs of notes in a cross-validation sample based on content analysis of the tone of the notes. Tedlock (2007) measured the positivity and negativity of a popular *Wall Street Journal* column by using the GI's Harvard Psycho-sociological Dictionary and found that high or low negativity of the column's content predicted high market trading volume. For decades, the GI had been applied to different social science domains including finance, sociology, political science, psychology, and cross-cultural studies (Hai, 2003; Loughran & McDonald, 2011; Tetlock, Sarr-Tsechansky, & Macskassy, 2008).

Weather Variables

This study employed the Air Pollution Index (API), temperature, and cloudiness as a comprehensive measurement of the Beijing weather. The API is a number used by government agencies around the world to characterize air quality in a city or a given location. When the API number goes up, it indicates that the air quality goes worse (see the appendix). In Beijing, an unpleasant day was almost always associated with higher API numbers, where air pollution was contributed mainly by five atmospheric pollutants measured in the API. The five pollutants, according to China's State Environment Protection Agency, were sulfur dioxide (SO_2), nitrogen dioxide (NO_2), suspended particulates (PM_{10}), carbon monoxide (CO), and ozone (O_3), which were measured at the monitoring stations throughout each city and published in newspapers every day. The detrimental effects of air pollution have a significant effect not only on health (e.g., severe headache) but also on people's mood (e.g., a positive or negative mood; Brandstatter, Fruhwirth, & Krichler, 1988; Bullinger, 1989, 1990; Mukamal, Wellenius, Suh, & Mittleman, 2009). The information of cloudiness was provided by China Meteorological Administration, which was published in Beijing's newspapers every day as, for instance, "sunny," "overcast," or "rainy," along with the temperature in Celsius degrees.

RESEARCH QUESTIONS

Based on the literature reviewed, people in good moods should find positive material more salient and psychologically available than negative materials. This evidence suggests that on dim, dull, dreary, depressing days with heavy air pollution, journalists might experience negative mood and thus frame news events by using more negative words, whereas cherry, bright days with better air quality will boost them to use more positive words. On the other hand, some studies found that weather did not influence much of people's mood. In this view, journalists might not be affected much by their daily mood or weather as they have been trained to view weather or mood effects antithetical to good journalism. Thus the following research questions were proposed:

RQ1: Does Beijing's weather—measured by the API, temperature, and cloudiness—have an effect on the tone of U.S. newspapers' coverage of the 2008 Beijing Olympic Games?

RQ2: Are there any differences between the four U.S. newspapers regarding the weather effects on the tone of their Olympic reports?

Among international correspondents, there is a saying that many correspondents tend to become more positive about what they cover regardless of their previous attitude, especially in a foreign country. The phenomenon was evident among some embedded journalists during the 2003 Iraq War. Researchers found that the longer these journalists were embedded within the military, the tone of their reports was more positive about U.S. military in Iraq (Artz & Kamalipour, 2005; Fahmy & Johnson, 2005; Pfau et al., 2004, 2005). To test whether such an attitude might exist among U.S. journalists who covered the Beijing Olympics, this study thus divided the news reports in August 2008 into three periods: (a) before the Games (August 1–8) when most international correspondents went to Beijing and began to form an initial impression of the capital and its preparation for the Olympics; (b) first half of the Games (August 9–15) when correspondents know more about China and the Games; (c) second half of the Games plus the final days in Beijing (August 16–31), a period when the reporters might have a more complete impression about China and the Games. To examine whether the tone of the Olympic stories fluctuated during the three periods, the following research question was formulated:

RQ3: Does the tone of the Olympic coverage differ over the three periods: before the Games (August 1–8), the first half of the Games (August 9–15), and second half of the Games plus the final days U.S. journalists filed reports from Beijing (August 16–31)?

METHOD

By using GI, this study examined the tone of four U.S. newspapers' Olympic reports that were filed from Beijing. The four newspapers were selected because they are the most circulated papers in the United States with a worldwide influence. A total of 289 news reports were collected from the newspapers, that is, the *New York Times* ($n = 88$), *Washington Post* ($n = 70$), *Wall Street Journal* ($n = 64$), and *USA Today* ($n = 67$). The reports were divided into two country categories: China-related reports ($n = 166$), covering Chinese athletes, sports teams and other China-related Olympic news (e.g., China's preparation for the Games), and U.S.-related reports ($n = 102$), covering U.S. athletes, sports teams and other U.S.-related Olympic news (e.g., The NBA News' plan of broadcasting the Games).

The reports covering both countries were excluded in either China or U.S. category.

Criteria for Selecting Reports

All the news reports included for analysis came from the print versions of the four newspapers. They were published from August 1 to 30, 2008, bearing either a deadline of "Beijing" or could be obviously identified that they were filed from Beijing. Any Olympic-related reports that could not be clearly identified being filed from Beijing were excluded in the analysis. Non-news reports such as columns, opinions, and letters to the editor were also excluded from the analysis.

Measures

Air Pollution Index. The API numbers published by the State Environment Protection Agency were collected by the first author from Beijing newspapers, ranging from 28 to 111 in August 2008 ($M = 57.73$, $SD = 24.82$). Higher API numbers suggested a higher pollution level in the capital.

Temperature and cloudiness. Beijing's temperature and cloudiness data in August 2008 came from China's National Meteorological Centre (NMC) located in Beijing, which were published in all Beijing newspapers. The NMC provides the press a daily weather reporting service including both forecasted high and low temperature for the day and previous day' actual high and low temperature in Celsius degrees. The actual high temperature data were used for this study because they were more accurate and had a stronger effect on people than low temperature in summer time. For temperature, the mean was 30.30°C (86.54°F; $SD = 2.45$). A higher number indicated a hotter day in Beijing. Beijing's cloudiness in that month was categorized into five categories by the NMC: rain (coded as 5), cloudy with rain (coded as 4), mostly cloudy (coded as 3), partly cloudy (coded as 2) and sunny (coded as 1). With $M = 3.13$, $SD = 1.04$ for cloudiness, more than half of the days in that August were cloudy in Beijing, and higher numbers suggested gloomier days in the capital.

Positivity and negativity. To calculate the positivity and negativity of the coverage, all the 289 reports on the Olympics were input into the GI, which compared all the words in the news stories with the embedded GI dictionary. The primary measure of the coverage of the Beijing Olympics was the standardized fraction of positive and negative words in each news story.

A story's tone was measured according to the relative frequency of positive or negative words used in it. Variables were generated based on the GI output showing the percentage of all words that were positive and the percentage of all words that were negative in each article. These procedures conform to prior studies using the Harvard-IV-4 dictionary (e.g., Tetlock, 2007; Tetlock et al., 2008). The positivity and negativity percentages from the 289 reports were then aggregated to form a model of time series data, an ordered sequence of values of the variables measuring the ups and downs of the positivity or negativity from August 1 to 31, 2008. Time series analysis was employed because it could help identify the nature of the phenomenon represented by the sequence of observations and, more important, explore any interaction between the weather and the tone of the Olympic coverage.

As a result, six variables were generated—"overall negativity or positivity," "negativity or positivity on China," and "negativity or positivity on U.S." The "overall positivity and negativity" variables refer to the aggregated positivity and negativity of the four newspapers' reports. They were calculated by adding up each report's negativity (or positivity) percentage, and then dividing by the total number of the articles published on the same day. The other variables were calculated in the same method. Larger numbers indicate higher percentage of positive or negative words used.

FINDINGS

A series of multiple regression, correlation, and multivariate analyses of variance (MANOVA) analyses were employed to investigate how the weather might influence the four U.S. newspapers' coverage of the 2008 Beijing Olympics.

RQ1: Weather Effects on Four U.S. Newspapers' Olympic Reports

Hierarchical multiple regression analyses disclosed a significant relationship between the weather and the overall negativity of the four U.S. newspapers' coverage of the Olympics, $F(4, 24) = 3.71$, $p < .01$, $\beta = .46$, $R^2 = .38$, $p < .01$. The model as a whole is significant, and the API and temperature emerged as predictors of using negative words in the Olympic reports, but not the cloudiness (see Table 1). Specifically, as shown in Table 1, when the weather got worse in Beijing, that is, the API (air pollution) went higher and temperature rose, U.S. journalists used more negative words in reporting the Olympics. The cloudiness was not found to have any effect on choices of negative words, though the combined effect of the API, temperature, and cloudiness could significantly predict the negativity of the Olympic reports.

TABLE 1
Hierarchical Regression Analyses Predicting Negativity of the Four U.S.
Newspapers' Coverage of the 2008 Beijing Olympics

	B	SE B	β
Step 1			
Constant	1.15	4.94	
API	.38	.14	.47**
Temperature	.32	.19	.45*
Cloudiness	−.48	.45	−.25
Step 2			
Constant	−6.52	5.89	
API × Temperature × Cloudiness	.21	.12	.46**

Note. For Step 1, $R^2 = .27$, $p < .01$; for Step 2, $\Delta R^2 = .38$, $p < .01$. API = Air Pollution Index.
*$p < .05$. **$p < .01$.

No interaction was detected between the weather and using more or fewer positive words. The nonsignificant relationship indicated that none of the three weather variables—the API, temperature, and cloudiness—influenced much how U.S. journalists used positive words in their stories.

A multicollinearity problem exists when two or more predictor variables in a multiple regression model are highly correlated. The highest condition number in the current regression model is 21.74. Belsley, Kuh, and Welsch (1980) proposed that a condition index of 30 to 100 indicates moderate to strong multicollinearity. Hence, multicollinearity may not be a big concern in this case.

The data disclosed that the API was also significantly correlated to the negativity of U.S. journalists' reports on China, $r(28) = .38$, $p < .05$, but not on U.S.-related reports, $r(19) = .25$, *ns*. The temperature was found to have a significant relationship with the negativity of the U.S.-related reports, $r(19) = .52$, $p < .05$, but not on the negativity of China-related reports, $r(28) = .10$, *ns*. Again the cloudiness was not found to have any relation with either positivity or negativity of the reports. This suggests that U.S. journalists tended to use more negative words in reporting China-related news as Beijing's air pollution level increased. They also used more negative words in U.S.-related stories when the temperature rose.

RQ2: Differences Between the U.S. Newspapers Regarding the Weather Influence

To investigate this research question, a correlation analysis was run between the weather variables (the API, temperature, and cloudiness) and positivity/negativity variables from each of the four newspapers, that is, overall positivity or negativity of the reports, positivity or negativity of the reports on China, and positivity or negativity of the reports on the United States. The results showed that the API had an effect on the negativity of two newspapers: the *Washington Post*, specifically the negativity of its overall Olympic reports, $r(25) = .45$, $p < .05$, and the *Wall Street Journal*, the negativity of its reports on China, $r(22) = .43$, $p < .05$. This means that the reporters from the *Washington Post* and the *Wall Street Journal* used more negative words in reporting the Olympics as the air pollution became worse.

The temperature was found to have a significant association with the negativity of the *New York Times*'s overall coverage of the Olympics, $r(26) = .40$, $p < .05$, and its reporting on China-related news, $r(21) = .48$, $p < .05$. The temperature also had a significant relationship with the *Washington Post*'s China-related reports, $r(21) = .46$, $p < .05$. These suggested that as the temperature went higher (less comfortable in summer), U.S. journalists used more negative words in their reports. But the temperature had little effect on how journalists used positive words in the same reports.

There was only one significant relationship involving the cloudiness. Analyses showed that Beijing's cloudiness was significantly associated with the overall positivity of the *Wall Street Journal*'s Olympic reports, $r(21) = .44$, $p < .05$, suggesting that its journalists used more positive words when it was sunny, but they did not use as many positive words when it was cloudier or raining.

RQ3: Changes of the Tone of the Olympic Coverage During the Olympics

The coverage of the Olympics was divided into the beginning (August 1–8; i.e., reports filed before the Games started); the middle (August 9–15), or the first half of the Games; and the ending (August 16–31), or the second half of the Games, plus the final days the U.S. journalists reported from Beijing. MANOVA analyses showed that Beijing's temperature had a significant difference between the three periods, $F(2, 29) = 5.61$, $p < .01$. But the air quality had little difference between the three periods, $F(2, 29) = 2.20$, $p = .13$, nor was the cloudiness different, $F(2, 29) = 2.23$, $p = .13$.

The positivity of the *Wall Street Journal* reports on the United States demonstrates a significant difference across the three periods, $F(2, 28) = 10.79$, $p < .01$. The Tukey's Honestly Significant Difference post hoc test indicates that the *Wall Street Journal* used significantly more positive words in its reports on the United States in the first period ($M = 6.76$, $SD = 1.27$) than the second period ($M = 4.23$, $SD = .48$, $p < .01$) or the third period

($M = 3.71$, $SD = .54$, $p < .01$). No other relationship was detected. This may suggest that the pattern of using positive or negative words did not change much among the four newspapers over the three periods.

DISCUSSION AND CONCLUSION

This study aims to investigate the weather effect on the tone of U.S. newspaper coverage of the 2008 Beijing Olympics by using the GI. Given the fact that the GI has been used in various disciplines except communication-based disciplines, the current research is breaking new ground in using it in communication studies. The results showed some significant associations between weather (especially air pollution and temperature) and the negativity of U.S. newspapers' reporting of the sports event. Specifically, as the temperatures rose and pollution levels increased, more negative words were found in U.S. journalists' stories. The same trend was also observed between the temperature and the negativity of China-related reports, that is, as the temperature rose, more negative words were found in the stories.

The analyses also discovered that the weather effect was not consistent across the four U.S. newspapers. By examining the weather effect on each newspaper, this study found that weather influenced the reports in the *Wall Street Journal*, the *Washington Post* and the *New York Times*, but not the *USA Today*. Specifically, as the API number went higher, more negative words were found in the news reported by the *Washington Post* and the *Wall Street Journal*. As the temperature rose, more negative words were found in the *New York Times* and the *Washington Post* reports. The findings may bring working journalists a cautionary note that their news decisions might be influenced by a greater variety of factors than they thought. Some exogenous factors beyond known patterns of journalistic practices (e.g., weather conditions as shown in this study) might also play an implicit role in news decision making.

The phenomena disclosed in this study may not be easily explained by existing theories of journalism studies. There are two reasons for the difficulty. On one hand, we are not so sure that the weather influences the negativity of news reports directly via affecting the journalists' mood states, or via some other social, physiological mechanisms. On the other, it is possible that using more or fewer positive and negative words in news reports might covary with certain unknown activities that in turn depend on the weather. Could it be that individual differences in the covariation between internal factors such as the anxiety of covering the Olympics in a foreign country, pressures of heavy workload and deadline, and excitement or disappointment caused by the ongoing sports competition, on one hand, and some external factors such as weather, a new working environment, and peer competition, on the other hand, caused a spurious interaction or correlation between weather and news reporting? Obviously traditional journalism theories do not provide much help here. But rather than offering a largely theoretical case, this research could serve as a unique opportunity to bridge the human–mass communication divide with some human communication theory as an underpinning.

It must be noted that any relations between Beijing's weather and the tone of U.S. newspapers' coverage of the Beijing Olympics could be equivocal in terms of causation. The findings did not provide any support for a causal relationship between weather and the tone of news stories. The correlations in this study may suggest an association between the two variables, but no causal relation between them. Any attempt to assume that good or bad weather is *directly* linked to either positivity or negativity of news coverage could simply be wrong. An association between weather and word choices represents, however, a result of the not-yet-understood link between weather and news decision making.

Some may argue that the widespread negativity of U.S. newspaper coverage discovered in the present research could be due in large part to the fact that the Beijing Olympics was an event that had received extensive criticism from U.S. media because of various air-pollution-related issues prior to the Games. The negativity in the coverage could also be due to some ideological biases, personal biases, or other reasons—not necessarily indicating the U.S. correspondents were physically "under the weather." The data in the current study did not provide good answers, which could become the direction of future research in this line. Future studies in this vein may consider excluding any news articles that explicitly mention air quality, temperature, or cloudiness into the analysis for a better validity of the weather-related influence on news reporting. Such studies should shed more light on the relations between weather and news decision making including choices of positive or negative words.

The findings in this study suggest some broader implications for news decision making, especially international news reporting. In addition to other more familiar factors in journalism studies, weather could be one of the many influences on the tone of news reports. On-scene reporters, gathering news from "ground zero," might be especially vulnerable to various exogenous influences such as air pollution and other weather conditions, which were yet to be systematically studied.

The process of news decision making is complex and can be influenced by numerous factors, explicit or implicit. We may never explain in fully satisfactory accounts why an individual journalist chooses more or fewer negative or positive words, and what factors may influence the choices and how.

But we argue that to better understand how journalists make decisions, it is necessary to explore not only known patterns of journalistic practice but also some exogenous factors. This study represents such an effort, the findings of which provide evidence that journalists' news decision making may be influenced by a greater variety of factors than we previously thought.

ACKNOWLEDGMENTS

We gratefully acknowledge the editors, Stephen D. Perry and Kim Bissell, and three anonymous reviewers for their valuable comments and suggestions to improve the manuscript, although any errors are ours.

REFERENCES

Allen, M., & Fischer, G. (1978). Ambient temperature effects on paired association learning. *Ergonomics, 21,* 95–101.

Artz, L., & Kamalipour, Y. R. (Eds.). (2005). *Bring 'em on: Media and politics in the Iraq war.* Lanham, MD: Rowman & Littlefield.

Bales, R. F. (1970). *Personality and interpersonal behavior.* New York, NY: Holt, Rinehart & Winston

Bales, R. F., & Cohen, S. P. (1979). *SYMLOG: A system for the multiple level observation of groups.* New York, NY: Free Press

Barnton, A. G. (1988). The effect of weather on mood, productivity, and frequency of emotional crisis in a temperate continental climate. *International Journal of Biometeorology, 32,* 134–143.

Belsley, D. A., Kuh, E., & Welsch, R. E. (1980). *Regression diagnostics: Identifying influential data and sources of collinearity.* New York, NY: Wiley.

Berkowitz, D., & TerKeurst, J. V. (1986). Community as interpretive community: Rethinking the journalist–source relationship. *Journal of Communication, 49,* 125–136.

Brandstatter, H., Fruhwirth, M., & Krichler, E. (1988). Effects of weather and air pollution on mood: An individual approach. In D. Canter, J. C. Jesuino, L. Soczka & G. M. Stephenson (Eds.), *Environmental social psychology* (pp. 149–159). New York, NY: Springer.

Bullinger, M. (1989). Psychological effects of air pollution on healthy residents: A time-series approach. *Journal of Environmental Psychology, 9,* 103–118.

Bullinger, M. (1990). Environmental stress: Effects of air pollution on mood, neuropsychological function and physical state. In S. Puglisi-Allegra & A. Oliverio (Eds.), *Psychology of stress* (pp. 241–250). Boston, MA: Kluwer Academic.

Clark, L. A., & Watson, D. (1988). Mood and the mundane: Relations between daily life events and self-reported mood. *Journal of Personality and Social Psychology, 54,* 296–308.

Cohn, E. G. (1990). Weather and crime. *British Journal of Criminology, 30*(1), 51–64.

Cunningham, M. R. (1979). Weather, mood and helping behavior: Quasi-experiments with the sunshine Samaritan. *Journal of Personality and Social Psychology, 37,* 1047–1056.

Denissen, J. J., Butalid, L., Penke, L., & van Aken, M. A. G. (2008). The effects of weather on daily mood: A multilevel approach. *Emotion, 8,* 662–667.

Fahmy, S., & Johnson, T. (2005). How we performed: Embedded journalists' attitudes and perceptions toward covering the Iraq War. *Journalism and Mass Communication Quarterly, 82,* 301–317.

Faust, V. (1977). *Biometeorologies.* Stuttgart, Germany: Hippokrates.

Goldstein, K. M. (1972). Weather, mood, and internal–external control. *Perceptual Motor Skills, 35,* 786.

Hai, Y. (2003) *Exploring positivity and negativity: Its measurement, validation and application in a study of leadership (Unpublished doctoral dissertation).* University of London, London, UK.

Haigh, M. M., Bruce, M., & Craig, E. (2008). Mad cow coverage more positive in Midwest papers. *Newspaper Research Journal, 29*(1), 50–62.

Hartmatz, M. G., Well, A. D., Overtree, C. E., Kawamura, K. Y., Rosal, M. C., & Ockene, I. S. (2000). Seasonal variation of depression and other moods: A longitudinal approach. *Journal of Biological Rhythms, 15,* 344–350.

Hirshleifer, D., & Shumway, T. (2003). Good day sunshine: Stock returns and the weather. *Journal of Finance, 58,* 1009–1032.

Howarth, E., & Hoffman, M. S. (1984). A multidimensional approach to the relationship between mood and weather. *British Journal of Psychology, 75,* 15–23.

Keller, M. C., Fredrickson, B. L., Ybarra, O., Cote, S., Johnson, K., Mikels, J., & Wager, T. (2005). A warm heart and a clear head: The contingent effects of weather on mood and cognition. *Psychological Science, 16,* 724–731.

Kumata, H., & Schramm, W. (1956). A pilot study of cross-cultural meaning. *Public Opinion Quarterly, 20,* 229–238.

Len-Rios, M. E., Park, S-A., Cameron, G. T., Duke, D. L., & Kreuter, M. (2008). Study asks if reporter's gender or audience predict paper's cancer coverage. *Newspaper Research Journal, 29,* 91–99.

Loughran, T., & McDonald, B. (2011). When is a liability not a liability? Textual analysis, dictionaries, and 10-Ks. *Journal of Finance, 66,* 35–65.

Mayer, J. D., Gaschke, Y. N., Braverman, D. L., & Evans, T. W. (1992). Mood-congruent judgment is a general effect. *Journal of Personality and Social Psychology, 63,* 119–132.

Mukamal, K. J., Wellenius, G. A., Suh, H. H., & Mittleman, M. A. (2009). Weather and air pollution as triggers of severe headaches. *Neurology, 72,* 922–927.

Ogilvie, D. M., Stone, P. J., & Kelly, E. F. (1982). Computer-aided content analysis. In R. B. Smith & P. K. Manning (Eds.), *Handbook of Social Science Methods* (pp. 219–246). Cambridge, MA: Ballinger.

Ogilvie, D. M., Stone, P. J., & Shneidman, E. S. (1966). Some characteristics of genuine versus simulated suicide notes. In P. J. Stone, D. C. Dunphy, M. S. Smith & D. M. Ogilvie (Eds.), *The General Inquirer: A computer approach to content analysis* (pp. 527–535). Cambridge, MA: MIT Press.

Osgood, C. E. (1959). The representational model and relevant research methods. In I. d. S. Pool (Ed.), *Trends in content analysis* (pp. 33–88). Urbana, IL: University of Illinois Press.

Osgood, C. E. (1963). Language universals and psycholinguistics. In J. H. Greenberg (Ed.), *Universals of language* (pp. 299–322). Cambridge, MA: MIT Press.

Parrott, W. G., & Sabini, J. (1990). Mood and memory under natural condition: Evidence for mood incongruent recall. *Journal of Personality and Social Psychology, 59,* 321–336.

Pennebaker, J., Mehl, M. R., & Niederhoffer, K. G. (2003). Psychological aspects of natural language use: Our words, our selves. *Annual Review of Psychology, 54,* 547–577.

Persinger, M. S. (1975). Lag responses in mood reports to changes in the weather matrix. *International Journal of Biometeorology, 19,* 108–114.

Pfau, M., Haigh, M., Gettle, M., Donnelly, M., Scott, G., Warr, D., & Wittenberg, E. (2004). Embedding journalists in military combat units: Impact on newspaper story frames and tone. *Journalism and Mass Communication Quarterly, 81,* 74–88.

Pfau, M., Haigh, M. M., Logsdon, L., Perrine, C., Baldwin, J. P., Breitenfeldt, R. E., & Romero, R. (2005). Embedded reporting during the invasion and occupation of Iraq: How the embedding of journalists affects television news reports. *Journal of Broadcasting & Electronic Media, 49,* 468–487.

Psathas, G. (1969). The general inquirer: Useful or not? *Computers and the Humanities, 3,* 163–174.

Rotton, J. (2000). Weather, disorderly conduct, and assaults. *Environment and Behavior, 32,* 651–673.

Sanders, J. L., & Brizzolara, M. S. (1982). Relationships between weather and mood. *Journal of General Psychology, 107*(1), 155–156.

Saunders, E. M. (1993). Stock prices and Wall Street weather. *American Economic Review, 83,* 1337–1345.

Scheier, M. E., & Carver, C. S. (1993). On the power of positive thinking: The benefits of being optimistic. *Current Directions in Psychological Science, 2*(1), 26–30.

Schwarz, N., & Clore, G. L. (1983). Mood, misattribution and judgment of well-being: Informative and directive function of affective states. *Journal of Personality and Social Psychology, 45,* 513–523.

Seib, P. M. (2002). *The global journalist: News and conscience in a world of conflict.* Lanham, MD: Rowman & Littlefield.

Shoemaker, P. J., & Reese, S. D. (1996). *Mediating the message: Theories of influences on mass media content* (2nd ed.). White Plains, NY: Longman.

Sinclair, R. C., Mark, M. M., & Clore, G. L. (1994). Mood-related persuasion depends on (mis)attributions. *Social Cognition, 12,* 309–326.

Stone, P. J., Dunphy, D. C., Smith, M. S., & Ogilvie, D. M. (1966). *The General Inquirer: A computer approach to content analysis.* Cambridge, MA: MIT Press

Sundar, S. S. (2003). News features and learning. In J. Bryant, D. Roskos-Ewoldsen & J. Cantor (Eds.), *Communication and emotion: Essays in honor of Dolf Zillmann* (pp. 275–296). Mahwah, NJ: Erlbaum.

Taylor, S. E. (1991). Asymmetrical effects of positive and negative events: The mobilization-minimization hypothesis. *Psychological Bulletin, 110*(1), 67–85.

Tetlock, P. C. (2007). Giving content to investor sentiment: The role of media in the stock market. *Journal of Finance, 62,* 1139–1168.

Tetlock, P. C., Sarr-Tschansky, M., & Macskassy, S. (2008). More than words: Quantifying language to measure firms' fundamentals. *Journal of Finance, 63,* 1437–1467.

Tromp, S. W. (1980). *Biometeorology: The impact of the weather and climate on humans and their environment (animals and plants).* Philadelphia, PA: Heyden.

Watson, D. (2000). *Mood and temperament.* New York, NY: Guilford.

Weaver, D. H., & Wu, W. (1998). *The global journalist: News people around the world.* Cresskill, NJ: Hampton.

Weber, R. P. (1990). *Basic content analysis* (2nd ed.). Newbury Park, CA: Sage.

Zhong, B., & Newhagen, J. E. (2009). How journalists think while they write: A transcultural model of news decision-making. *Journal of Communication, 59,* 584–605.

APPENDIX

TABLE A1
Air Pollution Index (API) and Health Implications

API	Level of air pollution	Health implications
0–50	Excellent	No health implications.
51–100	Good	No health implications.
101–150	Slightly polluted	Slight irritations may occur, individuals with breathing or heart problems should reduce outdoor exercise.
151–200	Lightly polluted	Slight irritations may occur, individuals with breathing or heart problems should reduce outdoor exercise.
201–250	Moderately polluted	Healthy people will be noticeably affected. People with breathing or heart problems will experience reduced endurance in activities. These individuals and elders should remain indoors and restrict activities.
251–300	Heavily polluted	Healthy people will be noticeably affected. People with breathing or heart problems will experience reduced endurance in activities. These individuals and elders should remain indoors and restrict activities.
300+	Severely polluted	Healthy people will experience reduced endurance in activities. There may be strong irritations and symptoms and may trigger other illnesses. Elders and the sick should remain indoors and avoid exercise. Healthy individuals should avoid out door activities.

Note. Source: China's State Environment Protection Agency.

When Symbols Clash: Legitimacy, Legality and the 2010 Winter Olympics

Karen-Marie Elah Perry
Department of Anthropology
University of Victoria

Helen Hyunji Kang
Department of Sociology and Anthropology
Simon Fraser University

In February 2010, the Olympics descended on Vancouver, British Columbia. Between athletes competing for gold and a provincial venue with the highest poverty rate in Canada, a clash of symbols arose: those deemed legitimate by the Vancouver Olympic Organizing Committee (VANOC) and those deemed illegitimate. The Games not only transformed the city's landscape, municipal laws, infrastructure, and social relations but also resulted in the concurrent transformation of the city's visual culture. As an explicit tactic, Aboriginal; antipoverty; environmental; anarchist; and lesbian, gay, bisexual, and transgender activists employed countersymbols to disrupt VANOC's plans. Through qualitative discourse analysis of photos and visual imagery, this article addresses social, historical, political, and economic issues tied to this clash of symbols, including the use of Aboriginal cultures in representations of Canadian nationalism; infringements upon civil liberties and freedom of speech that resulted from surveillance of activists and constraints to the arts;

and visual counter-discourse produced by activists through demonstrations, posters, and art.

INTRODUCTION

During the months leading up to February 2010, an extensive repertoire of images, texts, and visual practices were mobilized to build an iconography of the Vancouver Winter Olympics. The Vancouver Olympic Committee (VANOC) produced mascots, clothing labels, bumper stickers, and license plates en masse to adorn the facades of buildings, the bodies of residents and visitors to the city, and the surfaces of vehicles. At the heart of this iconography was an effort to portray a certain type of Vancouver-ness, British-Columbia-ness, and Canadian-ness, fused with visual narratives of global celebration, friendship between nations, and the glories of competitive sport that are associated with the Olympic Games. However, these images concealed more troubling aspects of the Games: VANOC had purchased a monopoly on outdoor advertising space during a 10-week period surrounding the Games, stifling not only business competitors but, as the British Columbia Civil Liberties Association (BCCLA) emphasized, "the ability of anyone else to engage in free speech" (BCCLA, 2008, p. 1). The freedom to express dissent toward the Olympic Games in Vancouver became a pressing concern for activists and citizens, who contested the billions of dollars spent on preparations for the Games (Auditor-General of British Columbia as cited in the *Vancouver Sun*, 2006), while the British Columbia (BC) Provincial Government undertook severe cutbacks to healthcare, the arts, education, and social assistance (Coalition for a Better BC, 2010). The financial and physical scale of the Olympics invited intense criticism from diverse groups, resulting in a week-long demonstration in downtown Vancouver during the Games.

Aboriginal activists were some of the first to organize in the anti-Olympic movement, notably helping to block expansion of the Sea-to-Sky Highway, a project promised in the original Olympic bid (Office of the Auditor General of British Columbia, 2003), which endangered the Eagleridge Bluffs, a fragile and unique ecosystem (Srivastava, 2006). After months of occupation, on May 25, 2006, 20 activists were arrested on site. Among them was respected Pacheedaht Elder Harriet Nahanee (Tsibeot), who died of complications due to pneumonia and cancer soon after her release from prison. Many blamed inhospitable conditions in prison as a contributing factor to her death, including Nahanee's lawyer Lyn Crompton, who reported "racist and violent" treatment during her incarceration. (The Province, 2007, para. 6). Despite a call for an independent public inquiry by local Member of Legislative Assembly, Jenny Kwan, the province refused to investigate the issue further (British Columbia Legislative Assembly, 2007). On March 6, 2007, the Native Warrior Society stole VANOC's 16×16 ft. Olympic flag from the City Hall "in honor of Harriet Nahanee" and "in solidarity with all those fighting against the destruction caused by the 2010 Winter Olympic Games" (p. 1).

Another large contingent was Vancouver's highly organized antipoverty activists, who challenged government spending on the Games and emphasized inadequately met promises for more social housing; poverty rates in BC, the highest in Canada for 11 years running (First Call, 2011); and conditions in the Downtown Eastside, a community known for its distinction as the "poorest postal code in Canada" and an HIV transmission rate of 30% (Poverty Olympics Organizing Committee, 2010b). For these and other activists who represented environmental; anarchist; and lesbian, gay, bisexual, and transgender contingents, the extravagance of the Olympics underscored a broader model of governance and morality that prioritizes the economic bottom-line and punitive measures against the poor over and above social equality, social programs and services, and environmental protection. As part of their efforts to highlight these social, political, and economic issues and to disrupt the popular narratives of the Games as merely a national celebration of cultural exchange, diverse activist groups subverted symbols associated with the Games, such as the mascots and the five interlocked rings, as part of their public protests. In this article, we examine the claims of legitimacy and illegitimacy that underpinned the exercises of power and resistance in visual narratives of the Olympics as they unfolded through the social, geographic, and visual transformation of Vancouver.

ANALYTIC FRAMEWORK

The visual politics of legitimate versus illegitimate representations of the Vancouver Winter Olympic Games can be understood in relation to critical works written on sports, activism, and surveillance. Given the scale of sponsorship opportunities, associated marketing, television network packages, promotional prospects, and tourist dollars associated with the Games, the Olympics represent a highly sought-after multibillion dollar industry (Rowe, 2004). Sociologist David Rowe (2004) characterized Olympic sporting events as "orgies of nationalism and commodification"—or, more aptly put, "commodified nationalism" (p. 24). Commodified nationalism depends on the erasure of complex socio-political issues, such as poverty, social inequality, homelessness, and contentious land claims with Aboriginal communities. Critical sports theorist Helen Lenskyj (2000) emphasized, "In the face of this image-making rhetoric, those engaged in grassroots resistance to

Olympic hegemony [face] the difficult task of moving public discourse away from urban and national chauvinism" (p. 98). Furthermore, the Olympics' symbolic value as an intensified expression of nationalism places opponents of the Olympics in a precarious position as antipatriots, creating challenges for activists not only in terms of media representation and public support but also in terms of heightened state surveillance.

Although the arts have historically played a pivotal role in critiques of the existing socio-political order, such as Surrealist and Dadaist movements in the mid-20th century (Arnason, 1986), the visual power of the arts was largely channeled in a single direction during the Vancouver Olympics: to produce an image of celebration that obscured the economic and political contexts in which the arts were being produced and practiced in the Province. Commenting on Tommie Smith's and John Carlos's defiant visual protest against racial segregation during the 1968 Mexico City Olympic Games, Avery Brundage once stated, "They violated one of the basic principles of the Olympic games: that politics play no part whatsoever in them" (as cited in Zirin, 2005, p. 76). As president of the International Olympic Committee from 1952 to 1972, an avid Nazi supporter, and outspoken critic of women participating in Olympic events (Zirin, 2007, p. 125), Brundage's argument for depoliticizing the Olympics erases his own position as political and, more broadly, obscures the centrality of politics to the Games. Internationally, it is erasure that has been the central focus of anti-Olympic activist/artists in their efforts to render visible that which is made invisible by the Olympic machine.

Visual protest tactics in a variety of forms have long been adopted in anticipation of Olympic events, informing an international vocabulary of resistance. These actions have ranged from the whimsical—for example, the United Kingdom's "I Love 2.3 Billion" mock bus tour highlighting London's gentrification and heightened security in the wake of the 2012 Games (Forkert, 2011, pp. 58–159)—to macabre "die-ins" hosted by Berlin's anti-Olympic group in anticipation of Berlin's bid for the 2000 Olympics (Lenskyj, 2000, p. 120). The quest for visibility by anti-Olympic activists has been met with aggressive campaigns of state surveillance, ranging from the use of closed-circuit television (CCTV) cameras to wiretapping (Boyle & Haggerty, 2009). In their report to the Privacy Commissioner of Canada regarding the Vancouver Olympics, sociologists Philip J. Boyle and Kevin D. Haggerty (2010) argued that Olympic surveillance has played a key role "in expanding, intensifying and normalizing surveillance practices" more broadly (p. 8).

Recent critical works on surveillance are largely influenced by Michel Foucault's (1975) work on the panopticon. Foucault famously explored Jeremy Bentham's prison structure, the panopticon, which houses inmates in cells constantly made visible to an obscured viewer in a central tower. Assumed to be under surveillance, the prisoners discipline themselves without the explicit action of an enforcer. In an age of digital technologies, the 19th-century model of the panopticon remains startlingly relevant. According to David Lyon (2006), it "still functions as an ideal, a metaphor and a set of practices" and "the idea of omniscient visibility lies behind many schemes from urban planning to military intelligence" (p. 5). The normalization of surveillance raises concerns for democratic politics: They can more readily bypass due process and accountability simply by making a vague claim to prevent an indeterminate threat (Hier, Walby, & Greenberg, 2006). The gaze of these technologies also falls disproportionately on youth, people of color, and the poor (Hier et al., 2006). CCTV cameras may be installed and justified under claims that everyone and anyone is subject to relatively harmless surveillance to ensure security and safety, but these cameras are, in fact, more closely aligned with the panoptic ideals of incarceration.

Discourse Analysis and Semiotics

To analyze the plethora of images and text that circulated in the years leading up to and during the Vancouver Games, we turn to Foucault's (1972) notion of discourse, particularly his understanding of statements as events that draw on an archive of what was said before, what is possible to say, and what is not (pp. 128–129). Hence, we situate the representations of the Games within the history of Canadian nationalism, the funding conditions of the artistic sector during the Games, and the criminalized surveillance of anti-Olympic activists. The combination of these forces made certain representations possible while rendering others impossible with respect to the Olympics. Foucault's approach to discourse is also attentive to the question of who may legitimately claim the right to speak, a methodological and theoretical position that highlights the ways in which various regimes of power shape what can be legitimately said or represented, how, and by whom. Foucault (1972) advised social researchers to look for shifts and breaks in exclusionary discourses in order to disrupt not only their claims to truth but their claims to have developed continuously and progressively, which serve to justify their exclusionary and limiting practices (pp. 220, 231–232). For example, Foucault (1972) found that psychiatric and medical discourses in the 19th century merely altered sexual taboos of previous eras into forms of illness, and thereby justified and lent scientific credibility to existing exclusionary and limiting cultural practices (p. 232). Moussa and Scapp (1996) argued that Foucault's methodology provides "a political clearing" by "creating spaces, within a discourse, where a counter discourse can emerge" (p. 92). Likewise, we pay attention to both the authoritative discourses produced by VANOC and the counterdiscourses produced by activists, and we position the two sides in terms of legitimate and illegitimate discourses, mandated as such by the law, by the media, and by other regimes of power, such as "commodified nationalism" (Rowe, 2004, p. 24). To analyze the range of counterimages produced by activists, we take up the semiotic analysis of American pragmatist Charles S. Peirce (1868). A Peircean sign is based on a triad: an object (that which is perceived), an interpretant (a sign created in the mind of the observer upon perceiving the object), and the ground (an idea of the person conveying the sign). Peircean semiosis is thus useful for analyzing the ways in which anti-Olympic activists resignified official Olympic iconography using parody and humor to convey their political ideas with respect to the Olympics. In this article, we engage in a Foucaultian discourse analysis of news stories related to the Games and the practices of representation enacted by VANOC and its sponsors, as well as activists and protesters, and apply semiotic analysis to specific visual images produced by these groups.

Many of the images explored in this article were photographed by the authors who agreed to carry cameras for the duration of the Games (from February 12 to February 28, 2010). By virtue of residence, our daily commutes to and from work in downtown Vancouver, errands, and social activities afforded opportunities to capture day-to-day transformations in Vancouver's landscape, but particularly street art and posters. In total, 68 photos were taken, with photographs indicating a range of anti-Olympic movements selected for this article. Visual sociologist Barbara Harrison (2002) emphasized that "practices which are part of everyday photography can be seen as forms of story-telling and provide access to both narratives and counter-narratives" (p. 87). We take up photography to largely document what were considered to be illegitimate representations of the Games— images and visual practices by anti-Olympic activists—that were skirted over or ignored in mainstream media. In addition, many of the anti-Olympic posters presented here were torn or removed within days or even hours. Hence, our photographic practices are an effort to make visible counterdis-courses to the Games. Qualitative visual analysis focuses less on the positivist assumption that the camera is an objective lens, but rather emphasizes interpretation, including meanings, representations, and how different claims to truth are produced and legitimized or delegitimized (Prosser, 1998). Thus, our methodological goal is not to portray a balanced representation (in a journalistic sense) of Vancouver's visual culture in the wake of the Games. Instead, our aim is to present the ways in which accepted social and media norms situated the Games as apolitical, historically sanitized, and celebratory (Lenskyj, 2000; Zirin, 2007), and thereby delegitimized and made impossible other more critical representations of the Games. Hence, this project demonstrates the ways in which relations of power may operate at the discursive level at the nexus of the Olympics, media, and society.

WHEN SYMBOLS CLASH

Spectacles of Nationalism, Aboriginal Peoples and the Olympic Spirit

In its original bid for the Olympic Games, the city of Vancouver had emphasized its cultural diversity: "Canada brings together the cultures of the world, as well as an ancient and rich First Nations culture, in one harmonious society: a living embodiment of the Olympic ideal" (Government of Canada, 2002, p. 3). This position was also reflected in the choice of logo for the 2010 Olympics, the Ilanaaq, which is an artist's interpretation of the inuksuk (a communicative symbol built from stacked stones) adopted from the Inuit, who are largely people of the North, not of the Pacific Northwest of BC (Forkert, 2011). Both the Ilanaaq and the notion of "an ancient and rich First Nations culture" homogenized over 630 diverse First Nations (Assembly of First Nations, 2010, para. 4), Inuit and Métis communities[1] that comprise the total Aboriginal population in Canada into a singular "culture." Such reductionism is a discursive practice that is intimately linked to the objectification and dehumanization of Aboriginal peoples in its level of generalization (L. Smith, 1999), a central aspect of the projects of colonialism that still operate in contemporary narratives of Canadian nationhood.

In the years leading up to the Olympics, Tourism BC televised a commercial with the slogan "Super, Natural British Columbia" with speaking parts delegated only to White English-speaking Canadian celebrities, whereas others in the commercial, including Aboriginal dancers and a young Aboriginal woman looking up at a totem pole, remain silent. These scenes appear side by side with sweeping shots of BC's natural and city landscapes and clips of downhill skiers, cowboys, Chinese New Year celebrations, sushi restaurants, sea kayakers, and golfers. This montage flattens historical and contemporary racial relations in Canada into a narrative of the happy meeting of diverse peoples of the world, including Aboriginal peoples who have been and continue to be subjected to physical and legislative violence and

---

[1]Many terms such as "Indian," "Aboriginal," "Métis," and "Native" adopted in Canada are highly legalistic, initially designed for Provincial and Federal Government control, monitoring and categorization of local indigenous populations with little relationship to traditional cultural distinctions or the preferences of communities (Sawchuk, 1998).

attempts at cultural erasure. Indeed, the 2010 Winter Olympics arrived just 14 years after the last federally run residential school[2] closed (Health Canada, 2011), 50 years after First Nations were able to vote in the 1962 federal election (University of Saskatchewan, 2011), and 20 years after the Oka crisis.[3] Although cultural revival is on the rise among Aboriginal communities and Vancouver is home to a rich Aboriginal youth movement involved in the arts and local leadership (Urban Native Youth Association, 2011), the discourse of multiculturalism, which is central to Canadian nationalism, erases—and thus renders insignificant—ongoing struggles for equity, sovereignty, land claims, and access to healthcare and education, which also characterize Aboriginal relations in Canada today. The history of colonial violence remained outside of what was possible to speak of in relation to Aboriginal communities during the Olympics; only what was celebratory and positive with respect to Canada as a liberal and multicultural nation could be legitimately depicted.

Indigenousness played a key role in VANOC's iconography, particularly in marketing and merchandising. VANOC marketed an array of "authentic" Aboriginal products to be sold through the Hudson's Bay Company (HBC), a multibillion dollar department store and North America's oldest company, which played a critical role in early colonial expansion across Canada (Royle, 2011). During the Games, the company provided uniforms for the Canadian Olympic team and was the purveyor of official Olympic merchandise. Although the Canadian Olympic team often donned the motifs of West Coast First Nations, their uniforms were in fact manufactured overseas. A group of Aboriginal artisans, led by Coast Salish artist and lawyer Shain Jackson, criticized VANOC for stealing Aboriginal art under false pretenses and for undermining the livelihood of local Aboriginal artisans (Kelly, 2010). In another highly publicized controversy, the Cowichan First Nation accused the HBC of stealing their traditional sweater design for the Olympic clothing line. The HBC produced mixed statements, denying that its sweaters were a Cowichan design but also admitting that it had declined the First Nation's offer to produce them on the basis that the handmade process made the sweaters unsuitable for mass production (Hume, 2009). These episodes demonstrate that First Nations' iconography and artistry were valuable commodities for the Olympic machinery, but this

---

[2]Beginning in the 1800s, Aboriginal children were forcibly removed from their homes and placed into residential schools for "reeducation." Mortality rates at the schools were extremely high, and many children were subject to physical and sexual abuse (Kelm, 1998).

[3]A highly publicized 78-day armed standoff between the Government of Canada and Mohawks from the Kanesatake Reserve, who were defending a burial ground from golf course development (York & Pindera, 1991).

was at the expense of First Nations artisans, ironically stripping the objects of their supposed authenticity.

There was also widespread Aboriginal support for the Games, demonstrated in agreements made with Olympics organizers by the Four Host First Nations, including the Musqueam, Tsleil-Waututh, Squamish, and Lil'wat (Government of Canada, 2010), with hopes for mutually beneficial economic arrangements, Aboriginal youth sports programs and cultural exchange in an international venue. There were also varying levels of agreement and disagreement about the impact of the Games in these communities themselves. What is important here is that there was hardly a monolithic Aboriginal perspective on the Olympic Games, yet the complexity of Aboriginal political, social, and economic perspectives, and the diversity of First Nations communities themselves, were buried under the veneer of celebration, cultural exchange, and commodified nationalism. The only legitimized ways in which Aboriginal people could participate in the Olympics was through agreement, endorsement, and contribution of their arts and cultures. Dissent and opposition were considered illegitimate and criminal, as in the case of Elder Harriet Nahanee at the Eagle Ridge Bluff protests.

Cuts to Arts and Culture

Despite the original Olympic bid's emphasis on the arts and cultural diversity in BC, the arts sector and community organizations were severely degraded during the period leading up to the Olympics (Pablo, 2009). In the fall of 2009, the Provincial Ministry of Tourism and Culture announced cuts to the arts, suddenly and unexpectedly obliterating $20 million in funding (Werb, 2009). The catastrophic losses for the arts took place while the Vancouver's Cultural Olympiad was under way. In a questionable fiscal parallel, the "$20 million" Cultural Olympiad became one of the more viable and immediate sources of money for arts and community groups while they waited in limbo for the restructuring of provincial arts funding (Wong, 2010). While Robert Kerr, the program director of the Cultural Olympiad, boasted that the Olympiad producers "partnered with 150 different local organizations to develop and deliver programming" (Wong, 2010, para. 5), the partnership proved to be based more on patronage. Vancouver poet laureate Brad Cran publically refused to participate in the Olympiad because he disagreed with a clause in the artist contract that read, "The artist shall at all times refrain from making any negative or derogatory remarks respecting VANOC, the 2010 Olympic and Paralympic Games, the Olympic movement generally, Bell and/or other sponsors associated with VANOC" (VANOC, as cited in Canadian Broadcasting Corporation, 2010, para. 3). The combination of cuts to arts funding and the imposition of the clause for artists contracted through the Olympiad meant that arts communities were limited in the ways in which they could articulate any view of the Olympics other than as a celebration.

Perhaps the most visible articulation of this turn of events was a street gallery of lantern sculptures in the heart of Downtown Vancouver. The LunarFest exhibit, erected by the Asian-Canadian Special Events Association as part of the Cultural Olympiad, celebrated the collaboration between Canadian and Taiwanese artists and featured a forest of trees adorned with lanterns made by Taiwanese school children. The main tower that advertised the exhibit's corporate sponsor and the organizers' name was composed of three brilliantly colored lantern sculptures in distinctive West Coast First Nations' motifs. The street gallery began at the intersection of Granville and Georgia Streets where the HBC's downtown store stands. At the time, the store was decked in giant posters of the VANOC logo and Olympic athletes wearing official merchandise. A huge Canadian flag also enveloped a commercial building on the other side of the street. This street intersection contained an interplay of signs—Taiwanese lanterns (signifying multiculturalism), West Coast First Nation motif, the Bay's athletes (signifying corporate sponsorship), and the Canadian flag—that were grounded in corporatized nationalism, resulting in an interpretant of Olympic spirit, which rendered any dissent or opposition to the Games virtually impossible, unpatriotic, and even irrational, all the while masking the dire state of the provincial arts sector and the fragility of the right to artistic freedom.

Surveillance and Transparency

Public spaces were seen as ripe with dangers of mob behavior that follow public festivities, but especially expressions of dissent by Canada's own citizens through protests and demonstrations. In fact, one Member of the Legislative Assembly of BC, Harry Bloy, stated that Olympic protesters were "terrorists" (British Columbia Legislative Assembly, 2009), a comment reflecting a not-uncommon view that protestors threatened the established order and were criminals. This discursive connection between protesters and "terrorists" or criminals made possible and justified the installation of almost one thousand CCTV surveillance cameras in Vancouver's downtown core (Integrated Security Unit [ISU], as cited in Vonn, 2010, p. 598), "brand[ing] protesters as dangerous" (Vonn, 2010, p. 600). The compulsion to see, in order to maintain law and order, not only resulted in the visualization of public spaces in ways that butted up against civil rights but also transformed private spaces, particularly the homes and lives of well-known and suspected activists in the city whom the ISU—composed of 6,000 police officers, 4,500 military personnel, and 5,000 private security guards[4]—perceived to be a threat. These measures were not only the largest security endeavor in Canadian history but "likely the most expensive security setup in the history of the Winter Olympics" (Wiebe, 2010, p. 21). In the months leading up to the Olympics, stories surfaced of police officers visiting the homes, associates, and neighbors of known or suspected activists and others who publically disagreed with the Olympics, including University of British Columbia professor and neurological researcher Dr. Chris Shaw (2009), the author of *Five Ring Circus* (Dembicki, 2009b). Everyday citizens were also encouraged to keep watch: Posters on college campuses told students to report "terrorism," and the local transit authority prompted commuters to "Report the suspicious, not the strange." The ISU justified these practices, stating, "What we seek to do is either confirm or disregard individuals as potential threats to the safety and security of Canadians and visitors to Canada who will be here during the Games" (Canadian Broadcasting Corporation, 2009, para. 11), thereby confirming the state's desire to distinguish between a threat and nonthreat at the expense of the privacy of its citizens and their civil liberties. The recent release of United States Diplomatic Cables pertaining to the 2010 Games on the website WikiLeaks (2011) indicates that the perceived threats of terrorism significantly outweighed the actual documented threats posed to the Olympics, which included an inert hand grenade, a plot to hang-glide over Olympic ceremonies by a mentally ill man, and a box of fishing gear at first thought to be a bomb.

Disrupting the direction of this panoptic gaze of the state and VANOC were the watchful eyes of individuals and groups in the city who opposed the Olympics as a whole or were specifically concerned about the level of police presence in the city. Most notable among these efforts were the hundreds of volunteer Legal Observers who underwent training by the BCCLA and Pivot Legal Society (BCCLA, 2010). The Legal Observers' role was to provide eyewitness documentation of the actions of the ISU in case of legal actions for instances of police misconduct: "Observers are the watchful eyes that will be focused on police, military and private security conduct to ensure accountability" (Eby & Rice, 2009, p. 5). The Legal Observers reversed the panoptic gaze and made visible the invisible hands of the state, the police, and VANOC. The protection of fundamental civil rights, such as freedom of speech and peaceful assembly, were at odds with the charter of the International Olympic Committee, which, executive director of the BCCLA David Eby (2009) pointed out, prohibited the expression of

---

[4]See the Government of Canada's Vancouver 2010 Integrated Security Unit Factsheet: http://www.canada2010.gc.ca/mmedia/kits/fch-6-eng.cfm.

political "propaganda" (para. 2) of which virtually any anti-Olympic discourse could be accused. This contradiction produced a tension for the City of Vancouver and Olympic organizers who faced criticism and scrutiny from activist groups and citizens to observe civil liberties and yet were also pressured to minimize visible protests against the Olympics.

Battle of Signs

VANOC worked at various levels of government (federal, provincial, and municipal) to enact legislation and bylaws that would ensure its control over the visual space of the city during the Games. In December 2007, as part of VANOC's contract with the International Olympic Committee, the federal government passed the Olympic and Paralympic Marks Act (2007) to protect VANOC and its official sponsors from "ambush marketing" by nonsponsoring companies using Olympics iconography (para. 6). This law resulted in several bizarre cases where long-standing small businesses in Vancouver bearing Olympic references, such as Olympia Pizza and Olympic First-Aid Services, faced legal warnings by VANOC to remove the unauthorized use of the Olympic brand (Nagy, 2006). Another city bylaw enabled the suppression of criticism of VANOC and its sponsors as unauthorized use of Olympic property, authorizing only celebratory signs until civil liberties activists intervened, resulting in a revision of the bylaw to remove this condition (Dembicki, 2009a). In addition, in October 2009, a provincial bill amended the Municipalities Enabling and Validating Act to allow police to enter private homes in Vancouver in order to remove anti-Olympic signage (BCCLA, 2009).

Anti-Olympic activists navigated these legal and judicial barriers in creative ways to express their critiques of the Games. On Commercial Drive in East Vancouver, an area of the city identified with the political Left and where one of the authors lives, two officers approached Patricia Salmond, the owner of retail store Urban Empire, requesting that she remove anti-Olympic merchandise from her store, including buttons and bumper stickers. Patricia refused, suggesting rather that they buy the entire stock of merchandise, which the officers did. She continued to sell anti-Olympic merchandise throughout the duration of the Games, even creating a full anti-Olympic window display (see Figure 1) and entering it in the Commercial Drive Business Association's Olympic Window Display Contest (P. Salmond, personal communication, February 15, 2010). Other activists resignified VANOC's iconography, such as the five interlocking rings and the mascots, through art in order to disrupt the prevailing discourse of celebration and to highlight the social, political, and economic costs of the Games. One of the most recognizable of these resignifications was Jesse

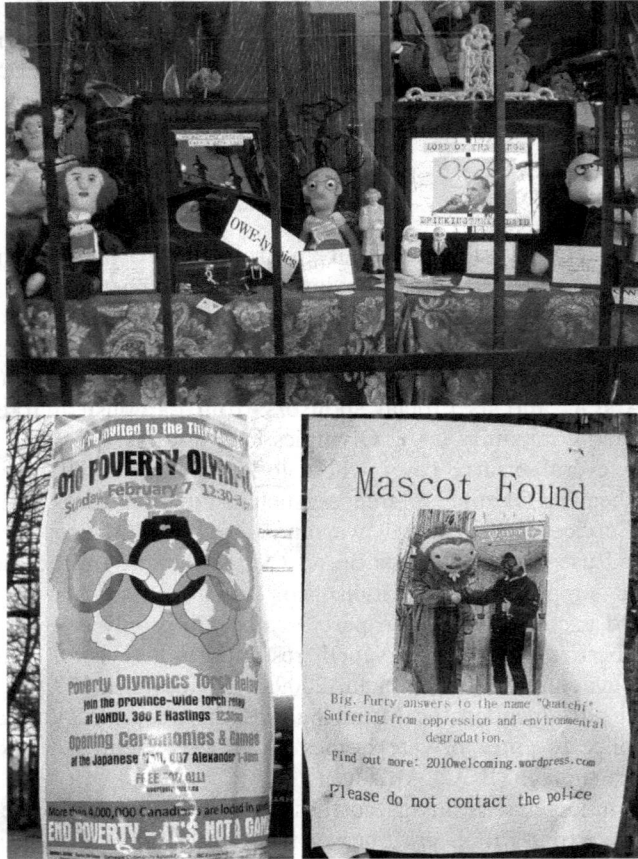

FIGURE 1   Counter-clockwise from top: Patricia's anti-Olympic window display; the Poverty Olympics' logo, "locked in poverty"; The 2010 Welcoming Committee's plea to not contact police.

Corcoran's visual parody of the Olympic rings as four unhappy faces and one happy face, grounding the iconographic rings in the Vancouver's Downtown Eastside where Corcoran also worked in a homeless shelter (C. Smith, 2009) to produce an interpretant that signifies the lack of support and funding for this neighborhood. In a 2010 Winter issue, Vancouver's lesbian, gay, bisexual, and transgender newspaper *Xtra-West* published John Crossen's (2010) "Twatchi, Smegma, and Dumi," which depicted satirical variations of the original Olympic mascots engaged in an orgy with the caption, "If you think THEY'RE getting SCREWED." Crossen's cartoon disrupted the childlike innocence of the mascots by grounding it in radical sexual imagery that highlights the costs of the games.

Antipoverty activists drew on the impact of the arts and visual culture to raise awareness and to exert pressure on politicians with regard to poorly met election promises for more affordable housing in downtown Vancouver. In 2008, 2009, and 2010, several community-based organizations organized the Poverty Olympics, which consisted of an array of visual parodies, in order to highlight Vancouver's "World Class Poverty" in the midst of the Games (Poverty Olympics Organizing Committee, 2010b). The organizers of the Poverty Olympics adopted Reporters Without Borders' image of five interlocking handcuffs (Forkert, 2011) to represent those "locked in poverty" (see Figure 1). The official mascots of the Poverty Olympics—Itchy the Bedbug, Creepy the Cockroach, and Chewy the Rat—are presented as humorous, yet subversive, resignifications that represent the living conditions in Vancouver's Downtown Eastside. Riffing off of Canada's national anthem, the Poverty Olympics even had its own anthem, beginning with "O Canada, our home on Native land" to highlight colonial violence (Van24sports, 2008). The promotional video for the 2010 Poverty Olympics, featured on the committee's website, is a biting satire of the Olympic Games and its legacy in Vancouver: "Poverty athletes will jump over housing hurdles and skate around poverty. We'll have Olympic wrestling: Community versus Mr. Condo" (Poverty Olympics Organizing Committee, 2010a). The video juxtaposes footage of the living conditions in the Downtown Eastside and homeless people sleeping outside with a sarcastic voice-over: "After a hard day working out, Poverty Olympic athletes can freshen up in the one bathroom on each floor. Athletes with no homes sleep here, in the great outdoors, in their very own second-hand tent." The Poverty Olympics functioned as a counterimage to that of the Olympics, disrupting the belief that Vancouver is a world-class and livable city by grounding official Olympics and Canadian national iconography in ideas of social justice and social inequality.

These acts of resignification and the subversion of VANOC's iconography were very risky for the artist/activists due to the Olympic and Paralympic Marks Act. This tension was evident in a poster produced by the "2010 Welcoming Committee," which portrays Quatchi, one of the official mascots of the Games, described to be "suffering from oppression and environmental degradation," shaking hands with a masked activist dressed in black. The playfulness of the poster is offset by a plea to the viewer, "Please do not contact the police," ominously hinting at the risk of being criminalized (see Figure 1). Activists, artists, and protesters worked within, through, around, and against the Vancouver ISU and associated legislation, which often contradicted the Canadian Charter of Rights and

Freedoms. The most successful way that they accomplished this subversion was through strength in numbers.

Visual Counterdiscourse

In an unprecedented convergence, Aboriginal groups, antipoverty activists, and civil-liberties advocates came together under the single banner of the "Anti-Olympic Convergence" chanting the slogan "No Olympics on stolen Native land" (Lopez, 2010, para. 8). Its logo depicts a thunderbird gripping and taking a bite out of the Olympic rings, a visual sign of opposition and dissent to the Games, which in turn contributes to the counterdiscourse to the idea of the Four Host First Nations, the Ilanaaq, and other Olympics-related imagery drawn from Aboriginal art. The Anti-Olympic Convergence logo is sandwiched between the words "Anti-colonial" and "Anti-capitalist" and is thus grounded in a political idea that the Olympics must be understood in relation to Canada's colonial history and social and economic disparities. Prior to February 10, the thunderbird image appeared in artwork produced by Riel Manywounds and Gord Hill, which included the words "Police Repression, Stolen Native Land, Homelessness, Huge Public Debt, Environmental Destruction" (Stimulator, 2011). The artists reported that they were pressured by their commissioners from Gallery Gachet, which was part of a project that received funding from the Cultural Olympiad, to remove the politically charged words (Stimulator, 2011). In opposition, the artists took the piece to be displayed instead at the Rhizome Café, a local restaurant known for its support for social justice initiatives. The image was also adapted as a logo for the Anti-Olympic Convergence movement, representing a concerted effort by diverse activist groups, each perceived to be concerned with different political issues and movements, to make conceptual and political connections across various forms of oppression and marginalization, such as poverty, colonial racism, and the suppression of free speech.

From February 10 to February 15, 2010, the Anti-Olympic Convergence demonstrated in various parts of downtown Vancouver, proclaiming a variety of goals: to disrupt the Torch Relay in the Downtown Eastside and on Commercial Drive, to "Take back our city!" from the ISU and VANOC by convening in front of the Vancouver Art Gallery, to obstruct streets in a "Heart Attack" demonstration, and to create a Tent City in protest of the lack of affordable and social housing promised by VANOC and the BC government (see Figure 2). The Annual Women's Memorial March, held every February 14 for murdered and missing women, also took place during this time as a separate protest to highlight the link between the disproportionate impact of poverty and sexual violence directed toward women in the Downtown Eastside (Women's Memorial March, 2012). The Anti-Olympic Convergence protests

FIGURE 2   Clockwise from top: Anti-Olympic Convergence's Thunderbird logo and the schedule of week-long demonstrations; additional anti-Olympic posters that link colonial history, government spending and constraints on free speech.

involved as many as 5,000 demonstrators but were predominantly peaceful, featuring marching bands, colorful banners, and costumes (Lopez, 2010). Indeed, the organizers used the word "festivals" to describe the peaceful demonstrations, a descriptor that fell in step with Olympic ideals; however, local, national, and international broadcasting networks focused on isolated incidents where a handful of demonstrators broke store windows, depicting them as hooligans, and underreported the size and political message of the more festive protesters and the targeted aspect of the vandalism directed specifically toward the HBC as an Olympic sponsor.

CONCLUSION

Drawing from Foucault's notion of discourse, we have argued that VANOC and the Canadian state framed the Olympics solely in terms of discourses of nationalism, multiculturalism, and celebration in such a way that any opposition to the Games would be considered unthinkable, illegal, and illegitimate. Against this highly organized cultural machinery, anti-Olympic activists produced demonstrations, festivals, parodies, posters, and graffiti art that subverted and resignified official Olympic iconography. Grounded in an alliance of anticolonial, anticapitalist, and antipoverty politics, these images and practices composed the visual counterdiscourse to the Games, interrogating the ways in which the celebratory discourse of the Olympics prevented a critical discussion of Canadian colonial history, government spending, and legal and criminal measures that undermined freedom of speech (see Figure 2). Our analysis of the authoritative discourses and counterdiscourses during the 2010 Vancouver Winter Olympics using Foucaultian discourse analysis and semiotic analysis is by no means exhaustive. For instance, media representations of demonstrators who broke store windows as problematic anarchists warrants critical investigation with regard to the criminalization of civic dissent. And although our visual examples as well as the historical and contemporary contexts are specific to Vancouver, we have developed a theoretical, methodological, and ethical framework that speaks more broadly to the relationship between mass communication, society, and the Olympics. We hope that other cultural scholars and activists will build on our framework as they contemplate, critique, and analyze the celebratory discourse of future Olympic events in various localities and find inspiration from the creativity and courage of Vancouver's activists and artists.

ACKNOWLEDGMENTS

In memory of Owen Idwal Taylor (1979–2010). We also acknowledge the assistance of Andrina Perry, Natasha Patterson, and Robert Smith?.

REFERENCES

Arnason, H. (1986). *History of modern art*. Los Angeles, CA: Times Mirror Books.

Assembly of First Nations. (2010). *About the AFN*. Retrieved from http://www.afn.ca/index.php/en/about-afn/description-of-the-afn

Boyle, P. J., & Haggerty, K. D. (2009). *Privacy games: The Vancouver Olympics, privacy and surveillance*. Edmonton, Canada: University of Alberta, Department of Sociology.

British Columbia Legislative Assembly. (5 March 2007). *Official report of the debates of the Legislative Assembly, 38 at 5748* (J. Kwan). online: Debates of the Legislative Assembly (Hansard). Retrieved from http://www.leg.bc.ca/hansard/38th3rd/H70305p.htm

British Columbia Legislative Assembly. (2 November 2009). *Official report of the debates of the Legislative Assembly, 39 at 1853* (H. Bloy), online: Debates of the Legislative Assembly (Hansard). Retrieved from http://www.leg.bc.ca/hansard/39th1st/H91102a.htm

British Columbia Civil Liberties Association. (2008). *Civil liberties group calls for government investigation and action against VANOC's unconscionable efforts to stifle free speech.* Retrieved from http://www.bccla.org/pressreleases/08vanoc.pdf

British Columbia Civil Liberties Association. (2009). *Civil liberties update.* Retrieved from http://www.bccla.org/pressreleases/09bill13.html

British Columbia Civil Liberties Association. (2010). *Launch of the first legal observers program in Olympic history.* Retrieved from http://www.bccla.org/pressreleases/10Media_advisory. html

Canadian Broadcasting Corporation. (2009). *RCMP using intimidation to silence Olympic protest, group says.* Retrieved from http://www.cbc.ca/news/canada/british columbia/story/2009/06/24/bc-olympic-protest-lawsuit.html

Canadian Broadcasting Corporation. (2010). *Vancouver poet denounces VANOC 'muzzle.'* Retrieved from http://www.cbc.ca/news/arts/books/story/2010/02/11/vancouver-poet-laureate-muzzle-clause.html

Coalition for a Better BC. (2010, 20 March). *Special report: Dialog on building a better BC.* Retrieved from http://www.betterbc.ca/wp-content/uploads/2010/03/Dialogue-Special-Report1.pdf

Crossen, J. (2010). *John Crossen Cartoon Company.* Retrieved from http://www.johncrossen. com/

Dembicki, G. (2009a). *Olympics critics file lawsuit against Vancouver.* Retrieved from http:// thetyee.ca/Blogs/TheHook/Olympics2010/2009/10/07/Vancouver-lawsuit-Olympics-bylaws/

Dembicki, G. (2009b). *Police question friend of Olympics critic Chris Shaw.* Retrieved from http://thetyee.ca/News/2009/10/05/OlympicsShawQuestioning/

Eby, D. (2009). *Queers should be concerned about Olympic censorship.* Retrieved from http:// www.xtra.ca/public/National/Queers_should_be_concerned_about_Olympic_censorship-7226.aspx

Eby, D., & Rice, C. (2009). *Legal observer information and training guide.* Vancouver, Canada: BC Civil Liberties Association and Pivot Legal Society.

First Call. (2011). *2011 Child poverty report card.* Vancouver, Canada: First Call Child and Youth Advocacy Coalition.

Forkert, K. (2011). Bread and five-ringed circuses: Art, activism, and the Olympic Games in Vancouver and London. In J. Cronin & K. Robertson (Eds.), *Imagining resistance: Visual culture and activism in Canada* (pp. 147–164). Waterloo, Canada: Wilfrid Laurier University Press.

Foucault, M. (1972). *The archaeology of knowledge & the discourse on language.* New York, NY: Pantheon Books.

Foucault, M. (1975). *Surveiller et punir [Discipline and punish].* Paris, France: Gallimard.

Government of Canada. (2002). *Bid book 1.* Retrieved from http://www.canada2010.gc.ca/docs/Vancouver_2010_Bid_Book_-_Volume_1.pdf

Government of Canada. (2010). *The four Host First nations.* Retrieved from http://www.canada2010.gc.ca/invsts/hnationsh/030401-eng.cfm

Harrison, B. (2002). Photographic visions and narrative inquiry. *Narrative Inquiry, 12,* 87–111.

Health Canada. (2011). *Indian residential schools.* Retrieved from http://www.hc-sc.gc.ca/fniah-spnia/services/indiresident/index-eng.php

Hier, S. P., Walby, K., & Greenberg, J. (2006). Supplementing the panoptic paradigm: surveillance, moral governance and CCTV. In D. Lyon (Ed.), *Theorizing surveillance: The panopticon and beyond* (pp. 3–20). Portland, OR: Willan.

Hume, M. (2009). *Cowichan leaders to meet with the Bay over sweater dispute.* Retrieved from http://www.theglobeandmail.com/news/national/british-columbia/cowichan-leaders-to-meet-with-the-bay-over-sweater-dispute/article1339454/

Kelly, M. (2010). *Artists, VANOC clash over Aboriginal art.* Retrieved from http://www.cbc.ca/news/arts/artdesign/story/2010/01/12/vanoc-art.html

Kelm, M. (1998). *Colonizing bodies: Aboriginal health and healing in British Columbia, 1900–50.* Vancouver, Canada: University of British Columbia Press.

Lenskyj, H. (2000). *Inside the Olympic industry.* Albany, NY: State University of New York Press.

Lopez, F. (2010). *Olympic resistance: Indigenous groups, anti-poverty activists, and civil liberties advocates protest 2010 Winter Games in Vancouver* [Video file]. Retrieved from_http://www.democracynow.org/2010/2/15/olympic_resistance_indigenous_groups_anti_poverty

Lyon, D. (2006). The search for surveillance theories. In D. Lyon (Ed.), *Theorizing surveillance: The panopticon and beyond* (pp. 3–20). Portland, OR: Willan.

Moussa, M., & Scapp, R. (1996). The practical theorizing of Michel Foucault: Politics and counter-discourse. *Cultural Critique, 33,* 87–112.

Nagy, S. (2006). *Olympic trademark battle snares small businesses.* Retrieved from http://www.theglobeandmail.com/report-on-business/olympic-trademark-battle-snares-small-businesses/article814075/page1/

Native Warrior Society. (2007). *Native warriors claim responsibility for taking Olympic flag.* Coast Salish Territory, Vancouver, Canada: Native Warrior Society.

Office of the Auditor General of British Columbia. (2003, January). *Review of estimates related to Vancouver's bid to stage the 2010 Olympic Winter Games and Paralympic Winter Games, 6,* online: Publications. Retrieved from http://www.bcauditor.com/files/publications/2003/report6/report/review-estimates-related-vancouver's-bid-stage-2010-olympic-winter-games-an.pdf

Olympics and Paralympic Marks Act. (2007). *Canada Gazette.* Retrieved from http://www.gazette.gc.ca/archives/p2/2007/2007-12-26/html/sor-dors294-eng.html

Pablo, C. (2009). *Arts community protests B.C. Liberal funding cuts at the Vancouver Art Gallery.* Retrieved from http://www.straight.com/article-256608/arts-community-protests-bc-liberal-funding-cuts-vancouver-art-gallery

Peirce, C. S. (1868). On a list of new categories. *Proceedings of the American Academy of Arts and Sciences, 7,* 287–298.

Poverty Olympics Organizing Committee. (2010a). *2010 Poverty Olympics* [Video File]. Retrieved from http://povertyolympics.ca/

Poverty Olympics Organizing Committee. (2010b). *Vancouver Poverty Olympics: World class province, world class poverty.* Retrieved from http://povertyolympics.ca/

Prosser, J. (1998). *Image-based research: A sourcebook for qualitative researchers.* Bristol, PA: Falmer Press.

Rowe, D. (2004). *Sport, culture and the media.* Berkshire, UK: Open University Press.

Royle, S. (2011). *Company, crown and colony: The Hudson's Bay Company and territorial endeavour in Western Canada.* London, UK: I. B. Tauris.

Sawchuk, J. (1998). *The dynamics of Native politics.* Saskatoon, Canada: Purich.

Shaw, C. (2009). *Five ring circus: Myths and realities of the Olympic Games.* Gabriola Island, Canada: New Society.

Smith, C. (2009). *Artist Jesse Corcoran says Olympic mural highlights suffering of the majority*. Retrieved from http://www.straight.com/article-274913/vancouver/artist-jesse-corcoran-says-olympic-mural-highlights-suffering-majority

Smith, L. (1999). *Decolonizing methodologies: Research and indigenous peoples*. Dunedin, New Zealand: University of Otago Press.

Srivastava, D. (2006). *The unique ecology of Eagleridge Bluffs and Larsen Creek Wetlands*. Vancouver, Canada: Lecture conducted from Simon Fraser University.

Stimulator. (2011). *The problem with W2: Co-option through capital* [Image]. Retrieved from http://vancouver.mediacoop.ca/blog/stimulator/6246

The Province. (2007). *Probe sought in Native Elder's death*. Retrieved from http://www.canada.com/story_print.html?id=ac62a19e-4d08-42b6-b451 31c1499b4c13&sponsor=

University of Saskatchewan. (2011). *Enfranchisement of Canada's First Nations*. Retrieved from http://www.usask.ca/diefenbaker/galleries/virtual_exhibit/enfranchisements_of_aboriginals/index.php

Urban Native Youth Association. (2011). *Welcome to UNYA*. Retrieved from http://www.unya.bc.ca/home

Van24sports. (2008). *Homes not podiums, say Poverty Olympics organizers* [Podcast]. Retrieved from http://povertyolympics.ca/?page_id=66

Vancouver Sun. (2006). *2010 Games in crisis*. Retrieved from http://www.canada.com/vancouversun/news/story.html?id=01fc5dbe-9e38-4573-9b07-696fd3144d3f

Vonn, M. (2010). Surveillance in public spaces and closed circuit television (CCTV): Spatial tactics and political strategies. *Case Western Reserve Journal of International Law*, *42*, 595–605.

Werb, J. (2009). *Confusion as BC Arts Council grants to be funded through gaming branch*. Retrieved from http://www.straight.com/article-253877/confusion-bc-arts-council-grants-be-funded-through-gaming-branch

Wiebe, J. (2010). Protecting the XXIst Winter Games will constitute the largest security operation in Canadian history. *Homeland Security Today*, *7*(1), 21–25.

WikiLeaks. (2011). *United States Diplomatic Cables*. Retrieved from http://wikileaks.org/

Women's Memorial March. (2012). *"Their spirits live within us."* Retrieved from http://womensmemorialmarch.wordpress.com/about/

Wong, K. (2010). *On with the show: What exactly is the point of the Cultural Olympiad?* Retrieved from http://www.cbc.ca/news/arts/media/story/2010/01/26/f-vancouver-cultural-olympiad.html

York, G., & Pindera, L. (1991). *People of the pines: The warriors and the legacy of Oka*. New York, NY: Little Brown.

Zirin, D. (2005). *What's my name, fool?: Sports and resistance in the United States*. Chicago, IL: Haymarket Books.

Zirin, D. (2007). *Welcome to the terrordome: The pain politics and promise of sports*. Chicago, IL: Haymarket Books.

Go "Heavy" or Go Home: An Examination of Audience Attitudes and Their Relationship to Gender Cues in the 2010 Olympic Snowboarding Coverage

Amy Jones

Department of Languages and Literature
University of West Alabama

Jennifer Greer

Department of Journalism
University of Alabama

This study uses a multimethod approach to examine links between societal attitudes about one extreme sport, snowboarding, and gender cues present in 2010 Winter Olympics broadcasts. Results of a nationwide survey of 718 adults found that viewing time emerged as the main predictor variable for attitudes. Respondents who watched more men's coverage rated the sport as more masculine, and those who watched more women's coverage rated the sport as more feminine. Attitudes toward the athletes were more complex, with heavy viewers rating both male and female boarders as possessing more of the masculine and feminine qualities success in the sport demands. Next, a content analysis was employed to examine visual and verbal cues present in 2 hours and 25 minutes of NBC's primetime coverage. Running time was equal for both sexes. Also, some cues present in the broadcasts did support traditional gender stereotypes, but other gendered cues were emphasized equally and amply for both sexes. The results provide evidence that gender cues in media coverage of the burgeoning area of extreme Olympic sports and audience attitudes may feed off each other.

INTRODUCTION

Millions worldwide tuned in to watch male and female snowboarders compete in the 2010 Winter Olympic Games in Vancouver, Canada, where ample primetime coverage was devoted to three snowboarding events (half-pipe, parallel giant slalom, and snowboard cross). In the United States alone, 30.1 million viewers tuned into NBC's coverage of the men's snowboard half-pipe final, a figure nearly double the audience for traditional ratings leader *American Idol* that night (Dillman, 2010). Since it was introduced as an official Olympic sport in 1998, snowboarding has garnered widespread media attention, grown its own superstars, including Shaun White and Lindsey Jacobellis, and launched multimillion dollar industries devoted to clothing lines, snowboard designs, and a punklike style among fans and riders. It has moved from a "sideshow" event to one of the core draws of the Games, clearing the way for a whole new genre of extreme Olympic sports in both winter (e.g., freestyle skiing) and summer (e.g., BMX) contests (Thorpe & Wheaton, 2011). Further, the "jazzed-up" formats used to present the sport brought younger audiences to the Vancouver Games, and the techniques used were being closely studied by organizers of the 2012 London Games looking at ways to showcase extreme sports (Thorpe & Wheaton, 2011).

Although they are garnering more attention, little is known about how extreme sports are covered and perceived by audiences, particularly in regard to gender issues. Snowboarding coverage and audience attitudes about the sport and its athletes demand attention from mass communication researchers interested in gender issues because of the unique combination of qualities needed to be successful in the sport. Like many extreme sports, snowboarding requires the traditionally masculine elements of power, strength, and risk, but it also relies on feminine elements of aesthetics and dexterity. Although snowboarding attracts fierce competitors of both sexes, like many extreme sports, it is typically gender-typed as more masculine (Hardin & Greer, 2009; Thorpe, 2010).

This study seeks to add to the body of literature on gender and sport by exploring media content and audience perceptions of a relatively new, increasingly popular extreme Olympic sport. Little is known about gender markers in extreme or "action" sports, and even less is known about media coverage of and attitudes toward snowboarding. Only a handful of studies have examined the snowboarding on any level, and no mass-communication-oriented study has examined the coverage of the sport and audience attitudes simultaneously. This research seeks to expand the body of research by focusing on one extreme sport and analyzing how gender stereotypes carry over from the snowboarding culture to televised media content and then to societal attitudes of the sport and its athletes. Does media coverage perpetuate the masculine frame noted by the few scholars who have examined snowboarding (Anderson, 1999; Heino, 2000; Humphreys, 1997; Thorpe, 2010)? Past studies have relied on depth interviews, ethnographies, and participant observation to examine gender in the snowboarding culture, but no published study to date has examined societal attitudes through analytical survey techniques. Further, other than qualitative analyses of magazines devoted to snowboarding, little study has been devoted to media coverage of the sport (Stone & Horne, 2008).

This study aims to fill gaps in our knowledge by taking a systematic, multimethod approach. We first examine societal attitudes about snowboarding and its athletes using an analytical survey with a national sample. Specifically, we examine how gendered attitudes are related to viewing the 2010 Winter Olympics snowboarding coverage. Next, we analyze the prime-time Olympics snowboarding broadcasts with quantitative and qualitative approaches to look for visual and verbal gender cues present in the coverage. The study aims to explore links between mediated content and societal attitudes about gender roles as the subfield of extreme sport grows in popularity, attracts more diverse participants, and makes more inroads into the Olympic Games.

LITERATURE REVIEW

Snowboarding and other extreme or action sports represent a unique "type" of sport because they include both masculine and feminine qualities (Hardin & Greer, 2009). Although snowboarding's participants tout equality and being beyond gender typing, researchers have dissected how male snowboarders construct their sport as a masculine activity through clothing and interaction as well as an emphasis on heterosexuality, violence, and aggression (Anderson, 1999; Thorpe, 2010). One 2009 exchange on Snowboardingforum.com illustrates this point. "I hear you all talk about the famous MALE snowboarders but never about female ones," one poster wrote. "Who are your favorite female snowboarders?" One senior member of the forum responded: "Women just can't rip like the guys can, so I base my decision of favourite female snowboarder on how attractive I find them and not how they ride, LOL" (iKimshi, 2009).

Examining coverage and attitudes of snowboarding is especially important today as the demographics of extreme sports shift. As Thorpe and Wheaton (2011) noted,

> While young, white, middle- and upperclass, heterosexual males often constitute a dominant force at the core of many action sport cultures, demographics are shifting, particularly on the margins of the sports, with increasing participation across different social classes and age groups, as well as females and minority groups. (p. 832)

Audience Attitudes and Gender Roles in Sport: Social Role Theory

Social role theory proposes that an individual's actions, thoughts, and behaviors are guided by expectations of social roles (Eagly & Johannesen-Schmidt, 2001). Furthermore, roles for women are specified as representing communality and roles for men are specified as representing agency. Research on social role theory defines communality as a concern for others, along with traits of affection, helpfulness, kindness, sensitivity, nurture, grace, and gentleness. On the other hand, agency is defined by aggression, dominance, strength, force, independence, confidence, and a competitive spirit (Cuneen & Claussen, 1999; Eagly & Chaiken, 1993).

Expected gender roles are related to attitudes about male and female interests. Attitudes are the tendency to evaluate an individual or situation as favorable or unfavorable. As a result, individuals and situations are "typed" (Perloff, 2003). Gender-appropriate behavior is often classified by attitudes in society. For example, girls are accepted if they play with dolls, whereas boys are rejected for the same behavior (Golombok et al., 2008). Research indicates that such attitudes about gender are learned socially from our relatives, mentors, peers, self-experience, and the media (Perloff, 2003). Therefore, not all individuals have the same attitudes about gender, but individuals with similar experiences and exposure to stimuli may form similar attitudes.

Historically, men have been significantly more interested in participating in sport, viewing sport media, attending athletic events, and learning about sport, leading many to label the sports industry as a masculine domain (Gantz & Wenner, 1995; Melby, 2010). However, research suggests that audiences do clearly type certain sports as masculine, extreme, gender neutral, and feminine based on different qualities emphasized in the sports themselves and the athletes who participate in them (Hardin & Greer,

2009). As a result of this gender-typing, sport can reinforce gender expectations in society. The unwritten value system in sport, which defines athletic events and athlete traits as either gender appropriate or gender inappropriate, has led to the formation and maintenance of gender stereotypes represented in societal attitudes (Hardin & Greer, 2009; Knight & Giuliano, 2001). Although the sports industry has been seen as a male domain, research indicates that women increasingly participate in sport and other male-dominated activities but prefer to participate and view more feminine-typed sports (Hanson & Kraus, 1999).

Arguably, the media play a part in guiding and reinforcing societal gender role expectations. Angelini (2008) argued that because the media portray sports in a stereotypical way, gender stereotypes are reinforced within the media audience and eventually in society. Because men are thought to be more interested in sport as a whole than are women, sport product advertising focuses on masculine social roles. Women often are portrayed as individual, leisure athletes, whereas men are portrayed as talented competitors (Koivula, 2001). Furthermore, experimental research found that women were perceived as being more agentic when portrayed playing masculine sports in the media, whereas men were perceived as being more communal when playing feminine sports (Harrison & Lynch, 2005). In other words, expected social roles may align not only with athlete sex but also the type of sport played. Recent research by Krane et al. (2011), however, found that girls' perceptions of female athletes may be less prone to be swayed by media images. After showing girls photographs of collegiate athletes, the research team noted little discussion of ideal body type or femininity among the participants. They concluded that the girls "were disrupting common social expectations about femininity and female athletes and were constructing their own messages about being athletic" (p. 765).

Using social role theory to explore how media content might be related to audiences' gender typing of a sport and perceptions of its athletes, the following hypotheses were proposed:

H1: Audience members who view more televised Olympic snowboarding event coverage will more strongly gender type the sport.

H2: Audience members who view more televised Olympic snowboarding event coverage will more strongly perceive agentic and communal traits of male and female snowboarders.

Gender Stereotypes in Snowboarding Culture

Snowboarding is considered an extreme, masculine, and highly dangerous sport; some contend a female competitor has to be "ballsy just to try it"

(Asthana, 2003, p. 22). Still, marketers increasingly have targeted women to sell equipment, and by the mid-1990s, about 1.8 million female snowboarders accounted for 30% of boarders worldwide (Walker & Gordon, 1994). Arguably, snowboarding differs from other masculine-typed sports because it contains both masculine and feminine elements. Snowboarding is an individual sport with judged aesthetic qualities (identified in past studies as feminine qualities), and it requires danger, risk, and speed (masculine qualities). In examining whether gender-typing of sport was still a valid concept, Hardin and Greer (2009) found that snowboarding was indeed typed by young audiences as more masculine but that it grouped distinctly with other extreme or action sports (e.g., skateboarding, motocross) rather than with team-oriented masculine sports (e.g., football, hockey).

Male snowboarders use distinct social practices to ensure that society perceives the sport as masculine, Anderson (1999) contended. They project a masculine image with baggy (punklike) clothing, frequently show violence and aggression during competition, and emphasize heterosexuality (Anderson, 1999). Thorpe (2010) studied male athletes who left the "fratriarchal group" of snowboarders for gender-inappropriate reasons other than competition (e.g., to get married, start a family, or pursue educational opportunities). She found that once they leave, they begin to reflect critically on the sport, recognizing how athletes celebrate injury and risk, marginalize women (including female boarders), and regularly engage in sexist and homophobic dialogue.

On the other hand, female competitors battle potential negative stereotypes associated with participating in this masculine sport. Koivula (2001) found that women who participate in gender-inappropriate (masculine) sports face negative portrayals in the media and society. Laurendeau and Sharara (2008) found through in-depth interviews that female boarders are reluctant to practice moves in the same spaces as male athletes, and they downplay their femininity through clothing choices used to disguise their sex.

Only a few studies have looked at media coverage and audience attitudes of the sport. Examining the audience characteristics and tendencies to sex type extreme sports, Hardin and Greer (2009) found that participating in personal fitness activities and holding traditional societal views of masculinity were linked to views of snowboarding and other extreme sports as less masculine. Of interest, viewing mediated coverage of extreme sports or general sports media use were not related at all to gender typing of extreme sports. An analysis of British media coverage found that snowboarding was gender stereotyped less than other sports. Stone and Horne (2008) contended that because male and female snowboarders wear similar clothing and speak a similar (sport-specific) language, female competitors are less likely to be stereotyped in print media coverage than female athletes competing in other sports. However, Thorpe (2008) interviewed female snowboarders, who reported feeling stereotyped in U.S. media. Female boarders said they felt pressured to conform to the "ideal" snowboarder image presented in the media—long hair flowing out of a "punklike" beanie and a matching (but slightly grungy) outfit. Other female boarders said they recognized that sex and femininity are used to sell the sport in the media, but they feel this image does not impact their athlete credibility. As one put it, "The only women in the snowboarding culture that get real respect are the ones that can ride well" (Thorpe, 2008, p. 215).

Gender Stereotypes in Sports Media Content

Research indicates that similar gender stereotypes are present across a variety of mass communications, including advertising, public relations campaigns, and prime-time programs (Hurtz & Durkin, 2004). Media transmit gender stereotypes through both amount of coverage and verbal and visual cues. Verbal cues involve scripts and spoken dialogue; visual cues emerge in photography and moving images.

Amount of media coverage. Research suggests that female athletes are underrepresented in sport media (Christopherson, Janning, & McConnell, 2002; Fink & Kensicki, 2002; Kim, Walkosz, & Iverson, 2006; Knight & Giuliano, 2003; Vincent, 2004). Female athletes receive significantly less media coverage than male athletes. In national newspapers, female college basketball players received only 27% of the collegiate basketball coverage (Kian, 2008). In collegiate newspapers, three fourths of the sport coverage featured male athletes, and in collegiate TV programs, male sports accounted for 82% of the coverage (Huffman, Tuggle, & Rosengard, 2004). Even when female athletes achieve athletic success, as in the 1996 Summer Olympic Games, they still receive less coverage than less successful male athletes competing in the same events (Fink & Kensicki, 2002). Furthermore, when women's and men's teams received equal amounts of coverage, the men's teams received significantly more commentary than the women's teams (Billings, Halone, & Denham, 2002). It should be noted, however, that recent research suggests that gender differences in amount of sport media coverage are lessened in international competition (Billings & Angelini, 2007). Hardin, Chance, Dodd, and Hardin (2002) noted that although sexual differences (visual gender cues) in media coverage still existed in the coverage of the 2000 Olympics, the amount of coverage was fair to both sexes.

Underrepresentation in coverage may suggest that sport media executives rate men's sports as more important than women's sports (Hardin, 2005; Huffman et al., 2004). Furthermore, it may influence audience opinions about gender and sport (Fink & Kinsicki, 2002; Kim et al., 2006). However, because the 2010 Winter Olympic Games involved international competition, the amount of media coverage may have been equal, as suggested by previous research (Billings & Angelini, 2007; Hardin et al., 2002). The first research question is designed to look at how prominently men's and women's snowboarding events were featured:

RQ1: Did the amount of primetime coverage of Olympic snowboarding events in 2010 vary by the sex of the athletes competing?

Visual cues. Gender cues in media coverage have been identified in video and still images of male and female athletes. When female athletes are portrayed, the focus on athleticism is often lacking (Bissell & Duke, 2007; Fink & Kensicki, 2002; Knight & Giuliano, 2003; Vincent, 2004). Instead, visual portrayals in the media focus on a female athlete's beauty and sexuality. Top female athletes in some sports must develop muscles and wear heavy athletic clothing, things society identifies as masculine. To counteract this, female athletes are often feminized and/or sexualized by the mass media, Knight and Giuliano (2001) argued.

Sport media often focus on female athletes' sexuality and sexual preference (Bissell & Duke, 2007; Christopherson et al., 2002; Kim et al., 2006; Perloff, 2003; Vincent, 2004). An analysis of video coverage of women's beach volleyball in the Olympic Games found that 20% of the camera shots focused on the athletes' chests and an additional 17% focused on the athletes' buttocks (Bissell & Duke, 2007). They argued that sexuality in sport media is used to sell female sport and to advance the popularity of the athletes. They posited that the frequency of body shots of female athletes indicates an intentional sexualized portrayal similar to portrayals in men's magazines (e.g., *Maxim* and *Playboy*). Furthermore, Hardin and colleagues (2002) found that visual cues differed even in coverage of photographs in international competition. However, it should be noted that research of the coverage of an international competition of men's and women's tennis found that online sources are less likely to minimize the athletic abilities of female athletes than traditional media sources, like newspapers (Kian & Clavio, 2011).

Studies of visual cues also have focused on production techniques such as editing, special effects, camera angle, and type of shot. One study of men's and women's Olympic track and field coverage found men's segments to contain more shots; a greater variety of angles; and more pans, zooms, and frequent close-ups than did women's. The authors concluded that this increased the excitement of the production (Greer, Hardin, & Homan, 2009). Studies have found female athletes to be shown as dependent upon others (e.g., coaches, teammates, and family members); therefore, camera shots of interactions with these individuals are more common (Fink & Kensicki, 2002). Differences in camera angles, number of cameras used, editing techniques, and pre/postgame production make coverage of men's athletics seem "historic," whereas the women's games are produced to look like "just another game" (Messner, Duncan, & Wachs, 1996).

To examine visual cues, the following research question was posed:

RQ2: Did visual gender cues present in the televised primetime network coverage of Olympic snowboarding events in 2010 vary by athlete sex?

Verbal cues.   Research also has found gender stereotypes transmitted by media commentary and scripted dialogue focused on athlete's gender roles, sexual orientation, appearance, and personality. Female athletes often are marginalized as competitors in media commentary, being described as "team players" and as "a part of a group" (Daddario, 1997). In magazine coverage of the Olympic Games, female Olympians often are portrayed as entertainers and performers rather than skilled athletes (Jollimore, 2002). As a result, female athletes are often described as mothers and wives, and male athletes are more likely to be described using masculine descriptors (e.g., aggressive, dominant, etc.; Christopherson et al., 2002).

In addition, media dialogue often focuses on a female athletes' appearance. Commentary during LPGA events found the verbal cues focused on female golfers' appearance and personality, by including rhetoric about a player's "pretty smile," physical attractiveness, or good looks (Kim et al., 2006). Christopherson et al. (2002) contended that textual focus on appearance subtlety promotes gender ideologies. In analyzing newspaper coverage of the 1999 Women's World Cup, they found frequent themes of femininity and sex appeal. Journalists focused on the athletes crying, hugging, and showing emotion, and the athletes were referred to as "smoldering" and "telegenic."

Finally, stereotypical roles have been found in verbal descriptions of an athlete's personality, which researchers contend leads to the marginalization of female athletes. Comments about male basketball players in the 2000 NCAA Final Four basketball tournament focused on athleticism and physical strength, whereas comments about female players focused on positive attitude, personality, looks/appearance, and personal background (Billings et al., 2002). Because verbal and textual cues have been linked to gender stereotypes of athletes and the sports they play, the final research question was posed:

RQ3a: Did verbal gender cues present in the televised primetime network coverage of Olympic snowboarding events in 2010 vary by athlete sex?

Scant research has examined the gender markers present in snowboarding coverage. Further, no study has examined the link between viewing this coverage and audience attitudes about gender. This research does both by using two studies (a nationwide survey and a content analysis) to examine how viewing is related to sex typing of the sport and its athletes found in Olympic snowboarding broadcasts.

STUDY 1: AUDIENCE ATTITUDES AND OLYMPIC VIEWING

Method

To examine how the viewing of mediated coverage of snowboarding was related to audiences' perceptions about the sport and its athletes, an analytical survey was employed.

Population and Sample

The theoretical population was all U.S. television viewers, whether or not they watched the 2010 Winter Olympic Games. Because this study examined amount of viewing in relation to attitudes, the population included non-viewers as well. A convenience sampling approach was used, an appropriate technique when the goal is to link behaviors (viewing level) to attitudes (gender typing) rather than to describe behaviors and attitudes in a larger population (Babbie, 2007). A link to an online survey was e-mailed to 350 personal and professional contacts of the researchers. Each contact was asked to distribute the survey to at least three additional contacts. In addition, links to the survey were posted on personal social media pages of the researchers and their acquaintances.

In all, 812 individuals started the survey, and 718 (88.4%) completed enough questions to be retained for analysis. Women comprised 58.8% of the sample, and age of respondents ranged from 19 to 84, with 59.1% younger than age 50. The median and mean age were both 45.0 ($SD = 15.11$). A vast majority of the participants (86.4%) identified themselves as White, 6.8% identified as African American, 2.9% as Hispanic, 1.7% as Asian American, 1.5% as American Indian or Other, and 0.7% declined to share their ethnicity. The sample included participants from 44 states, with the majority of respondents from South and the West, where they researchers had connections.

Variables

Olympic viewing. Participants were asked how many hours a day they spent watching the 2010 Winter Olympics broadcasts, with options ranging from *none* to 5+ *hours* in 30-minute intervals. Next, participants reported how frequently they watched broadcast coverage of men's and women's snowboarding events during the Games on a 7-point response format, from 1 (*never watched*) to 7 (*frequently watched*).

Sport participation. Respondents were asked about their participation in sports and fitness activities. They indicated how many hours each day they participated in competitive sports and in recreational activities or exercise. Responses ranged from *none* to 5+ *hours* with 12 options in 30-minute intervals.

Demographics. Participants reported their sex, age, ethnicity, and geographic location. Participant sex was a main construct of interest because of the established link between sex and attitudes about sport (Angelini, 2008; Gantz & Wenner, 1995).

Attitudes about snowboarding and snowboarders. Respondents indicated how masculine they viewed snowboarding as a sport overall on a single item with response options ranging from 1 (*masculine*) to 7 (*feminine*). Respondents then responded to two gendered character traits for the male and female athletes (aggression and grace) suggested by social role theory. For example, respondents read the statement "Male snowboarders are aggressive" and responded on a 1 (*strongly disagree*) to 7 (*strongly agree*) response format.

Results

Overall, respondents rated snowboarding as closer to the masculine end of the masculine/feminine continuum ($M = 2.9$, $SD = 1.08$), well below the midpoint on the scale (4.0). Therefore, those in the sample typed snowboarding as masculine. The first hypothesis predicted that viewing of the Olympic broadcasts would be linked to perceptions of snowboarding as a masculine or feminine sport. To test this, blocked hierarchical regression was run with gender typing of the sport as the dependent variable. Three

viewing variables were loaded in first, followed by three demographic variables and two sport participation variables.

As predicted, viewing behaviors were significantly related to differences
in how respondents viewed the sport. Hours spent watching Olympic broadcasts in general did not emerge as a predictor variable, but time watching
men's and women's snowboarding events did. As Table 1 shows, more hours
viewing men's events was linked to audiences seeing the sport as more masculine. Conversely, more hours spent viewing women's coverage was linked
to perceptions of the sport as more feminine. These viewing variables
remained the only significant predictors of variation in attitudes even when
demographic and sport participation variables were loaded into the model.
Therefore, Hypothesis 1 was supported. Time viewing snowboarding coverage related to how the audience gender typed the sport.

The second hypothesis predicted that audience attitudes of gendered
traits of individual snowboarders also would be related to time viewing
the event coverage. To test this, the variables related to male snowboarders
were tested collectively using a multivariate analysis of covariance. Respondents were split into three viewing groups: "No-viewing" participants were
those who reported watching no male snowboarding events or a 1 on the

TABLE 1

Blocked Hierarchical Regression Analysis for Gender Typing of Snowboarding
With Viewing, Demographic, and Sports Participation Variables as Predictors

Predictors	B	t
Block 1 Viewing		
Time viewing 2011 Olympic Games	−.051	1.13
Time viewing men's events	−.129	2.09*
Time viewing women's events	.348	5.87***
Adjusted R^2	.060	
Block 2 Demographics		
Sex (M = 1; W = 2)	.006	0.16
Age	.008	0.19
Ethnicity (Wh = 1; non-Wh = 2)	.009	0.23
Change in Adjusted R^2	−.003	
Adjusted R^2	.057	
Block 3 Sports participation		
Time spent on competitive sports	−.079	1.8
Time spent on fitness activities	.023	0.58
Change in Adjusted R^2	.002	
Adjusted R^2	.059	

Note. Dependent variable = sex typing of sport, 1 (*masculine*) to 7 (*feminine*).
Final model, Adjusted $R^2 = .059$, $F(8, 627) = 5.98***$. M = men; W = women;
Wh = White.

scale; "light-viewing" participants were those who watched limited coverage or a 2, 3, or 4 on the scale; and "heavy-viewing" participants were those who marked a 5 or higher on the 7-point scale. These groups did not differ on demographic traits, so age, sex, and ethnicity of respondent were loaded into the model as covariates. The dependent variables were attitudes toward the male snowboarders as aggressive (agentic, masculine trait) and graceful (communal, feminine trait). The analysis was repeated for time spent viewing women's events and gendered attitudes toward female athletes.

As Table 2 shows, significant models emerged for each of the four dependent variables. For the covariates, respondent sex and ethnicity were not linked to attitudes, but age was significantly linked to perceptions of aggression for both men and women. Older viewers saw both male and female snowboarders as more aggressive. The variable with the most explanatory power in the models, however, was viewing—the main variable of interest in the hypothesis. Across the board, time spent watching either men's or women's coverage was related to audience perceptions of male and female snowboarders as both more aggressive and more graceful. Of course, given the method, causality cannot be assumed in this relationship.

For male snowboarders, heavy viewers saw the men as significantly more aggressive ($M = 6.00$) than did light ($M = 5.20$) or nonviewers ($M = 4.78$). Heavy viewers also saw the men as more graceful than did light or nonviewers ($M = 4.87$ compared to $M = 4.13$ and $M = 3.95$).The same pattern held for attitudes toward female boarders. Heavy viewers saw the female

TABLE 2

Multivariate Analysis of Covariance Results for Perceptions of Agentic and Communal Traits of Male and Female Snowboarders Based on Time Spent Viewing Coverage for Each Gender

| | Male snowboarders | | | | Female snowboarders | | | |
| | Aggression | | Grace | | Aggression | | Grace | |
	F	η^2	F	η^2	F	η^2	F	η^2
Corrected model	18.53***	.14	7.69***	.06	20.81***	.15	5.20***	.04
Covariates:								
Age	32.09***	.05	ns	.00	27.07***	.04	ns	.00
Sex	ns	.00	ns	.00	ns	.00	ns	.00
Ethnicity	ns	.00	ns	.01	ns	.00	ns	.00
Main effect:								
Viewing	28.30***	.09	16.68***	.05	34.49***	.11	12.60***	.04

Note. η^2 = Partial η^2 for covariates and main effects.
***$p < .001$.

athletes as significantly more aggressive ($M = 6.06$) than did light ($M = 5.08$) or nonviewers ($M = 4.81$). The same was true for gracefulness ratings ($M = 4.88$ compared to $M = 4.28$ and $M = 4.02$).

Therefore, the second hypothesis was supported. Viewing Olympic coverage was related to stronger attitudes about masculine and feminine traits of both male and female snowboarders. Of interest, though, viewing was not linked to straight gender typing of the male athletes as having more agentic traits and the female athlete as having more communal traits. Rather, viewing was linked to audiences seeing the athletes as possessing more of both traits, with heavy viewers seeing the athletes, regardless of sex, as having more masculine and more feminine traits than did the light viewers.

STUDY 2: MEDIA COVERAGE OF SNOWBOARDING

Method

The results of Study 1 found links—but not a causal relationship—between more time spent viewing the men's and women's coverage and stronger gender-related perceptions of the sport and its athletes. Therefore, we next examined the content of the 2010 Olympic snowboarding coverage to see what gendered markers were present in visual and verbal aspects of the broadcasts.

Population and Sample

The prime-time (defined as 6 to 11 p.m. CST) coverage of 2010 Winter Games on the official Olympic network (NBC) was recorded on a digital video recorder from opening ceremonies to closing ceremonies. In total, 85 televised hours over 17 days starting Friday, February 12, 2010, were captured. All live or taped snowboarding coverage, including feature segments, interviews, competition, and medal ceremonies, was analyzed, totaling 2 hours, 24 minutes, and 59 seconds.

Unit of Analysis

Coders first identified segments of snowboarding coverage. Based on past work (Billings et al., 2002; Greer et al., 2009), a segment was defined as coverage in between interruptions such as commercial breaks, a shift from snowboarding to another sport or to non-Olympic coverage (e.g., news, promos), a shift from one athlete/group of athletes to another, or a shift from one type of coverage to another (e.g., live event to a feature).

Coders classified each segment by the sex of the dominant athlete. Because more than one athlete could be featured in a segment, the dominant athlete was defined as the one with the most obvious focus visually (in number and length of shots) and verbally (in amount of commentary or dialog). Because men's segments were significantly shorter ($M = 140.69$ seconds) than women's segments ($M = 156.84$), $t(52) = 6.38$, $p < .05$, minute of coverage became the unit of analysis. For the following variables, the number of tallies for each cue present per segment was divided by segment length in minutes so each could be reported per minute of coverage.

Content Categories

Visual cues. Coding categories were developed for 11 visual cues linked to gender stereotypes and roles in previous literature (Cuneen & Claussen, 1999; Harrison & Lynch, 2005). Five cues measured the number of interactions shown between the dominant athlete and others (family member, significant other, friend, coach, and other athlete). Two camera angle cues were noted: high and low. Using coding schemes from past studies (Bissell & Duke, 2007; Greer et al., 2009), these two camera angles were tallied because high camera angles have been liked to femininity and lower angles to masculinity. Medium angles (eye level) were used for the majority of the shots; these were noted but not analyzed because they have not been linked to gender cues. Finally, coders tallied the number of shots per segment focused on four specific parts of the body (face, chest, buttocks, and back), areas of emphasis associated with femininity.

Verbal cues. Coding categories were developed for 10 verbal cues spoken by the commentators or interviewers. The same two commentators were used for both the men's and women's snowboarding events in the 2010 Olympic Games, and both were men. To be analyzed, comments had to be directed at the dominant athlete in the segment being coded. Comments from the athletes themselves, coaches, family members, and the like were not included.

Verbal cues examined were divided into theme and social role descriptor variables and were based on previous studies (Billings et al., 2002; Kim et al., 2006). Coders categorized comments into four feminine or masculine themes, tallying the number of times a theme was used in a segment. The two feminine themes were physical appearance and aesthetic ability; the two masculine themes were performance and athletic injury. Social role descriptors (adjectives and adverbs) were developed from past studies (Cuneen & Claussen, 1999; Harrison & Lynch, 2005). While social role descriptors and commentary themes may overlap, descriptors are more direct than themes, which may not be as obvious to viewers. Coders tallied the presence of six social role descriptors, three feminine (aesthetic beauty, emotion, physical beauty) and three masculine (aggression, dominance, physical ability). The total number of feminine comments (the sum of feminine theme comments and descriptors) and masculine comments (the sum of masculine theme comments and descriptors) were then calculated.

Social role descriptors also were analyzed qualitatively. A list of every social role descriptor used was recorded by athlete sex. Words were first sorted into two categories: words used to describe the athlete and words used to describe the athlete's actions. The adjectives/adverbs were then grouped with like words (synonyms) within each of the descriptor categories.

Reliability. Two coders analyzed the data, and they both coded 12% of the sample to test for intercoder reliability. For the cue categories requiring tallies, agreement was defined matching within two tallies per segment across all variables in that category. For example, in one segment of more than 4 minutes, angle changed 20 times. If coders were within two angles total and not off by more than two in any subcategory (low, medium, high), it was counted as a match. Reliability using Cohen's Kappa was .88 for variables measuring visual cues and .80 for verbal cues.

Results

The first research question asked whether the amount of prime-time coverage of Olympic snowboarding events in 2010 varied by the sex of the athletes competing. Running time was virtually identical for male and female snowboarders. Women's events received 1 hour, 13 minutes, and 3 seconds of coverage; men's events received 1 hour, 11 minutes, and 56 seconds. Average segment time was longer for women, as previously noted, but no difference in coverage amount was found.

The second research question examined whether visual gender cues in the coverage existed and differed by athlete sex. For these continuous variables, a series of independent samples *t* tests were conducted to compare the average number of cues per minute for men and women boarders. Of the 11 visual gender cues examined, five varied significantly for men's and women's coverage. As Table 3 shows, male snowboarders were more likely to be shown using a low angle (emphasizing masculinity), and female boarders were more likely shown with high angles (emphasizing femininity). For body shots, cameras were twice as likely to focus on the face of a female boarder. Finally, female boarders were shown interacting with a coach or significant other four times more than male boarders. Interaction, as the literature indicates, suggests dependence on another for success. No differences were found on the three other variables measuring camera shots of the body or the three other variables for interaction with others.

TABLE 3
Mean Number of Visual Cues per Minute of Coverage for Male and Female Snowboarders

Visual cues	Male athlete		Female athlete		
	M	SD	M	SD	t
High camera angle	2.14	1.30	3.08	1.90	2.16*
Low camera angle	2.83	1.70	2.04	0.98	2.17*
Body shot/Face	1.21	1.72	2.68	1.82	3.06**
Interact with significant other	0.07	0.29	0.30	0.32	2.75**
Interact with coach	0.09	0.32	0.39	0.31	2.77**

$^*p < .05.$ $^{**}p < .01.$

The last research question examined differences in verbal gender cues in snowboarding coverage. Two of the four commentary themes (one masculine and one feminine) and two of the six social role descriptors (one masculine and one feminine) significantly differed by athlete sex. Further, the total number of masculine and feminine verbal cues differed by athlete sex, as shown in Table 4.

For commentary theme, female snowboarders received significantly more comments about their aesthetic ability, whereas male boarders received significantly more comments about their athletic performance, following gender stereotypes. For social role adjectives, female boarders and their moves were significantly more likely to be described as aesthetic, whereas male boarders and their moves were significantly more likely to be described as aggressive, again, following gender stereotypes. Finally, the men received twice as many masculine comments than the women, and the women received more than four times the amount of feminine comments than the

TABLE 4
Mean Number of Verbal Cues per Minute of Coverage for Male and Female Snowboarders

Verbal cues	Male athlete		Female athlete		
	M	SD	M	SD	t
Aesthetic theme	0.70	0.26	2.00	1.41	7.23***
Performance theme	3.72	1.44	2.00	1.12	4.86***
Aesthetic social role descriptors	0.10	0.31	0.48	0.65	2.77**
Aggressive social role descriptors	0.31	0.71	0.00	0.00	2.18*
Total masculine cues	6.38	2.50	3.72	1.88	4.36***
Total feminine cues	1.17	1.10	4.28	2.57	5.91***

$^*p < .05.$ $^{**}p < .01.$ $^{***}p < .001.$

men. It should be noted that for six of the role descriptors, no differences were found.

An additional qualitative analysis on the social role descriptors was conducted by grouping adjectives and adverbs into categories. Overall, male snowboarders were described as either dominant (e.g., "untouchable," "the master," "the great," "a leader") or aggressive (e.g., "a fighter," "tenacious," "digs deep," "clutch"). Their actions either were described as sizeable (e.g., "big," "deep," "heavy," "massive," "huge") or dangerous (e.g., "insane," "aggressive," "explosive," "risky"). Each descriptor emphasized the masculinity of the male athlete.

The descriptors used to describe the female snowboarders, in contrast, emphasized much of the same traits, but commentators included a feminine twist. Women's moves were described as sizeable, but the terms had a softer feel (e.g., "glamorous," "generous," "big and beautiful," "showboat-ish"). Comments about the female athletes focused on their technical performances (e.g., "clean," "conservative," "soft-spoken") or on their personalities (e.g., "charismatic," "generous spirit," "poised," "feeling the pressure").

Discussion

Collectively, the results from the attitudinal survey and the broadcast content analysis present a complex picture of audiences' gendered perceptions and media coverage of snowboarding and snowboarders. Viewing of the Olympic coverage of the sport was clearly linked to variances in attitudes, in some ways in line with traditional gender stereotypes and in other ways departing from these norms. Further, although some visual and verbal cues present in the broadcasts clearly supported traditional gender roles of male athletes as masculine and female athletes as feminine, no differences were found on other variables. Media portrayals of the sport and its athletes, then, fall in line with the perceptions of those who reported watching large amounts of the Olympic telecasts of snowboarding in 2010. Some findings support past research suggesting that audience attitudes and coverage would be in line with traditional gender stereotypes in U.S. society. Other findings suggest that snowboarding, or at least coverage and attitudes related to the 2010 Olympic Games, may join a growing body of recent literature finding more gender equality in sports media content and views toward athletes.

Traditional Gender Stereotypes in Attitudes and Coverage

Amount of time viewing the 2010 Olympic snowboarding coverage emerged as the main predictor variable that explained audience sex typing of snowboarding and to attitudes about male and female snowboarders. Audiences who watched a lot of coverage of men's snowboarding typed the sport in general as more masculine; conversely those who watched more women's coverage saw the sport as more feminine. Further, some of the findings on attitudes about the athletes followed traditional societal gender stereotypes. Watching more men's coverage was related to perceptions of male snowboarders as more masculine, whereas watching more women's coverage was linked to seeing female snowboarders as more graceful. It should be noted, however, that heavier viewing also was linked to attitudes that countered traditional patterns, a finding discussed in the next section.

Only controlled experimental research can establish causation; however, this study provides evidence that the coverage was in many ways in line with audience attitudes about the sport and its athletes. Visually, the camera angles and shot content portrayed female athletes as more feminine and male athletes as more masculine, a finding in line with past research (Bissell & Duke, 2007; Greer et al., 2009). Female athletes were portrayed as smaller (with use of high camera angles), as more emotional and aesthetically pleasing (with an emphasis on facial shots), and as more dependent (with shots showing athletes interacting with coaches or significant others, most of which were men) than were male snowboarders. Men were shot significantly more often from lower camera angles than women, giving them the appearance of size and might.

The same stereotypical patterns were found through some verbal commentary themes and the descriptors used for snowboarders. The commentary about the female competitors emphasized their aesthetic ability (a feminine trait), whereas the commentary about the male boarders emphasized their athletic performances and aggression (both masculine traits). Furthermore, the qualitative analysis of the commentary showed that the words used to describe female athletes used a feminine twist for constructs typically considered masculine (size and power). Again, no differences were found on other variables, as noted in the next section.

The significant differences between men's and women's coverage on some variables in this study indicates that the masculine "culture" of snowboarding described in the literature is reflected in part in media content—and in attitudes of those who report watching a lot of men's and women's coverage. Arguably, the backgrounds of the snowboarding commentators used in 2010 play a role for the verbal gender cues present. Both were men with a history in the sport either as snowboarding competitors or seasoned action broadcasters, and the same commentators were used for both the men's and women's events. Therefore, both likely have been socialized in a male snowboarding culture, one known to emphasize violence, aggression, heterosexuality, and the marginalization of women (Anderson, 1999; Thorpe, 2010). Still, commentator background and socialization explains the presence of stereotyping in coverage—and perhaps in heavy viewers' attitudes—only in part. Visual cues also had stereotypical markers that, together with commentary, painted a picture of female boarders as more feminine and male boarders as more masculine. These cues could have been noted either consciously or subconsciously by heavy viewers, leading them to see the sport as more masculine when they watched more men's coverage and more feminine when they watched more women's coverage.

Gender Equality in Some Areas

For each finding that supported traditional disparities in content and societal attitudes about sport or male and female athletes, another finding disputed these patterns. First, both the men's and women's snowboarding events received equal amounts of coverage in 2010 primetime broadcasts, a finding that lined up with previous research suggesting that amount of coverage in international competitions does not differ by athlete sex (Billings & Angelini, 2007; Hardin et al., 2002). It is important to note that this finding now expands to include a masculine/extreme sport (snowboarding).

Further, although gender stereotyping of the sport of snowboarding was clearly supported, attitudes toward the athletes themselves were more complex. Heavy viewers of men's and women's coverage did give the athletes featured in those segments higher ratings of traditional gender roles (men as aggressive and women as graceful), but these viewers also gave the athletes higher ratings of gender incongruent roles (men as graceful and women as aggressive). In short, more time spent viewing men's events was linked to higher ratings of the men as both aggressive and graceful, and more time spent viewing women's events was linked to higher ratings of women on both agentic and communal traits. In line with another recent study (Krane et al., 2011), this study found that audiences are clearly constructing more complex attitudes about individual athletes, especially those who are highly involved in viewing the sport.

At first, the perceptions among heavy viewers that male and female athletes possessed more of both traits was unexpected, but clues to what might be driving these dual perceptions again can be found in the content cues. As previously noted, men's and women's coverage did not differ on all the cues. For six of the 11 visual cues and six of the 10 verbal cues, no differences by gender were found. For those cues, male and female snowboarders received coverage marked with equal and ample masculine and feminine cues. Therefore, it is not surprising that audiences that spent a lot of time viewing the events would see all boarders as possessing both masculine and feminine traits. The findings that men's and women's coverage didn't differ in running time or in some content cues supports a growing recent body of literature finding more gender equality in sports media coverage (Billings & Angelini, 2007; Kian & Clavio, 2011).

Limitations and Implications for Future Research

These findings clearly apply only to one narrow slice, snowboarding, of a singular sporting phenomenon, the 2010 Winter Olympic Games. In different sporting contexts, the athletes, successes/failures, commentators, regulations, spectators, and venues will differ. Results may be specific to this sport at this clearly defined moment in Olympic history. Further, attitudes and their links to viewing behaviors are based on a convenience sample of U.S. viewers. Although the goal was not to describe attitudes held by a larger population, clearly these viewers are not representative of all Olympic viewers worldwide.

The fact that this study, by nature of its design, cannot establish causation is perhaps the biggest limitation. Cues found in televised content clearly are reflected in audience attitudes about snowboarding, a sport growing in popularity, and its athletes. Although time spent viewing the coverage is the only variable linked to variation in gendered attitudes, we stop short, however, of saying the coverage is driving attitudes. The coverage and the attitudes may mirror each other because those who watch a lot of snowboarding and those who produce broadcasts and comment on snowboarding may be socialized to view the sport and the athletes in similar ways. Further, the producers and commentators may simply be responding to what they know heavy snowboarding viewers want to see.

Correcting for the limitations, however, provides a road map for further research that expands the scope of this study to other Games, other extreme sports, and other audiences is sorely needed. Further, more experimental and longitudinal approaches squarely aimed at establishing causation may help directly link content cues to audience attitudes.

CONCLUSION

Snowboarding, a sport gaining in popularity and media attention, is unique in its identity as an extreme sport with both masculine and feminine qualities. In the 2010 Winter Olympics, audience attitudes about the sport and parts of the coverage reflected a sport grounded in traditional gender roles and norms. The more audiences watched men's coverage, which emphasized masculinity of the boarders in some areas, the more masculine they rated the sport. The more respondents watched women's coverage, which emphasized femininity in some areas, the more feminine they rated the sport. Attitudes toward the athletes themselves, however, were more complex, with heavy viewers seeing both men and women as possessing greater masculine and more feminine traits than did light viewers. In short, those who watched more coverage of men's or women's snowboarding saw the participants as more complete athletes, possessing more of the masculine and feminine qualities success in snowboarding demands. Some gendered content cues were emphasized equally and amply, which again could explain attitudes. In this way, our study of the 2010 Olympic snowboarding coverage breaks new ground. Societal gender stereotypes found in televised broadcasts are mirrored in audiences' perceptions of the sport and its athletes. Further, clues about why some nonstereotypical beliefs exist can be explained by patterns in content. The results provide evidence that content cues and attitudes are related and may feed off each other.

REFERENCES

Anderson, K. L. (1999). Snowboarding: The construction of gender in an emerging sport. *Journal of Sport and Social Issues, 23*(1), 55–79.

Angelini, J. R. (2008). How did the sport make you feel? Looking at the three dimensions of emotion through a gendered lens. *Sex Roles, 58*, 127–135.

Asthana, A. (2003, September 14). Focus: Extreme sports: Girls just want to have fun too. *The Observer*, pp. 20–23.

Babbie, E. (2007). *The practice of social research* (11th ed.). Belmont, CA: Thomson.

Billings, A., & Angelini, J. R. (2007). Packaging the games for viewer consumption Gender, ethnicity, and nationality in NBC's coverage of the 2004 Summer Olympics. *Communication Quarterly, 55*(1), 95–111.

Billings, A., Halone, K., & Denham, B. (2002). Man, that was a pretty shot: An analysis of gendered broadcast commentary surrounding the 2000 men's and women's NCAA final four basketball championships. *Mass Communication & Society, 5*, 295–315.

Bissell, K. L., & Duke, A. M. (2007). Bump, set, spike: An analysis of commentary and camera angles of women's beach volleyball during the 2004 summer Olympics. *Journal of Promotion Management, 13*, 35–53.

Christopherson, N., Janning, M., & McConnell, E. D. (2002). Two kicks forward, one kick back: A content analysis of media discourses on the 1999 Women's World Cup Soccer Championship. *Sociology of Sport Journal, 19*, 170–188.

Cuneen, J., & Claussen, C. L. (1999). Gender portrayals in sports-product point-of-purchase advertising. *Women in Sport & Physical Activity Journal, 8*, 73–80.

Daddario, G. (1997). Chilly scenes of the 1992 winter games: The mass media and the marginalization of female athletes. *Sociology of Sport Journal, 11*, 275–288.

Dillman, L. (2010, February 21). Snowboarding's 'X Games vibe' an unlikely but profitable fit with Olympics tradition. *The Los Angeles Times*. Available from http://www.cleveland.com/olympics/index.ssf/2010/02/snowboardings_x_games_vibe_an.html

Eagly, A. E., & Chaiken, S. (1993). *The psychology of attitudes*. Orlando, FL: Harcourt Brace.

Eagly, A. H., & Johannesen-Schmidt, M. C. (2001). The leadership styles of women and men. *Journal of Social Issues, 57*, 781–797.

Fink, J. S., & Kensicki, L. J. (2002). An imperceptible difference: Visual and textual constructions of femininity in *Sports Illustrated* and *Sports Illustrated for Women*. *Mass Communication & Society, 5*, 317–339.

Gantz, W., & Wenner, L. A. (1995). Fanship and the television sports viewing experience. *Sociology of Sport Journal, 12*, 56–74.

Golombok, S., Rust, J., Zervoulis, K., Croudace, T., Golding, J., & Hines, M. (2008). Developmental trajectories of sex-typed behavior in boys and girls: A longitudinal general population study of children aged 2.5–7 years. *Child Development, 79*, 1583–1593.

Greer, J. D., Hardin, M., & Homan, C. (2009). "Naturally" less exciting? Visual production of men's and women's track and field coverage during the 2004 Olympics. *Journal of Broadcasting and Electronic Media, 53*, 173–189.

Hanson, S. L., & Kraus, R. S. (1999). Women in male domains: Sport and science. *Sociology of Sport Journal, 16*, 92–110.

Hardin, M. (2005). Stopped at the gate: Women's sports, reader interest and decision making by editors. *Journalism & Mass Communication Quarterly, 82*(1), 62–77.

Hardin, M., Chance, J., Dodd, J. E., & Hardin, B. (2002). Olympic photo coverage fair to female athletes. *Newspaper Research Journal, 23*(2/3), 64–78.

Hardin, M., & Greer, J. D. (2009). The influence of gender-role socialization, media use and sports participation on perceptions of gender-appropriate sports. *Journal of Sport Behavior, 32*, 207–226.

Harrison, L. A., & Lynch, A. B. (2005). Social role theory and the perceived gender role orientation of athletes. *Sex Roles, 52*, 227–236.

Heino, R. (2000). What is so punk about snowboarding? *Journal of Sport and Social Issues, 24*, 176–191.

Huffman, S., Tuggle, C. A., & Rosengard, D. S. (2004). How campus media cover sports: The gender-equity issue, one generation later. *Mass Communication & Society, 7*, 475–489.

Humphreys, D. (1997). Shredheads go mainstream? Snowboarding and alternative youth. *International Review for the Sociology of Sport, 32*, 147–160.

Hurtz, W., & Durkin, K. (2004). The effects of gender-stereotyped radio commercials. *Journal of Applied Social Psychology, 34*, 1974–1992.

iKimshi. (2009). Favorite female snowboarder [Discussion forum]. Retrieved from http://www.snowboardingforum.com/snowboarding-general-chat/14628-favorite-female-snowboarder.html

Jollimore, M. (2002). "Yes, but how many tattoos does she have?" A review of the portrayal of Olympic sportswomen in *Sports Illustrated* magazine, 1980–2002 (Unpublished master's thesis). Mount Saint Vincent University, Halifax, Canada.

Kian, E. M. (2008). Study examines stereotypes in two national newspapers. *Newspaper Research Journal, 29*, 38–49.

Kian, E. M., & Clavio, G. (2011). A comparison of online media and traditional newspaper coverage of the men's and women's U.S. Open Tennis Tournaments. *Journal of Sports Media, 6*(1), 55–84.

Kim, E., Walkosz, B. J., & Iverson, J. (2006). *USA Today's* coverage of the top women golfers, 1998–2001. *The Howard Journal of Communications, 17*, 307–321.

Knight, J. L., & Giuliano, T. A. (2001). He's a Laker; she's a "looker": The consequences of gender-stereotypical portrayals of male and female athletes by the print media. *Sex Roles, 45*, 217–229.

Knight, J. L., & Giuliano, T. A. (2003). Blood, sweat, and jeers: The impact of the media's heterosexist portrayals on perceptions of male and female athletes. *Journal of Sport Behavior, 26*, 272–284.

Koivula, N. (2001). Perceived characteristics of sports categorized as gender-neutral, feminine and masculine. *Journal of Sport Behavior, 24*, 377–393.

Krane, V., Ross, S. R., Miller, M., Ganoe, K., Lucas-Carr, C., & Barak, K. (2011). "It's cheesy when they smile:" What girl athletes prefer in images of female college athletes. *Research Quarterly For Exercise & Sport, 82*, 755–768.

Laurendeau, J., & Sharara, N. (2008). "Women could be every bit as good as guys": Reproductive and resistant agency in two "action" sports. *Journal of Sport and Social Issues, 32*(1), 24–47.

Melby, T. (2010). What's it mean to be a man? *Contemporary Sexuality, 44*, 1–5.

Messner, M., Duncan, M., & Wachs, F. (1996). The gender of audience building: Televised coverage of women's and men's NCAA basketball. *Sociological Inquiry, 66*, 422–439.

Perloff, R. M. (2003). *The dynamics of persuasion: Communication and attitudes in the 21st Century* (2nd ed.). Mahwah, NJ: Erlbaum.

Stone, J., & Horne, J. (2008). The print media coverage of skiing and snowboarding in Britain: Does it have to be downhill all the way? *Journal of Sport and Social Issues, 32*, 94–112.

Thorpe, H. (2008). Foucault, technologies of self, and the media: Discourses of femininity in snowboarding culture. *Journal of Sport and Social Issues, 32*, 199–229.

Thorpe, H. (2010). Bourdieu, gender reflexivity and physical culture: A case of masculinities in the snowboarding field. *Journal of Sport and Social Issues, 34*, 176–214.

Thorpe, H., & Wheaton, B. (2011). 'Generation X games,' action sports and the Olympic movement: Understanding the cultural politics of incorporation. *Sociology, 45*, 830–847.

Vincent, J. (2004). Game, sex, and match: The construction of gender in British newspaper coverage of the 2000 Wimbledon Championships. *Sociology of Sport Journal, 21*, 435–456.

Walker, C., & Gordon, J. (1994, December 19). Boarding's year of the woman. *Newsweek*, pp. 76–77.

"The More Things Change, the More They...": Commentary During Women's Ice Hockey at the 2010 Olympic Games

Kelly Poniatowski

Department of Communications
Elizabethtown College

Marie Hardin

Department of Communications
The Pennsylvania State University

This research uses textual analysis rooted in cultural studies to investigate how commentary constructed women hockey players during the 2010 Olympics, one of the biggest mediated sporting events in the world. Games were aired on NBC's cable affiliates during non-prime-time hours, a departure from previous Olympic studies. Hockey is a sport that is traditionally violent, and women are often viewed as intruders to this male world, breaking up male hegemony. Results indicate that women have both male and female role models, are compared to both their male counterparts, succeed after having played on North American college teams, and gain entry into the sport through boys' teams. Despite the positive finding of women as role models, commentators never define the heroine. The other traditional presentations of women are set against the backdrop of progress for women's sports also framed as reliant on men's sports, reflecting a strategy of *ambivalence* that marginalizes the female athlete and reinforces sexual difference.

INTRODUCTION

Title IX, the 1972 federal law that guarantees girls and young women in the United States the same access to sports in public institutions as boys and young men, has been the catalyst for explosive growth in female athletic participation that has not abated since the law was signed (Carpenter & Acosta, 2005; Suggs, 2005). In 1971, fewer than 300,000 girls, constituting about 5% of high school athletes in the United States, participated in school sports. By 2002, the number had jumped to 2.8 million girls—56% of U.S. high school athletes (Carpenter & Acosta, 2005). In 1997, the NCAA predicted it would take at least 10 years to achieve equal participation rates in women's and men's sports, but the next year the NCAA cut the number of years to 5 (Betancourt, 2001). During the 10-year span from 1995 to 2005, women's participation in sports increased more than 60% (Cheslock, 2007).

Canada's Charter of Rights and Freedoms has sometimes been compared to Title IX (Stevens, 2006). The Charter became law in 1982, and an Equality Rights section was added several years later (Abols & Dunkley, 1986; Department of Justice Canada, 1982). Legal victories in the fight for girls' and women's access to sports in Canada have been associated with the Charter (Hall, 1992). Sports participation rates for Canadian girls have also grown in some age groups, and the overall gap for male and female participation rates in sport has narrowed in recent years (Ifedi, 2005).

One sport that has enjoyed increased participation as doors have opened to female athletes is hockey, generally viewed as a masculine sport (Theberge, 1997). For instance, participation among girls and young women in the United States has steadily grown since the late 1990s. Girls' participation in USA Hockey programs jumped 45% between 2001 and 2007 (Clark, 2009). Women have been playing hockey for more than 100 years (Theberge, 2000). Lord Stanley, founder of the Stanley Cup, had a daughter who played hockey and was one of the first women photographed with a stick and puck, in 1890. Women's hockey games were common in the early 1900s in Canada, and women's leagues were formed. Women's hockey was also played at colleges and universities (Theberge, 2000).

Titles IX in the United States and the Canadian Charter of Rights and Freedoms, although to a lesser degree, have opened doors for girls and

143

women to pursue hockey via the same avenues as boys and men (Stevens, 2006). In 1998, the United States won the gold medal at the Olympics, and that medal is considered a catalyst for women's interest in hockey participation in the United States (Clark, 2009). Canadian and U.S. teams have typically dominated international competition, falling into the top echelon of women's hockey. As with many other women's sports, media attention for women's hockey has been waning; however, for the first time in 2006 and again in 2010, NBC aired all women's hockey games along with the men's, signaling, perhaps, that it saw the sport as deserving of equal billing.

Media coverage of masculine sports such as hockey and football is important because these types of sports are "vigorously contested" where competiveness may turn into violence, at least in the male versions (Gunter, 2006). In regards to hockey, the male version allows fighting and body checking, the purposeful throwing of the body into another player, whereas the women's game does not, thus ultimately constructing the women's game as inferior (Stevens, 2006; Theberge, 2000). Other sports such as soccer and basketball may be defined as masculine sports but are not vigorously violent because the violence is not built in; rather, as is the case with soccer, the violence tends to occur within the fan subcultures and not the athletes themselves (Gunter, 2006). Therefore, sports such as hockey and football with violence built in are viewed as less acceptable for women and therefore constructed as less exciting than women's participation in other socially defined masculine sports such as basketball and soccer, where the violence is not naturally part of the game.

It is important then to understand how commentators construct female athletes in traditionally violent sports such as hockey on a world stage such as the Olympics in order to gain a better understanding of how both gender and nationality are managed. In addition, most research regarding the Olympics has looked at prime-time coverage (Billings & Eastman, 2002, 2003; Eastman & Billings, 1999; Greer, Hardin, & Homan, 2009; Stevens, 2006). Women's hockey primarily appears on NBC's cable affiliates during non-prime-time hours. Billings (2008) called for more research of the Olympics via the cable network broadcasts rather than prime time. This is particularly important because NBC focuses most of its resources on the prime-time hours and hires freelance commentators to cover events during non-prime-time hours, trusting those commentators to fulfill the NBC vision on their own (Poniatowski, 2011).

This research uses textual analysis to evaluate commentary during women's hockey games during the 2010 Olympics. The commentary, although celebrating women's hockey and its athletes as markers of progress in women's sports in the United States and Canada, simultaneously positions female players as substandard (with the standard as masculine) in several key ways. Thus, it ultimately reflects a strategy of *ambivalence* that undermines the credibility of the athlete and women's participation in the sport.

MEDIA COVERAGE OF WOMEN IN SPORT

Mediated sporting events, although wildly popular (the Super Bowl, for instance, is the most-watched television event in the United States each year), also serve as one of the most predominant and powerful platforms to reinforce gender norms (Duncan, 2006). Studies indicate that female athletes remain marginalized in the media, struggling to gain the same recognition as men for their accomplishments (Billings & Eastman, 2002, 2003; Duncan & Messner, 1998; Eastman & Billings, 1999; Weiller, Higgs, & Greenleaf, 2004). They are also presented in ways that are distinctly different from the norms for representation of men in sport (Duncan, 2006). Female athletes have historically been underrepresented and misrepresented in overall coverage, despite increases in their opportunities and participation. The marginalization of women in sports media is one way to reinforce the notion that women are "naturally" less interested in and suited for sport than are men (Duncan & Sayaovong, 1990).

Hegemonic Masculinity and Femininity

Hegemonic masculinity is a gender ideal reinforcing patriarchy and the dominant position of men over women within the culture (Connell, 2005). Hegemonic masculinity is idealized masculinity, and it is positioned against its "opposite": idealized (hegemonic) femininity (Connell, 1990). Characteristics of hegemonic masculinity include physical force, heterosexuality, pain, competitiveness, initiative, strength, power, aggression, and confidence (Beal, 1996; Duncan, 2006; Trujillo, 1991).

In contrast, characteristics of hegemonic femininity include exhibition of emotion, passivity, dependence, motherhood, domesticity, and fragility (Craig, 1993; Duncan, 2006; Krane, 2001; Rusk, 2000). Femininity is at the bottom of the gender hierarchy and is further marginalized (Connell, 2005). The military and sport are two social institutions that reinforce the ideals of hegemonic masculinity (Beal, 1996).

Hegemonic masculinity is rooted in the form of the hero (Connell, 1987; Hargreaves, 2000). The male hero is strong, aggressive, and brave, and he usually completes a feat using muscular strength (i.e., slaying a dragon). This makes male athletes the perfect sports heroes, because they are viewed as using muscular strength to succeed. In contrast, characteristics of the female heroine pertain to being selfless, kind, motherly, and moral (Hargreaves, 2000). This leaves an inconsistency when describing the female athlete, who might be heroic according to the male definitions of a hero but who is being held to feminine standards. As a result, mediated sports emphasize the male hero.

Reinforcement of Gender Ideals in Mediated Sports

Mediated sports serve as an ideological narrative of culture, portraying various ideas on social relations and cultural meanings (Boyle & Haynes, 2000). Perhaps the most potent messages are about gender relations, where men are the center of interest and women are literally along the sidelines in the roles of cheerleaders and spectators, for instance (Trujillo, 1991). This creates and reinforces "sexual difference" (also called "gender difference"), which is the notion that women are less suited to sport (and, ultimately, to all activities in the public sphere) because of their natural differences from men (Hardin, Dodd, Chance, & Waldorf, 2004). Sexual difference is reinforced in the culturally constructed differences or stereotypes between men and women depicted in media (Duncan, 1990; Hardin, Chance, Dodd, & Hardin, 2002; Hardin, Lynn, Walsdorf, & Hardin, 2002). These differences are presented as natural and biological, not as manufactured to reinforce gender relations that empower men (Hardin, Lynn, et al., 2002).

Sex-appropriate sports. One way sexual difference is reinforced is through a hierarchy of sporting activities based on the understanding of sports as appropriate for either men or women based on their ability to reflect masculine or feminine ideals (Hardin, Lynn, et al., 2002). The social construction of sex-appropriate sports promotes the idea that some sports like figure skating or gymnastics, which rely on the overt demonstrations of grace and flexibility, are more appropriate for women. Sports like football and hockey, which call for strength and aggression, are more appropriate for men (Adams, 2006; Jones, Murrell, & Jackson, 1999; Kinnick, 1998; Tuggle & Owen, 1999). Sexual difference is reinforced through the media, which tend to "emphasize those sports, which are seen as 'sex appropriate'" for men and for women (Kinnick, 1998, p. 215).

Greer et al. (2009) defined the qualities of masculine sports as force, contact, strength, speed, and risk. Furthermore, "the more of these features a sport has, the more masculine it (is) perceived" (Koivula, 2001, p. 388). Koivula also noted that hockey is characterized as a masculine sport. Poniatowski (2011) argued that only when body checking has been removed from the women's hockey game and full face masks are required do women become legitimate hockey players. But the problem is that women's hockey is constructed as less exciting when this happens. Women are viewed as too frail and weak to sustain body checking or not be required to wear full face masks (Lenskyj, 2003). Of interest, women have been cited as wanting body checking in hockey; Angela Ruggiero, Hillary Knight, and Cassie Campbell, all Olympians, have said they wish body checking was allowed in women's hockey (Ramsey, 2010; "Women's Hockey," 2010). Theberge (2000) noted that players in a professional women's team in Canada also indicated that the game was more enjoyable to play when body checking was allowed.

Representations of women in sports. Because masculinity is so aligned with sports, it is no surprise that mediated depictions of female athletes generally position them as not measuring up to the (male) standard. For instance, research suggests women are more likely to be compared to their male counterparts in the same sport, whereas men are not compared to their female counterpart (Eastman & Billings, 2000; Jones et al., 1999; Weiller et al., 2004). In addition, commentators have tended to focus on women athletes as needing male role models and male support (Poniatowski, 2008). The media also present women in sports as sexually different (i.e., inferior to men) by portraying them as emotionally vulnerable and dependent on men (Kinnick, 1998).

Women who traverse sporting territory through participation in highly masculine sports that have unambiguously been marked as men's, like hockey or rugby, are generally dismissed or presented as deviant or comic (Duncan, 2006). For instance, the media portrayed Hailey Wickenheiser as a "comic sideshow" and inferior to European male players after she played men's professional hockey in Finland and returned to Canada to join the women's national team (Stevens, 2006).

Commentary in coverage of men's and women's sports. Commentators play a large role in the way audiences view sporting events as well as provide a framework for the audience to view and interpret events (Bryant, Comisky, & Zillman, 1977; Tudor, 1992). Most research on the way commentary reinforces ideology has focused on issues of racial difference and binary dualism. Far fewer studies have examined gender as a factor, and even then, the gender of the commentators has been a primary focus (Billings et al., 2002; Duncan & Messner, 2005; Rada & Wulfmeyer, 2005). However, some research has examined differences in the ways that male and female athletes are presented by commentators. An example of a difference noted by scholars is that of a "hierarchy of naming" that positions women as subordinate to men by the casual use of competitor's first names (Bruce, 2004; Duncan, 2006; Duncan & Brummett, 1987; Halbert & Latimer, 1994; Messner, Duncan, & Jensen, 1993). Other research has noted that there is generally less chatter by commentators during women's games, which may characterize women's games as less important and less interesting (Billings et al., 2002).

Mixed messages. Although research has confirmed consistent packaging of women's sports in ways that reinforce gender norms, researchers acknowledge that, in recent years, some changes in the ways female athletes are presented might provide reason to hope that overall coverage may become more equitable. In recent years, mediated women's sports have been characterized as "contested terrain," implying the possibility that coverage of women's sports could reach a tipping point (Messner, 2002). For instance, the notion of "women's empowerment" through sports has been noted as an important theme in coverage (Duncan, 2006). Duncan summarized a number of recent studies that have noted the emergence of portrayals of women that may be considered positive. The problem, however, has been in the conflicting messages contained in a single media production: those of women's empowerment undercut by imagery that reinforces sexual difference and, ultimately, masculine hegemony. Thus, the *ambivalence* running through mediated women's sports does not challenge stereotypes and general themes that have guided coverage for decades (Duncan, 2006).

THIS RESEARCH

As Messner (2002) suggested, mediated coverage of women may someday reach a tipping point. Following on this idea, this study was designed to explore the representation of women in a sport that, although considered highly masculine for its emphasis on speed, aggression, and strength, has seen growing participation rates in North America among girls and women, and, perhaps subsequently, it has also seen increased media coverage of women who play, at least at the Olympic level. The goal of this research was to explore the ways women were constructed via commentary and to consider how empowerment and hegemony were reinforced on a world stage during non-prime-time hours in a traditionally violent and masculine sport.

Methods

Purposeful sampling was used to include both U.S. and Canadian women's and men's 2010 Olympic hockey games. NBC and its affiliates aired all nine women's games and all 12 men's games. Both the U.S. and Canadian women played a total of five games each—both the United States and Canada played in the gold medal game. The Canadian men played seven games. Canada had an extra qualification game, and the U.S. and Canadian men played against each other in the gold medal game. All U.S. and Canadian games for both genders were analyzed with the exception of the extra qualification game for Canada due to a DVR malfunction. Canadian and U.S. games were picked because both teams are North American and both competed on an equal level in the 2010 Olympics. Regarding the women's teams, both teams fall into the top echelon of women's hockey and both have enjoyed success due to legislature that has opened doors for female athletes. The men's games were used simply as a baseline to compare the commentary in the women's games.

All of the games were recorded from television at the time of broadcast. The game constituted the commentary from the time the broadcast began and ended after the postgame commentary went to commercial break. Interviews with players were included. Games were coded via video using NVivo software. NVivo software allowed different documents to be linked together in order to store the information in one central location (Walsh, 2003). The coders watched the games in NVivo and, as themes became apparent, coded those themes in the software. The "tree nodes" function was used to help organize the data. The software also allowed for more efficient coding and organization of the data (Smith & Hesse-Biber, 1996; Welsh, 2002). The gender of each commentator making a comment was noted along with if the comment referred to a North American athlete or a non–North American athlete. The software simply allowed the coders to keep track of the information more easily in the software and pull final reports for each node.

A cultural studies approach was used to conduct thematic textual analysis of the Olympic hockey commentary. Cultural studies serves to realign dominant and nondominant cultures while serving to criticize cultural texts, such as mediated sports (Andrews, 2002; Fiske, 1991). Cultural studies is rooted in theory even though questions are open-ended; this serves to make connections between culture, context, and power (Grossberg, 1995; Hall, 1992). Media images help shape our identities and reveal who has power in society (Kellner, 1995).

Themes were rooted in the literature and previous research (Poniatowski, 2008, 2011). One broad research question was asked (How were female athletes constructed in the commentary?) so that we could remain open to the text and not have too narrow a vision. Open coding was conducted, and we reworked the themes several times until agreement with a peer evaluator was met.

Thematic textual analysis, also referred to as qualitative content analysis, is a systematic and replicable process to analyze texts based on certain rules of coding within the context of communication (Braun & Clarke, 2006; Mayring, 2000; Stemler, 2001). In some cases, recoding as new themes emerged took place. Some initial themes that did not become relevant were eliminated such as sacrifices women make to play hockey, emotion, playing through pain, previously playing sports other than hockey, and only playing hockey. The strongest themes were role models for women and teams girls play on. Thematic textual analysis preserves the rigor and advantages of quantitative content analysis in a qualitative manner. Textual analysis is a way to unpack meanings of text in order to understand the larger cultural significance those texts hold (Kellner, 2001).

Commentators

The core group of commentators for the women's games (United States and Canada) was consistent through the Olympic tournament, and all commentators were either American or Canadian. Former NHL player Bill Clement and former Olympian Cammi Granato provided in-studio reports before the game, during intermissions, and postgame. Either Mike Emrick or Kenny Albert served as play-by-play announcers for all the games. Both Emrick and Albert are longtime hockey commentators; neither have played hockey professionally. A.J. Mleczko served as the color commentator for all the games. She is a former two-time Olympian like Granato. Finally, either Joe Micheletti or Pierre McGuire was the "sideline" reporter, referred to in broadcast as "the third man on our crew." Both Micheletti and McGuire are former NHL players like Clement. All three frequently serve as hockey announcers for various NHL and Olympic games.

FINDINGS

Three main themes emerged for consideration: role models for women, comparisons of women, and teams girls play on. These themes, some of which emphasized dependency on men, emerged against a backdrop that emphasized the advancement of women's sports in North America ultimately sending mixed messages about female athletes. Ninety percent of the comments regarding "role models," and 87.5% regarding "who women were compared to" focused on North American athletes. Of the comments for the theme of "teams girls play on," 65.2% were about North American teams, suggesting that overall commentators created a North American sense of ideology.

Role Models for Women

Both men and women were almost equally positioned as role models for women. In comparison, there were no instances of men as role models for other men in the games. Regarding role models for women, comments constructed men as role models for women 47.2% of the time, and women were role models 52.8% of the time. This might be viewed as a positive finding, as it suggests that although women are still compared to men, women also have other women role models to look up to. It should be noted that all the female athletes who were mentioned as having male heroes were 22 years or older; those born in 1987 would have been about 10 years old when women's hockey premiered in 1998. Because 2006 marked the 1st year equal coverage of women's Olympic hockey took place, older women most likely had only male role models to follow (Poniatowski, 2011).

In comments regarding men as role models for women, 94.1% were made by male commentators. Perhaps male commentators use male role models more frequently because they are more familiar with those male players from the NHL. However, in doing so they reinforce ideologies about what a male hero is, further marginalizing the female role model. During the game between Canada and Finland Kenny Albert said, "A look at Hayley Wickenheiser, the team captain for Canada, grew up skating on an outdoor rink imagining she was Mark Messier or Wayne Gretzky." In a different Canadian game, Albert again stated, "[Hayley Wickenheiser] taught herself how to play hockey back on an outdoor rink. . . . She imagained she was either Mark Messier or Wayne Gretzky." Hayley Wickenheiser is one of the most experienced veterans for Team Canada. The 2010 Olympics were her fourth at age 31, meaning that while she was growing up there were no famous women hockey players to look up to. Today, by contrast, younger players might actually look up to Wickenheiser as a heroine.

U.S. player Jesse Vetter (age 24) wanted to meet former New York Ranger Mike Richter. One commentator said, "She said if we could throw it out there on the air, [if] Mike Richter is watching, Jesse would love to speak with you." Mike Richter, along with Wayne Gretzky and Mark Messier, were all players known for their quickness, speed, and strength, along with being "good guys" and family men, all characteristics that define the male hero. However, it was not supposed that Vetter was any of these things since she was female.

A new finding was that women were also equally constructed as role models for other women. More significant is that 63.2% of these comments were made by male commentators, whereas 36.8% were made by female commentators. This suggests that even though more male commentators mentioned men as role models, they also mentioned women as role models too. In addition, those women serving as role models were all older than 28 and were part of the initial 1998 teams competing in the Olympics. Those who looked up to these heroines were all younger than 23. For instance, a comment about two Finnish players was, "Noora Räty [20] looks up to Emma Laaksonen [28] and knows what she offers." U.S. player Erika Lawler [23] initially did not want to play on a women's team until "she was playing in 2002 for Cushing Academy for Paul Kennedy whose daughter, Courtney [Kennedy, 30] was on that team in 2002 so she watched and from that point on was inspired."

One commentator said of a U.S. player, "In fact, Hillary Knight [20] told a story that when she was ten she was in the doctor's office she picked up a magazine, read an article about Cammie Granato [38], Angela Ruggiero [30], Jenny Potter [31] and she said to herself, I want to be like them." The commentators went on to note that now Hillary Knight was playing in the Olympics with Angela Ruggiero and Jenny Potter "right alongside her heroes."

This research found similar findings to Poniatowski (2008), who discovered that men served as role models to women in the 2006 Olympics. However, these data have departed from previous findings because women are now equally viewed as role models for each other, particularly veteran players as role models to young lesser experienced players. Thus, masculine hegemony is not preserved because women have seemingly gained equal footing.

As 2010 marked the fourth time in 12 years that women played hockey in the Olympics, the increase of female role models makes sense; women's hockey is now at a point where veteran players—the heroines—are now playing alongside those women who looked up to them as children. This is a positive step in the construction of women athletes, particularly in a masculine sport.

What is unclear from the commentary is how exactly these women serve as role models. Hargreaves (2000) stated that heroines are traditionally shown as selfless, kind, motherly, and moral, but it is hard to discern these traits from this commentary. This ultimately leaves the female heroine undefined, which ultimately creates ambivalence toward her.

Comparisons of Women

Commentators constructed female athletes in comparison to their male counterparts, which were positioned as the standard, 93.3% of the time. Throughout the women's games, female athletes were compared with such players as Sidney Crosby, Dominik Hašek, Henrik Lindquist, and twins Daniel and Henrik Sedin—all well-known NHL players. In contrast, there was only one instance of a male player compared to another male player. Overall, 64.3% of these comments were made by male commentators compared to 35.7% by female commentators. Male commentators may unintentionally compare women to men simply because they are more familiar with the men's players. In addition, because of the lack of media coverage of women's hockey, except for the Olympics, audiences are also more familiar with male players who are covered seasonally in the NHL. This reinforces masculine hegemony. Men are the "natural" athletes or the standard. The problem is it serves to construct sexual difference because women can never actually live up to the male standard.

For instance, during the gold-medal game between the United States and Canada, American Jesse Vetter was compared to Dominik Hašek. At one point Pierre McGuire stated, "And here is a Dominik Hašek impersonation by Jesse Vetter. . . . I know she got picked twice on the glove side, but she's shown some quickness." This comment suggests that she impersonated Dominik Hašek and failed while he succeeded. This type of comment reinforces male heroism—speed and strength—but also reinforces sexual difference. Vetter is naturally not as strong or fast as Hašek because she is a woman.

Comparisons to men were often, by implication, favorable. For instance, McGuire also compared U.S. player Erika Lawler to Mats Zucarello Hossa from Norway during the same game: "She is the female version of Mats Zucarello Hossa."

During the gold medal game, Emrick stated about Marie Philip-Poulin, "She is described as a female Sidney Crosby. I don't think if you are a Canadian young woman you'd want a better description of your talent than to be compared to Sidney Crosby." McGuire responded, "She handles the puck very much like Sidney Crosby. I'd agree with that." This is the type of comment that audiences can relate to if they are frequent viewers of hockey. Crosby is considered one of the best goal scorers in the NHL, and by extension Philip-Poulin can be viewed as the same. But it also insinuates that male players are the standard for women to be compared, leaving women to try and "catch up" with the men but never being able to because of socially constructed natural differences.

Teams Girls Play On

A final theme that emerged was the teams women played on, with 82.6% of the comments relating to women playing on North American teams, particularly U.S. college teams, which comprised 93.4% of the comments. The remaining comments focused on professional women's teams. Only 17.4% of the overall comments were of girls or women playing on boys' or men's teams.

References to women playing on North American college teams focused on the success they endured as a result of playing college hockey. Of interest, 74.5% of these comments were made by male commentators. These types of comments served to preserve a sense of North American ideology. Nationalistic hegemony was not maintained due to the fact that both North American and non–North American players benefited.

Often comments were made about where a player was from. For instance, "Stefanie Marty holds up through traffic; plays for Syracuse University" or "Holly Engstrom one of the seven Wisconsin Badgers on this team."

Comments such as these simply give audience members a reference point of where these women play. This is no different to male hockey players and references to the NHL teams. Commentator Mike Emrick made several statements in different games about the number of women's teams in the United States, for instance, "But 131, by my count, teams in the United States that are women's college hockey teams. That's club teams, as well as Division 1 and Division 3." In another similar reference Emrick invites the audience to attend a women's college game "near you" to see these Olympians play. Comments such as this construct women hockey players in a positive manner, suggesting that these are Olympians worth watching, they are easily accessible, and each player is quite possibly the "girl next door."

It was also often mentioned that both Team USA and Team Canada contained a large number of college hockey players. For instance, Emrick stated during a Canadian game, "That [Team USA] is a team that has everyone who has played college hockey. It is remarkable to know that 17 of the 21 Canadians are playing or have played college hockey either in the United States or in Canada." These types of comments reoccurred frequently, reinforcing the message that there was a connection to playing college hockey and being on one of the two top-tier teams in women's Olympic hockey, all of which exist in North America. These types of comments reinforced North American hegemony. The fact that all of the commentators were from North America further reinforced those ideologies.

Comments about where the players typically played hockey also served to reinforce North American ideology. Women were constructed as elite players—enjoying success—for having played on North American college teams. For instance, "Pernilla Winberg who played for Minnesota Duluth...she has five goals here in Vancouver," and "Stefanie Marty who plays for Syracuse has two hat tricks in this tournament." American player Jesse Vetter was said to have "won three titles playing for Mark Johnson at the University of Wisconsin." Although both North American and non–North American players were seen to have success from playing on college teams, these comments reinforced the elite status of North American hockey and further preserved the construction of the echelons in women's hockey with the United States and Canada being at the top. It suggested that North American hockey was the best.

Girls Playing on Boys' Teams

In discussions about girls playing on boys' teams, commentators positioned the boys' game as the "gateway" for girls to enter the sport. From that foundation, girls had been able to progress into college and Olympic hockey. These comments were split 50% for men and women commentators.

During the Canada and Switzerland game Emrick stated, "Shannon Szabados getting her first-ever Olympic experience and her first time completely on a women's team." Szabados was 23 years old at the time of the 2010 Olympics. Later in the game Emrick referenced this again:

> The young lady that is playing her very first Olympic game here today in Canada is Shannon Szabados and also the first time if you are just joining us to be on a completely women's team... and in so many cases they had to play on boys' teams in order to compete at the level in order to be accepted for the Olympics.

In a sense Emrick is acknowledging that there were no other options for a lot of women, particularly the more veteran players who simply did not have girls' hockey teams to play on. But Emrick's comment also suggests a certain hint that girls still must play on boys' teams to become good enough to play in the Olympics. Comments like this reinforced hockey as a sex appropriate sport for men.

Again Mleczko made another reference to Shannon Szabados in the same game: "She's only played in men's leagues as we talked about. She's very calm and it's a good skill, a great skill." Granato reinforced this sentiment about Szabados in-studio: "She's played with the boys. She's a very good goaltender and talking to the players, they feel confident." The last two comments by Mleczko and Granato, both former women's Olympic hockey players, suggest a sense that the only reason Szabados has great skill and is calm is because she has competed with men, allowing her to excel against women who are not as strong.

An example of another female hockey player who began on a boys' team was U.S. player Erika Lawler. Throughout different games, commentators mentioned that in 1998 "she didn't even want to watch the game because she played boys' hockey and she claimed she never wanted to play girls' hockey." These comments showed Lawler traditionally rejecting women's hockey before finally accepting it.

DISCUSSION AND CONCLUSIONS

Duncan (2006), in her summary of recent research on mediated women's sports, recognized the concept of *ambivalence* as a key way to understand modern presentations of women's sports, where legal remedies such as Title IX and the Canadian Charter have literally empowered female athletes, but at the same time mediated depictions have generally reinforced traditional power relations. This ultimately leads to the marginalization of the female athlete within the media (Duncan & Sayaovong, 1990). Messner (2002) noted that at some point women's sports might reach a tipping point; this research shows many mixed messages in constructing women athletes and suggests that we are only on the brink of the tipping point.

Our analysis of commentary during women's hockey games in 2010 is underscored, in some places more than others, by the concept of ambivalence and ultimately marginalization of the female athlete. Women were more often compared to men than other women suggesting that the men's game is the dominant game, and the women need to strive to be more like the men. This reinforces not only masculine hegemony but sexual difference where women are compared to men but can never catch up because of their biological differences.

Although a new finding—women are equal to their male counterparts in serving as role models for young women—is positive step in the construction of the female athlete in a vigorously violent sport, it also misses the definition of what a heroine actually is. This leaves audiences wondering why these women are called heroines, ultimately creating a sense of ambivalence and ultimately marginalization. Men were role models because they were good guys and had speed and strength, all definitions of the male hero. However, according to Hargreaves (2000), heroines are defined differently but were never defined or constructed in this commentary.

The fact that men were not shown to have role models and almost never compared to other men served only to reinforce men as the standard. Women become intruders to man's game, ultimately breaking up the male hegemony that previously existed. Women must constantly be compared to men in order to prove themselves and gain acceptance, creating not only sex-appropriateness of the sport but also sexual difference. In this sense women are always striving to catch up but never can.

Finally, mixed messages were constructed by NBC's commentators regarding the teams women played for. Many references to women playing for women's college teams in North America might be viewed as a positive finding, especially given that commentators also noted that audiences could watch these women in their hometowns. But in a sense it is really no different than commentators stating the NHL team of a men's player, which audiences might also see at home. In contrast, playing North American women's college hockey was equated with success and ultimately the prize—the top echelon of women's hockey, which only the United States and Canada have achieved.

Female athletes were positioned as moving from boys' hockey into women's hockey, which only then legitimated them. Instead, girls playing on boys' teams threaten the male hegemony of ice hockey. Women were compared only to men, thereby insinuating that the game is masculine. Real power, then, ultimately was conferred where it has always been: with men, men's sports, and male athletes. This reinforces sexual difference (Duncan, 1990) and ultimately serves to marginalize the female hockey player during Olympic coverage.

All three themes are only more complex when considering the North American sense of superiority overshadowing all of the themes. Comments about role models and women being compared to men overwhelmingly focused on North American players.

We observed that commentators recognized the progress of women's sports and the elite-level ability of female Olympians, particularly if those athletes were from North America. Of course, it would have been difficult to do otherwise, as the athletes they watched and discussed were the product of improved opportunities for girls and they were at the top of the sport. However, given that so-called equal-opportunities have been afforded Americans and Canadians through Title IX and the Canadian Charter of Rights and Freedoms, comments reflect a standard view that girls must play on boys' teams to become better players and that announcers regularly compare them to men in this particular sport.

It is important to understand the ambivalence underlying the construction of the female athlete in Olympic ice hockey. Not only are the Olympics the most mediated sporting event, but media have the power to construct reality for television viewers (De Moragas Spà, Rivenburgh, & Larson, 1995). The fact that most research has been conducted on prime-time Olympic coverage where NBC controls more of its content, rather than on affiliate networks where freelancers are used, makes ice hockey ideal in looking at the results that occur when there is less control over the commentators. The fact that ice hockey, in the traditional sense, contains both body checking and fighting sets it apart from other masculine sports such as soccer and basketball, which lack the built-in violence. After 12 years of inclusion in the Winter Olympics, women's ice hockey should have reached a tipping point in the media but still fails in some areas to do so.

Limitations and Further Research

This research must be understood in light of its limitations. We did not aim to generalize about all commentary of women's sports—not even all commentary about women's Olympic hockey. Instead, we looked in great depth at the commentary for games during the 2010 Olympics that involved North American teams. Furthermore, we realize that with textual analysis, even though measures are taken to increase the validity of the project, our identities as women with an interest in sport are the lenses through which we understood this commentary and, as such, keep us from making claims to "objective truth" in our conclusions. In other words, we recognize that there are other ways to understand these media texts.

Even so, we believe this research is a step in understanding the "contested terrain" of women's sports (Messner, 2002) and how new understandings of women's sports as empowering are still significantly challenged and recast in ways that preserve traditional gender relations and social power structures. Research that would continue the trajectory of this study might involve exploration of the ways in which male and female sports fans understand women's hockey through coverage, and how they reconcile images of women in the sport with cultural understandings of hockey as a masculine endeavor. This kind of inquiry might provide insight into how messages of empowerment of women in sports are received and what the social implications of those messages are.

REFERENCES

Abols, I. J., Dunkley, K., & Canada Library of Parliament Research Branch. (1986). *The Charter of Rights and Freedoms. Equality rights.*

Adams, M. L. (2006). The game of whose lives? Gender, race and entitlement in Canada's national game. In D. Whitson & R. Gruneau (Eds.), *Artificial ice: Hockey, culture, and commerce* (pp. 71–84). Peterborough, Ontario, Canada: Garamond.

Andrews, D. L. (2002). Coming to terms with cultural studies. *Journal of Sport & Social Issues, 26,* 110–117. doi: 10.1177/0193723502261007

Beal, B. (1996). Alternative masculinity and its effects on gender relations in the subculture of skateboarding. *Journal of Sport Behavior, 19,* 204–220.

Betancourt, M. (2001). *Playing like a girl.* New York, NY: Contemporary Books.

Billings, A. C. (2008). *Olympic media: Inside the biggest show on television.* New York, NY: Routledge.

Billings, A. C., & Eastman, S. T. (2002). Selective representation of gender, ethnicity, and nationality in american television coverage of the 2000 Summer Olympics. *International Review for Sociology of Sport, 37,* 351–370.

Billings, A. C., & Eastman, S. T. (2003). Framing identities: Gender, ethnic, and national parity in network announcing of the 2002 Winter Olympics. *Journal of Communication, 53,* 569–586. doi: 10.1111/j.1460–2466.2003.tb02911.x

Billings, A. C., Halone, K. K., & Denham, B. E. (2002). "Man, that was a pretty shot": An analysis of gendered broadcast commentary surrounding the 2000 Men's and Women's NCAA Final Four Basketball Championships. *Mass Communication & Society, 5,* 295–315. doi: 10.1207/S15327825MCS0503_4

Boyle, R., & Haynes, R. (2000). *Power play: Sport, the media & popular culture.* New York, NY: Pearson Education.

Braun, V., & Clarke, V. (2006). Using thematic analysis in psychology. *Qualitative Research in Psychology, 3,* 77–101. doi: 10.1191/1478088706qp063oa

Bruce, T. (2004). Marking the boundaries of the "normal" in televised sports: They play-by-play of race. *Media, Culture and Society, 26,* 861–879. doi: 10.1177/0163443704047030

Bryant, J., Comisky, P., & Zillman, D. (1977). Drama in sports commentary. *Journal of Communication, 27,* 140–149. doi: 10.1111/j.1460–2466.1977.tb02140.x

Carpenter, L. J., & Acosta, R. V. (2005). *Title IX*. Champaign, IL: Human Kinetics.

Cheslock, J. (2007, June 5). *Who's playing college sports?: Trends in participation. Women's Sports Foundation Research Series*. Retrieved from http://www.womenssportsfoundation. org/home/research/articles-and-reports/school-and-colleges/trends-in-participation

Clark, J. (2009, March 20). *Women's hockey on a powerplay. Boston Herald*, p. 62.

Connell, R. W. (1987). *Gender & power*. Stanford, CA: Stanford University Press.

Connell, R. W. (1990). An iron man: The body and some contradictions of hegemonic masculinity. In M. A. Messner & D. F. Sabo (Eds.), *Sport, men and the gender order* (pp. 83–95). Champagne, IL: Human Kinetics.

Connell, R. W. (2005). *Masculinities* (2nd ed.). Los Angeles, CA: University of California Press.

Craig, S. (1993). Selling masculinities, selling femininities: Multiple genders and the economics of television. *The Mid-Atlantic Almanack*, *2*, 15–27.

De Moragas Spà, M., Rivenburgh, N. K., & Larson, J. F. (1995). *Television in the Olympics*. London, UK: John Libbey.

Department of Justice Canada. (1982). *Canadian Charter of Rights and Freedoms*. Retrieved from http://laws-lois.justice.gc.ca/eng/charter/page-1.html#l_I:s_15

Duncan, M. C. (1990). Sports photographs and sexual difference: Images of women and men in the 1984 and 1988 Olympic Games. *Sociology of Sports Journal*, *7*, 22–40.

Duncan, M. C. (2006). Gender warriors in sport: Women and the media. In R. Raney & J. Bryant (Eds.), *Handbook of sports and media* (pp. 231–252). Mahwah, NJ: Erlbaum.

Duncan, M. C., & Brummett, B. (1987). The mediation of spectator sport. *Research Quarterly for Exercise and Sport*, *58*, 168–177.

Duncan, M. C., & Messner, M. A. (1998). The media image of sport and gender. In L. A. Wenner (Ed.), *MediaSport* (pp. 170–185). London, UK: Routledge.

Duncan, M. C., & Messner, M. A. (2005). *Gender in televised sports: News and highlights shows, 1989–2004*. Retrieved from http://www.la84foundation.org/9arr/ResearchReports/tv2004.pdf

Duncan, M. C., & Sayaovong, A. (1990). Photographic Images and gender in *Sports Illustrated* for kids. *Play and Culture*, *3*, 96–116.

Eastman, S. T., & Billings, A. C. (1999). Gender parity in the Olympics: Hyping women athletes, favoring men athletes. *Journal of Sport & Social Issues*, *23*, 140–170. doi: 10.1177/0193723599232003

Eastman, S. T., & Billings, A. C. (2000). Sportscasting and sports reporting. *Journal of Sport & Social Issues*, *24*, 192–313.

Fiske, J. (1991). Cultural studies and the culture of everyday life. In L. Grossberg, C. Nelson & P. A. Treichler (Eds.), *Cultural studies* (pp. 154–165). New York, NY: Routledge.

Greer, J. D., Hardin, M., & Homan, C. (2009). "Naturally" less exciting? Visual production of men's and women's track and field coverage during the 2004 Olympics. *Journal of Broadcasting & Electronic Media*, *53*, 173–189. doi: 10.1080/08838150902907595

Grossberg, L. (1995). Cultural studies: What's in a name (one more time). *Taboo*, *1*, 1–37.

Gunter, B. (2006). Sport, violence, and the media. In R. Raney & J. Bryant (Eds.), *Handbook of sports and media* (pp. 383–395). Mahwah, NJ: Erlbaum.

Halbert, C., & Latimer, M. (1994). "Battling" gendered language: An analysis of the language used by sports commentators in a televised coed tennis competition. *Sociology of Sport Journal*, *11*, 298–308.

Hall, S. (1992). Cultural studies and its theoretical legacies. In L. Grossberg (Ed.), *Cultural studies* (pp. 277–294). New York, NY: Routledge.

Hardin, M., Chance, J., Dodd, J. E., & Hardin, B. (2002). Olympic photo coverage fair to female athletes. *Newspaper Research Journal*, *2*, 64–78.

Hardin, M., Dodd, J., Chance, J., & Walsdorf, K. (2004). Sporting Images in Black and White: Race in newspaper coverage of the 2000 Olympic Games. *The Howard Journal of Communications, 15*, 211–227. doi: 10.1080/10646170490521176

Hardin, M., Lynn, S., Walsdorf, K., & Hardin, B. (2002). The framing of sexual difference in SI for kids editorial photos. *Mass Communication & Society, 5*, 341–359. doi: 10.1207/S15327825MCS0503_6

Hargreaves, J. (2000). *Heroines of sport: The politics of difference and identity.* New York, NY: Routledge.

Ifedi, F. (2005). *Sport participation in Canada, 2005.* Ottawa, Canada: Culture, Tourism, and the Centre for Education Statistics.

Jones, R., Murrell, A. J., & Jackson, J. (1999). Pretty versus powerful in the sports pages: Print media coverage of U.S. women's Olympic gold medal winning teams. *Journal of Sport & Social Issues, 23*, 183–192. doi: 10.1177/0193723599232005

Kellner, D. (1995). Cultural studies, multiculturalism and media culture. In G. Dines & J. M. Humez (Eds.), *Gender, race and class in media* (pp. 5–17). Thousand Oaks, CA: Sage.

Kellner, D. (2001). *The Frankfurt School and British Cultural Studies: The missed articulation. Illuminations.* Retrieved from http://www.uta.edu/huma/illuminations/

Kinnick, K. N. (1998). Gender bias in newspaper profiles of 1996 Olympic athletes: A content analysis of five major dailies. *Women's Studies in Communication, 21*, 212–236.

Koivula, N. (2001). Perceived characteristics of sports categorized as gender-neutral, feminine and masculine. *Journal of Sport Behavior, 24*, 377–393.

Krane, V. (2001). We can be athletic and feminine, but do we want to? Challenging hegemonic femininity in women's sports. *Quest, 53*, 115–133. doi: 10.1023/B:SERS.0000018888.48437.4f

Lenskyj, H. J. (2003). *Out on the field: Gender, spot and sexualities.* Toronto, Canada: Women's Press.

Mayring, P. (2000, June). Qualitative Content Analysis [28 paragraphs]. *Forum: Qualitative Social Research, 1*(2). Retrieved from http://qualitative-research.net/fqs/fqs-e/2-00inhalt-e.htm

Messner, M. A. (2002). *Taking the field: Women men and sports.* Minneapolis: University of Minnesota Press.

Messner, M. A., Duncan, M. C., & Jensen, K. (1993). Separating the men from the girls: The gendered language of televised sports. *Gender & Society, 7*, 121–137. doi: 10.1177/089124393007001007

Poniatowski, K. (2008). *NBC's Portrayal of U.S. and Canadian hockey players on the Olympic Stage: A textual analysis of gender, race, and nationality issues in the commentary.* (Unpublished doctoral dissertation, The Pennsylvania State University, 2008). *Electronic Thesis and Dissertations.* Retrieved from http://etda.libraries.psu.edu/theses/approved/WorldWideIndex/ETD-2890/index.html

Poniatowski, K. (2011). "You're not allowed body checking in women's hockey": Preserving gendered and nationalistic hegemonies in the 2006 Olympic ice hockey tournament. *Women in Sport and Physical Activity Journal, 19*.

Rada, J. A., & Wulfemeyer, K. T. (2005). Color coded: Racial descriptors in television coverage of intercollegiate sports. *Journal of Broadcasting & Electronic Media, 49*, 65–85.

Ramsey, D. (2010, January 11). *Women hockey Olympians debate the values of checking. Colorado Springs The Gazette.* Retrieved from http://www.gazette.com

Rusk, D. L. (2000, Spring). *Feminizing the athletic body: Female athletes, self-empowerment, and media objectification. Deliberations*, 16–21. Retrieved from http://www.deliberations.org/pdf/deliberations2000idx.pdf#page=16

Smith, B. A., & Hesse-Biber, S. (1996). Users' experiences with qualitative data analysis software: Neither Frankenstein's monster nor muse. *Social Science Computer Review, 14*, 423–432. doi: 10.1177/089443939601400404

Stemler, S. (2001). An overview of content analysis. *Practical Assessment, Research & Evaluation, 7*(17). Retrieved from http://PAREonline.net/getvn.asp?v=7&n=17

Stevens, J. (2006). Women's hockey in Canada: After the "gold rush". In D. Whitson & R. Gruneau (Eds.), *Artificial ice: Hockey, culture, and commerce* (pp. 85–100). Peterborough, Ontario, Canada: Garamond.

Suggs, W. (2005). *A Place on the team: The triumph and tragedy of Title IX*. Princeton, NJ: Princeton University Press.

Theberge, N. (1997). "It's part of the game": Physicality and the production of gender in women's hockey. *Gender & Society, 11*, 69–87. doi: 10.1177/089124397011001005

Theberge, N. (2000). *Higher goals: Women's ice hockey and the politics of gender*. Albany, NY: State University of New York Press.

Trujillo, N. (1991). Hegemonic masculinity on the mound: media representations of Nolan Ryan and American sports culture. *Critical Studies in Mass Communication, 8*, 290–308. doi: 10.1080/15295039109366799

Tudor, A. (1992). Them and us: Story and stereotype in TV World Cup coverage. *European Journal of Communication, 7*, 391–413. doi: 10.1177/0267323192007003004

Tuggle, C. A., & Owen, A. (1999). A descriptive analysis of NBC's coverage of the Centennial Olympics: The "Games of the Woman"?. *Journal of Sport & Social Issues, 23*, 171–182. doi:10.1177/0193723599232004

Walsh, M. (2003). Teaching qualitative analysis using QSR NVivo. *The Qualitative Report, 8*, 251–256.

Weiller, K., Higgs, C., & Greenleaf, C. (2004). Analysis of television media commentary of the 2000 Olympic Games. *Media Report to Women, 32*, 14–21.

Welsh, E. (2002). Dealing with data: Using NVivo in the qualitative data analysis process. *Forum: Qualitative Social Research, 3*. Retrieved from http://www.qualitative-research.net/fqs/fqs-eng.htm

Women's Hockey: Will it be gold? Or silver? (2010). *The Vancouver Sun*. Retrieved from http://www.vancouversun.com/pdf/OlyHockeyWomensed.pdf

Index

Media and Social Inequality

Innovations in Community Structure Research

Edited by John C. Pollock

This book systematically explores the impact of community inequality on reporting political and social change. Although most journalism scholars are still fascinated by the impact of media on society, this book explores the reverse perspective: the impact of society on media. Using a 'community structure' approach, and rejecting the perspective that studies of media and audiences can be reduced to the individual level of psychological phenomena, all contributions examine connections between community-level 'macro' characteristics and variations in the coverage of critical issues.

This book was originally published as a special issue of *Mass Communication and Society*.

December 2012: 234 x 156: 192pp
Hb: 978-0-415-63118-1
£85 / $145

For Product Safety Concerns and Information please contact our EU
representative GPSR@taylorandfrancis.com
Taylor & Francis Verlag GmbH, Kaufingerstraße 24, 80331 München, Germany

www.ingramcontent.com/pod-product-compliance
Lightning Source LLC
Chambersburg PA
CBHW050714280326
41926CB00088B/3024

9 7 8 1 1 3 8 9 4 4 3 2 9